THEORIES AND NARRATIVES

THEORIES AND NARRATIVES

Reflections on the Philosophy of History

Alex Callinicos

Polity Press

First published in 1995 by Polity Press
in association with Blackwell Publishers Ltd.

Reprinted 1997

Editorial office:
Polity Press
65 Bridge Street
Cambridge CB2 1UR, UK

Marketing and production:
Blackwell Publishers Ltd
108 Cowley Road
Oxford OX4 1JF, UK

ISBN 0–7456–1200–8
ISBN 0–7456–1201–6 (pbk)

A CIP catalogue record for this book is available from the
British Library.

Typeset in 10½ on 12pt Sabon Symposia
by Apex Products, Singapore
Printed in Great Britain by Hartnolls Ltd, Bodmin, Cornwall

This book is printed on acid-free paper.

To Frederick, with love

I shall soon be fifty years old. I have spent thirty of them in these eternally agitated times, full of hopes and fears. I had hoped that we might be done with hope and fear. Now I must confess that everything goes on, and indeed is continually getting worse.

G. W. F. Hegel (1819)

Happy endings depend on stopping the story before it's finished.

Orson Welles (1985)

CONTENTS

PREFACE AND
ACKNOWLEDGEMENTS

This is a book about history. It is about history as a discourse and about what that discourse itself is about. If I concentrate more on the former aspect – historiography, history as a body of writing – this is because my concern is largely to disentangle some of the issues involved in debates – some recent, others longer-running – about how we represent to ourselves and interpret the past, and about the political and ideological significance of these representations and interpretations. The meaning of history has once again become quite a highly charged question over the past few years, for various reasons, which I seek to explore below. My main objective in taking all this on is to establish the respects in which it is legitimate to formulate large-scale theories about the historical process as a whole. Showing that such theories are philosophically respectable is, as I hope should become clear by the end of the book, politically important.

History and philosophy are my oldest intellectual loves, so this book probably has quite deep roots. It largely complements an earlier book of mine, *Making History*, which was concerned with outlining a satisfactory account of the relationship between social structure and human agency: any theory of history presupposes such an account. I have greatly benefited from the opportunities to set out some of the ideas developed in the present book provided by a number of venues, notably the Radical

Political Thought Conference held at the University of Sussex in November 1992; the Humanities Seminar at Manchester Metropolitan University; the Political Theory Workshop at the University of York; the Centre for Social Theory and Comparative History at the University of California, Los Angeles; and the European History Research Seminar at the University of East Anglia. I am grateful to all who participated in these events, but I should like especially to mention Joe McCarney, whose own work exploring the tensions and ambivalences present in Fukuyama's writing has been trail-blazing, and Gregory Elliott, with whom I share many interests, even if our views on them often differ.

Polity Press once again made the business of writing a book as pleasurable a process as it can possibly be. I would like to thank David Held, Debbie Seymour, Gillian Bromley and Gill Motley. I am also grateful to my colleagues at the Department of Politics at the University of York for allowing me the time in which to write this book.

Authors are probably the worst judges of those who have influenced them, but I would still like to name a few. First and closest are three comrades and friends, Chris Bambery, Chris Harman and John Rees. We have been discussing, and occasionally quarrelling over, the relationship between Marxism and history for as long as I can remember. At a somewhat further remove are Bob Brenner and Eero Loone, both of whose work has been an important stimulus even when I have disagreed with it. At a still greater, indeed suitably Olympian distance, there is Perry Anderson. His writing has been a major reference-point: I can say, like Chris Wickham, that often 'I started with his analysis – and with his bibliography – even if I have finished elsewhere.'

Last of all there is Frederick, to whom this book is dedicated, and who has been growing with terrifying speed all the time I have been working on it. He isn't exactly a source of intellectual inspiration, more a force of disruption. I especially remember the day we visited the Anasazi remains at Bandelier National Monument in New Mexico, when he suppressed any inclination I might have had, rather like Gibbon amid the ruins of the Forum, to ruminate on the destiny of civilizations, by nearly throwing himself into the river, twice.

A.T.C.

INTRODUCTION

Philosophy of history in the grand sense is decidedly out of fashion. The attempt, that is, associated above all with Hegel and with the *philosophes* of the eighteenth-century Enlightenment, to arrive at a comprehensive interpretation of the whole course of historical development is very widely discredited. When Jean-François Lyotard sought to define what he called the 'postmodern condition' he characterized it as 'incredulity toward metanarratives', toward discourses which sought to legitimize themselves by 'making an explicit appeal to some grand narrative, such as the dialectics of Spirit, the hermeneutics of meaning, the emancipation of the rational or working subject, or the creation of wealth'.[1] Despite the numerous disagreements which fuelled the apparently interminable debate on postmodernism provoked by Lyotard's announcement, few participants dissented from his assertion that the attempt to grasp theoretically a pattern underlying the flux of historical events is not simply philosophically untenable, but morally and politically flawed.

Philosophers in the English-speaking world have long treated this proposition as a truism. After all, Sir Karl Popper devoted the Second World War to writing two books, *The Open Society and its Enemies* and *The Poverty of Historicism*, which damned Hegel and Marx as the authors of all the miseries of the twentieth century, whose source lay in the attempt – common to both thinkers – theoretically to understand human societies as totalities subject to law-governed processes of development.[2] Philosophy

of history flourishes in the English-speaking world as an academic specialism whose founding texts are probably Maurice
Mandelbaum's *The Problem of Historical Knowledge* (1938)
and R. G. Collingwood's *The Idea of History* (1946). But this
is a discipline which was constituted precisely by the act of
differentiating itself from 'speculative' or 'substantive' philosophy
of history which seeks theoretically to master the whole course
of history. 'Analytical' or 'critical' philosophy of history, by contrast, confines itself to the epistemological task of establishing
the credentials of historical writing as a distinctive form of
knowledge subject to quite different protocols from those governing the physical sciences. The more recent emergence, first in
the work of analytical philosophers such as Arthur Danto and
W. B. Gallie, then much more radically in Hayden White's
Metahistory (1973), of what has come to be known as narrativism has strengthened Anglophone theorists' preoccupation
with the nature of historical discourse. The *differentia specifica*
of historical writing is now held to be that it is a species of
story-telling; from the perspective of the kind of exploration of
narrative conventions and the rhetorical tropes in which they are
embedded that White has pioneered, attempts to use the tools of
theory to make sense of historical processes appear hopelessly
jejeune and dated.[3]

There has thus, in the English-speaking world at any rate,
been a movement from one kind of reflection on history to
another. The first – speculative philosophy of history – is, as
Danto puts it, like 'ordinary historical inquiry', 'concerned to
give accounts of what happened in the past', but does so on
a much grander scale by trying 'to discover a kind of theory
concerned with the ... whole of history'.[4] The second has as
its object historical inquiry itself, which it increasingly seeks to
conceptualize as a form of writing. The transformation of philosophy of history into metahistory is typical of analytical philosophers' preoccupation (at least in the immediate postwar period)
with establishing the presuppositions of different forms of discourse. White's development of narrativism into the study of
the different 'modes of emplotment' employed by historians,
however, verges on relativism. The statement, for example, that
'the best grounds for choosing one perspective on history rather
than another are ultimately aesthetic or moral rather than epistemological' seems to express a scepticism that Ranke's injunction
to historians to show the past *wie es eigentlich gewesen* – as it
actually happened – can ever be observed.[5]

The point can be put another way, with the help of a metaphor provided by F. R. Ankersmit: 'Like a dike covered with ice-floes at the end of winter, the past has been covered by a thick crust of narrative interpretations; and historical debate is as much a debate about the components of this crust as about the past hidden beneath it.'[6] But what White, at times at least, seems to be saying is that, to use the fashionable parlance, it's crust all the way down. Any attempt to distinguish between historical discourse and the past as a reality existing independently of this discourse is futile; the past is a discursive construct, constituted in various forms of writing which purport to be 'about' it but which in fact provide forms in which we can collectively imagine and represent to ourselves the pasts appropriate to our present preoccupations. The convergence of this kind of historical anti-realism with the variant of poststructuralism which takes literally Jacques Derrida's announcement that '[t]here is no outside-text' ('*Il n'y a pas de hors-texte*') is evident enough.[7] The presence of these influences can be read, for example, in Patrick Joyce's declaration: 'The major advance of "post-modernism" needs to be registered by historians: namely that the events, structures and processes of the past are indistinguishable from the forms of documentary representation, the conceptual and political appro-priations, and the historical discourses that construct them.'[8]

Claims of this sort involve a further move. Whereas analytical philosophy of history insisted on the distinction between what Danto calls 'ordinary historical inquiry', which seeks to depict the past *wie es eigentlich gewesen*, and philosophy of history, which attempts to establish the cognitive status of such inquiry, now the two are collapsed into each other. Joyce enjoins histor-ians to study representations of the past, including 'the historical discourses' which they themselves produce. Metahistory swallows up history itself. Nor is this development simply a matter of programmatic statements of the kind cited from Joyce. The fashion-able mid-Atlantic historian Simon Schama recently published a book consisting of two narratives about (if putting it this way doesn't beg too many questions) two actual events. He explains that, '[t]hough these stories may at times appear to observe the discursive conventions of history, they are in fact historical novellas, since some passages ... are pure inventions, based, however, on what documents suggest.' Schama dissociates himself from the 'naively relativist position which insists that the lived past is *nothing* more than an artificially designed text'. The inter-weaving of fact and fiction is rather a device allowing us to 'play with the teasing gap separating a lived event and its subsequent narration'.[9] Though Schama is thus not prepared to go as far as Joyce and treat the past as a discursive construct, they share a preoccupation with the *representation* of the past.

A condition of possibility of this series of conceptual slides, in which metahistory ends up by absorbing what conventionally had been thought of as the independently existing referent of historical discourse, is that, as W. H. Walsh observes,

> the word 'history' is itself ambiguous. It covers (1) the totality of past human actions, and (2) the narrative or account we construct of them now. This ambiguity is important because it opens up at once two possible fields for philosophy of history. That study might be concerned, as it was in its traditional form, with the actual course of historical events. It might, on the other hand, occupy itself with the processes of historical thinking, the means by which history in the second sense is arrived at.[10]

This ambiguity (which the term 'history' shares with its counterparts in other European languages, such as *Geschichte* and *histoire*) thus leaves open whether theoretical reflection on history should focus on historical processes and occurrences or on their discursive representation.[11] The confluence of narrativism and poststructuralism I have been describing effectively resolves this ambiguity by treating what Walsh calls 'the processes of historical thinking' – or, more usually these days, of historical writing – as the object of historical inquiry itself. It is therefore entirely appropriate that events which Hegel would have had no hesitation in describing as 'world-historic' should be indelibly associated with the revival of philosophy of history of the most robustly speculative kind.

For it is, when one thinks about it, something of a paradox of recent intellectual history that the 1980s, the decade of postmodernism, should have ended with an attempt to rehabilitate the grandest of all secular narratives – Hegel's philosophy of history – in the shape of Francis Fukuyama's celebrated article and book.[12] Though first published before the events which made it notorious – the east European revolutions of 1989 and the disintegration of the Soviet Union after the failed Moscow coup of August 1991 – Fukuyama's thesis took its force from the process of which they were the culmination, the collapse of the Stalinist regimes. These upheavals marked, he claimed, not simply the definitive triumph of Western liberal capitalism, but also, since this system no longer faced any serious competitors, the end of history. Whatever one might think of this assertion, it certainly represented a willingness to reflect philosophically on the whole course of historical development, as if all the strictures made against such a way of proceeding by thinkers as different as Popper and Lyotard had never been uttered.

Some take Fukuyama's intervention and the debate it provoked as straws in the intellectual wind. Thus Gordon Marsden, editor of *History Today*, calls them 'a further indication – as was the impact of Paul Kennedy's *Rise and Fall of the Great Powers* – that grand sweep historical analysis is back on the agenda in our trying to make sense of our own times'.[13] A sceptic would be tempted to seize on the comparison Marsden makes between Fukuyama's texts and Kennedy's book. *The Rise and Fall of the Great Powers* (1988) and Fukuyama's original article 'The End of History?' (1989) appeared within less than two years of each other. Both provoked considerable debates in the United States, in each case centred on what is sometimes called the Washington foreign policy community and its extensive offshoots in the academic world and the mass media. Both Kennedy's and Fukuyama's central claims were elevated into 'isms', respectively 'Declinism' and 'Endism'. The intensity of the debates around these theses surely arises from the fact that they were taken to have a direct bearing on the future of the United States at a time of great uncertainty, though their implications seemed directly opposed: Kennedy set America's relative economic decline in the postwar era in the context of a long-run historical cycle in which Great Powers tend to undermine their economic bases by over-reaching themselves militarily, while Fukuyama by contrast apparently endorsed Ronald Reagan's prophecy that 'the best is yet to come' for the United States.

One might then dismiss Fukuyama's writing, like Kennedy's before it, as merely catering for a middlebrow demand for 'grand sweep historical analysis' in unsettled times. There is a striking parallel between the notoriety enjoyed by Fukuyama and the impact made by another philosopher of history, Arnold Toynbee, at the beginning of the Cold War era. His biographer, William H. McNeill, writes:

No other historian has ever enjoyed the status Toynbee achieved in the United States after 1947, for he suddenly became a professional wise man, whose pronouncements on

current affairs, on the historical past, and on religious and
metaphysical questions were all accorded serious attention by
a broad spectrum of earnest souls seeking guidance in a
tumultuous postwar world.[14]

Toynbee's standing was in part a consequence of the appearance
in 1947 of D. C. Somervell's abridgement of the first six volumes
of *A Study of History* (originally published in 1934 and 1936).
But this coincided with the appearance, on 17 March 1947, of
a cover story on Toynbee in *Time* magazine. Now, Toynbee's
gargantuan account of the rise and fall of civilizations as a cyclical process governed by the law of challenge-and-response has
typically been charged by his critics with fatalism and pessimism.
H. R. Trevor-Roper, for example, damns it as 'a doctrine of
messianic defeatism'.[15] This was not, however, how *Time* presented Toynbee's philosophy. The cover story was written by
Whittaker Chambers, an ex-Communist turned fanatical red-baiter
who was later to play a leading role in one of the great show
trials of the McCarthy era. Published within days of President
Truman's announcement that the United States would step into
the gap left by British withdrawal from Greece – a move often
regarded as the beginning of the Cold War proper – the article
offered Toynbee as a 'cultural legate from a Britain in crisis to a
US at the crossroads', and drew from the *Study* the conclusion
that 'since his [man's] capacity for response is infinitely varied, no
civilization, including our own, is inexorably doomed.' McNeill
observes: 'Thus *Time* presented Toynbee's vision of history as a
call to action – American action, accepting the challenge of defending a civilization that was not Western ... but specifically
Christian.'[16]
    It is tempting, then, to treat Toynbee and Fukuyama as
comparable figures, offering America philosophically sanctioned
reassurance in difficult periods of transition, respectively the beginning and the end of the Cold War. Whether or not Fukuyama's
argument can be reduced to its surface message of Reaganite
triumphalism is one of the issues considered in chapter 1 below.
That a market now exists for world-historical speculation is
nevertheless undeniable. Kennedy, for example, in a sequel to
The Rise and Fall of the Great Powers, conducts the rather
Toynbeean exercise of listing the problems facing humankind
in the next few decades – which come down, he argues, to the
final arrival of the crisis predicted by Malthus, in which world
population outstrips the capacity of the global economy and

environment to support it – and exploring possible responses.[17]
And the veteran Cold Warrior Samuel Huntington follows even
more closely the path laid down in Toynbee's *Study*, arguing in
one of the house organs of the US foreign policy establishment
that 'the fundamental source of conflict in this new world will
not be primarily ideological or primarily economic ... the principal conflicts of global politics will occur between nations and
groups of different civilizations. The clash of civilizations will
dominate global politics.'[18]

If all theorizing about the historical process took the form of
such speculations, then one might be forced to acknowledge the
victory of its opponents, that intellectually heterogeneous collection of poststructuralists, narrativists, analytical philosophers
and professional historians. Matters, however, are not so simple.
One can identify at least two counter-trends of great moment.
The first is the emergence of historical sociology. This is the
name that has come to be attached to a variety of studies which
have crossed the disciplinary boundary separating social theory
from substantive historical inquiry.[19] Perhaps the most important
stimulus to the development of this body of work has been the
reception in the English-speaking world of the work of the
Annales group of French historians, and in particular of Fernand
Braudel's great studies of the early modern world economy. But
arguably of even greater significance in the constitution of historical sociology has been the appearance in the 1980s of what
Perry Anderson describes as 'a series of large-scale theories of
history, comparable in scope to that adumbrated by Marx, and
conceived to outmatch it', which were produced independently
by four British sociologists, Ernest Gellner, Anthony Giddens,
Michael Mann and W. G. Runciman.[20] Representing, broadly
speaking, different versions of a fundamentally Weberian perspective which treats forms of political and ideological domination
as factors of explanatory importance coequal with that of class
exploitation, this formidable body of work collectively amounts
to a remarkably ambitious attempt to reaffirm the claim of theory
to comprehend the course of history.

These neo-Weberian historical sociologies, as Anderson notes,
were intended, among other things, as rivals to Marx's theory of
history. That theory – historical materialism, as it came to be
known – is still the most influential of the grand narratives.
Its continued vitality constitutes the second counter-trend to the
general disdain with which any attempt at a comprehensive interpretation of human development is now greeted. Recent years

have seen important philosophical work devoted to the exploration and elaboration of the conceptual structures of historical
materialism, thanks chiefly to the stimulus provided by the writing
of Louis Althusser and G. A. Cohen.[21] They have also seen
substantive historical investigations which have continued the
tradition established by the extraordinary group of Marxist historians who emerged in Britain after the Second World War –
Edward Thompson, Christopher Hill, Eric Hobsbawm, Geoffrey
de Ste Croix, Rodney Hilton and George Rudé – in which social
theory and empirical evidence continually interrogate each other.
Some of the books produced by younger Marxist historians over
the past few years, for example, Guy Bois's *La Mutation de l'an
mil* (1989), Peter Linebaugh's *The London Hanged* (1991) and
Robert Brenner's *Merchants and Revolution* (1993), demonstrate
that this tradition is a living one.

The contrast which thus arises between, on the one hand,
what Lyotard rightly describes as the widespread 'incredulity
toward metanarratives' and, on the other, the existence of powerful intellectual traditions which are not afraid theoretically to
comprehend the course of history forms the focus of this book.
In it I attempt to establish the scope of legitimate historical
theory. This does not amount to a general defence of the philosophy of history; on the contrary, I seek to develop a distinction
between philosophies and theories of history. There may seem to
be a Kantian ring about this – distinguishing the valid exercise
of historical reason from illicit metaphysical attempts to escape
its limits. These resonances are not wholly misleading: a central
issue of this book could be described as the conditions of possibility of historical knowledge. But I do not attempt anything so
ambitious as the Critique of Historical Reason which Dilthey
claimed was necessary to complete the Kantian enterprise. Nor
does the way in which I try to establish my case bear much resemblance to the transcendental arguments which were one of
Kant's main contributions to philosophy. Indeed, my own arguments are informed by a philosophical naturalism which, in
treating human beings as continuous with the rest of nature,
stressing the methods shared by the physical and the social
sciences, and seeking to explain human thought, language and
action as far as possible by setting them in their physical and
social contexts, must find itself at odds with any version of
Kantian philosophy.

The book takes the following form. In chapter 1 I explore the
issues raised by Fukuyama's rehabilitation of the idea of the

End of History, and seek to establish that it is a theme which belongs less, as he (following Alexandre Kojève) claims, to the traditions of Hegel and Marx, than to the aristocratic critique of modernity pioneered by Nietzsche and continued in the present century by German conservative-revolutionary thinkers, above all Spengler. One provisional conclusion which emerges from this discussion is that there exists an important distinction, already adverted to, between philosophies of history, whose concern is primarily with the meaning of the historical process, and theories of history, which, while they may range over a much wider expanse of time than the accounts given by ordinary historians, employ essentially the same kind of explanations as the latter.

Chapter 2 then begins the work of establishing that historical theory in the sense just clarified is not simply compatible with, but is required by, substantive historical inquiry. It does so by examining the claims of narrativism. I seek to show that the attempt to equate historical writing with story-telling misconstrues the specific character of modern historical discourse. Further, it can lead to a scepticism about historical knowledge which is neither philosophically nor ethically tenable. Finally, I contend, a satisfactory account of historical knowledge must include a recognition of the dependence of the explanations offered by historians on larger-scale theories of history.

These arguments naturally lead, in chapter 3, to a discussion of theories of history themselves. After offering an account of the features shared by all theories of history, I proceed to a comparison of the two main instances of such theories, namely Marxism and neo-Weberian historical sociology. I conclude by considering some of the difficulties internal to what I believe to be the more successful of these two research programmes, namely historical materialism.

Finally, in chapter 4, I confront one feature of theories of history since the Enlightenment, and more specifically of Marxism, namely that they tend to treat the course of history as a process of development, indeed as a tale of human progress. It is this, more than anything else, that has given support to the belief that any genuine radicalism must refuse to theorize about the historical process. The thought is that any attempt at a comprehensive account of the historical process must issue in an ethnocentric celebration of the transcendent virtues of Western civilization. I dispute this claim, seeking to establish that there are respects in which it is legitimate to talk about progress in history, and to consider the conditions under which theory can be an instrument of liberation rather than a tool of oppression.

The issues discussed in this final chapter may serve to highlight the fact that current debates surrounding history – both the discourse and its real object – are of more than purely intellectual import. A host of contradictory images and associations are today bound up with the idea of history. The convergence of narrativism and postmodernism represented by White's work can be seen as a continuation of the tradition which, as he himself puts it,

> from Valéry and Heidegger to Sartre, Lévi-Strauss, and Michel Foucault – [has] ... cast serious doubts on the value of a specifically 'historical' consciousness, stressing the fictive character of historical reconstructions, and challenged history's claims to a place among the sciences.[22]

The origins of this tradition lie, of course, in Nietzsche's essay 'On the Uses and Disadvantages of History for Life' (1874) and its great polemic against Hegel's philosophy of history and the German historical school for inculcating 'that admiration for the "power of history" which in practice transforms every moment into a naked admiration for success and leads to an idolatry of the factual'.[23]

Nietzsche's championing of 'the unhistorical and the suprahistorical', 'the natural antidotes to the stifling of life by the historical', has many contemporary exemplars, most obviously in the various forms of postmodernism which derive ultimately from his critique of modernity.[24] Others with different intellectual antecedents argue that behind the various contemporary appeals to history lies the same fear of change, the same flight into the past to escape the challenges of the present.[25] But the uses of history seem too diverse all to be characterized in this way. There are indeed plenty of cases where the study of the past is used for conservative political and ideological purposes: a good example is provided by the attempts of the Tory government in Britain to make the teaching of history in schools under the national curriculum a celebration of Britain's past greatness. More generally, the appeals made by the right on both sides of the Atlantic to 'family values' are intended to help rebuild their popular support by conjuring up the image of an organic society in which everyone had their place and evils such as street crime and child abuse were unknown – of a past which has been lost but may be regained by pursuing the right (in both senses of the word) policies.

Even this kind of direct political resort to nostalgic myth does not seem to me necessarily the most insidious of the present uses to which history is put. *The Pleasures of the Past* is the title of a recent collection of essays by David Cannadine, one of the best-known figures in the younger generation of British historians which is likely increasingly to assume the leadership of their profession. The phrase invites us (whether or not Cannadine intended us to respond in this way) to think of the past as something to be consumed, a luxury item perhaps, to be savoured, like a good glass of port, for its associations of high living and old-world elegance. It is not entirely surprising that Cannadine should have gone on to write a highly polemical biography of G. M. Trevelyan, which seeks to rehabilitate this historian's reputation by selecting for special praise his celebration of the unique virtues of England's historical development, his determination to write for a popular audience rather than for other academics and his efforts to preserve the English countryside.[26]

History in such usage comes to signify both a national past whose memory must be conserved and an item of consumption. Such developments as the emergence of the 'Heritage' industry in Britain are aspects of what one might call the commodification of history. Visitors to the Jorvik Centre in York see not merely an exhibition of artefacts dating from the Viking occupation of the city, but simulations of how people then lived. At Roaring Camp Railway near Santa Cruz in northern California one can spend a delightful day being pulled along through redwoods by an old steam locomotive; the climax of the trip comes when the train is held up by robbers whose outfits betray an effort meticulously to reconstruct the old West. History seems sometimes to become the raw material for a myriad of theme parks, fuel for the leisure industry. And what is one to make of the fact that there are now over ninety Holocaust museums in the United States? Do they represent an entirely appropriate attempt to keep alive the memory of an unspeakable crime, or the point at which even the artefacts of genocide become so many consumables?

It would be too easy – and, ultimately, elitist – to lapse into a disdainful dismissal of all popular interest in history as instances of a commercially driven transformation of the past into entertainment. Thus take the substantial non-specialist audience which exists for serious historical writing, shown, for example, by the success of journals like *History Today*, and by the existence of various history book clubs. The commodification of history is undeniably at work here. After all, modern techniques of photographic reproduction have transformed the history book from the dusty, closely printed, multi-volume work typical of nineteenth-century historical texts into an object that is aesthetically pleasing to handle and read. Schama's *Citizens*, Cannadine's *The Decline and Fall of the British Aristocracy*, even Braudel's avowedly non-narrative *Capitalism and Civilization* are all works whose claim to reproduce the past rests not simply on the accounts they give but on their lavish illustrations. But it is surely not simply this kind of *plaisir du texte*, or indeed that which, as its defenders stress, was always provided by traditional narrative historiography, which provides historians with their non-specialist readership. [27]

The connection between understanding the past and making the present intelligible has always been a strong one. *Historia magistra vitae* – history the teacher of life – said Cicero, and while modern historical discourse constituted itself in part by abandoning this pragmatic conception of its task, it has never fully broken the connection between knowing the past and acting in the present. [28] Thus the most politically significant recent debate among historians, the *Historikerstreit* in West Germany which broke out in the mid-1980s over what Jürgen Habermas described as 'apologetic tendencies' towards National Socialism displayed by conservative historians such as Andreas Hillgruber, Ernst Nolte and Michael Stürmer, centred on the relationship between interpretations of the Nazi past and the project of Helmut Kohl's government to rehabilitate German nationalism. [29] One striking feature of this debate was that it took place against the background of what Mary Nolan describes

as a perhaps unparalleled effervescence of interest in history [in Germany], in its most recent and troubled history. If the German fascination with *Heimat* suggests that such interest is romantic, not to say reactionary, much else testifies to a popular historical consciousness and culture that seems enviable from the perspective of Reagan's America. Thousands of high-school students enter yearly history competitions, doing projects on such themes as 'Everyday Life in the Third Reich'. The extensive grass roots history workshop movement has encouraged all sorts of local and oral history endeavours. Like its counterparts in other countries, it has taken history out of the academy and taught nonhistorians how to investigate-their own history. Local museums are thriving, and historical books and television programmes are enormously popular. The problem for the right is that all too much of this historical interest and analysis is sponsored by the left and tainted by its concerns and categories. It is unsuited to inculcate a positive and proud identity and to encourage the varied political projects of a Kohl, a Stürmer or a Hillgruber.[30]

As is suggested by the true story told by Michael Verhoeven's film *The Nasty Girl*, of how a young woman's attempt to uncover the history of her small Bavarian home town under the Third Reich brings her into conflict with the entire local establishment, this kind of popular investment of history can lead not to the worship of what Nietzsche calls 'the blind power of the actual', but to a critical confrontation with the past which has direct implications for the present.[31]

Events subsequent to the *Historikerstreit* have, of course, quite unexpectedly opened a new chapter of German history. The revolution in the German Democratic Republic in the autumn of 1989 and the state's absorption a year later into the Federal Republic have had consequences – economic collapse in the east and recession in the west, the largest-scale class conflicts for more than a generation, the emergence of the first serious fascist movements since the destruction of the Third Reich – which have revived images from Germany's terrible past. But then, developments in Germany represent one perhaps especially dramatic case of what is widely experienced as the world's – and especially Europe's – relapse since the end of the Cold War into not a New World Order but the old anarchy of fratricidal national hatreds. The wars in the Balkans and in parts of the former Soviet Union, the resurgence of the extreme right across Europe, coup and counter-coup in Moscow – all this conjures up the image, not of the End of History, but of history as the endless repetition of disaster, the 'one single catastrophe which keeps piling up wreckage after wreckage' on which, according to Walter Benjamin, the eyes of 'the angel of history' are fixed.[32] Reinhart Koselleck argues that one of the main features of the modern concept of history as it took shape in the eighteenth century was that history came to be experienced as 'acceleration', so that 'this accelerated time, i.e., our history, abbreviated the space of experiences, robbed them of their constancy, and continually brought into play new, unknown factors.'[33] The upheavals of

1989 and after suggest that this experience of history as acceleration is still part of the life-world of our times; now, however, it is likely to be interpreted not, as the *philosophes* proposed, as progress, but as a constantly revolving cycle of false hopes and real suffering.

The most appropriate reaction to history experienced in this way might seem to be that of Joyce's Stephen Dedalus, who says: 'History ... is a nightmare from which I am trying to awake.'[34] Whether this is in fact the right response, or whether even now, after all the catastrophes of the past century, there is still something to be said for the enterprise Hegel commended of seeking to discover 'the rose in the cross of the present', is ultimately the issue I seek to confront in this book.[35] Putting it as starkly as this is, of course, misleading – as if the only options were a despairing flight from history conceived as catastrophe or Hegel's secularized version of the Christian theodicy. Nevertheless, it still seems worth asking whether human reason can comprehend the historical process in whose making it is entangled. How one proceeds to address this question is not a neutral matter, and it is only right that I should make clear from the start my own predispositions, as a naturalistic realist in philosophy, a Marxist in social theory and a revolutionary socialist in politics. Naturally I have tried to construct my arguments so that they do not presuppose the beliefs on which these predispositions depend, and I therefore hope that this book will be of some use to those who share none of them. Certainly the issues with which I grapple here – how well, I leave it to the reader to decide – are ones which no one who reflects either on the nature of historical thinking or on the current state of the world can evade.

1
SYMPATHY FOR THE DEVIL? FRANCIS FUKUYAMA AND THE END OF HISTORY

Some people think the future means the end of history. Well, we haven't run out of history quite yet.

Captain James T. Kirk, in *Star Trek VI: The Undiscovered Country*

1.1 FUKUYAMA AND THE LEFT

One oddity of the debate first provoked by Francis Fukuyama's essay 'The End of History?', and then refuelled by his subsequent book *The End of History and the Last Man*, was that prominent figures on the left were among the few participants to express any sympathy with his basic argument. Fukuyama can best be understood as reviving an idea and advancing a claim. The idea is, of course, the concept of the End of History. Consider, for example, this formulation:

> an 'end of history' is implicit in the writing of all Universal Histories. The particular events of history can become meaningful only with respect to some larger end or goal, the achievement of which necessarily brings the historical process to a close. This final end of man is what makes all particular events potentially intelligible.[1]

Note that this passage implies the proposition, nowhere defended by Fukuyama, that historical explanation is necessarily teleological, and moreover teleological in the strong sense that, as the last sentence quoted asserts, it is the 'final end of man' which 'makes all particular events potentially intelligible'. All historical narrative is thus ultimately grand narrative; all historical explanation reduces to the philosophy of history. I discuss this ultra-Hegelian conception of historiography in section 1.4 below. More relevant for present purposes is the claim Fukuyama makes that this End of History, essential to making sense of the past, is now upon us, and that it takes the form of the triumph of liberal capitalism. History, on his somewhat bowdlerized version of Hegel, is the struggle of rival ideologies. The double revolution of 1989/91 – the collapse of the Stalinist regimes in Eastern Europe followed hotfoot by the disintegration of the Soviet Union – therefore amounted to the End of History, because the now defunct system of what is sometimes called 'historical Communism' – unlike other, surviving threats to the West's tranquillity such as Islamic fundamentalism and the varieties of nationalism – legitimized itself by appeal to a universalistic ideology, Marxism–Leninism. The discourse of the market economy and liberal democracy has turned out to be the final form in which aspirations potentially common to all human beings can be shared.

Now, many (perhaps most) people confronted with this claim are probably disposed to respond in much the same way as Dr Johnson famously dealt with Berkeley's idealism. Boswell tells the story:

> After we came out of the church, we stood talking for some time together of Bishop Berkeley's ingenious sophistry to prove the non-existence of matter, and that every thing in the universe is ideal. I observed, that though we are satisfied his doctrine is not true, it is impossible to refute it. I shall never forget the alacrity with which Johnson answered, striking his foot with mighty force against a large stone, till he rebounded from it, 'I refute it *thus*.'[2]

Similarly, the critic of Fukuyama might gesture at the panorama of instability that has spread across the world since 1989 and demand to know whether this really is the End of History.[3] But Fukuyama has an answer to what one might call this Johnsonian riposte to his claim: 'What I suggested had come to an end was not the occurrence of events, even large and grave events, but History: that is, history understood as a single, coherent, evolutionary process, when taking into account the experiences of all peoples at all times.'[4] This passage strongly recalls Braudel's famous dismissal of 'the history of events: surface disturbances, crests of foam that the tides of history carry on their strong backs'.[5] But can the Johnsonian riposte be so easily dismissed, when these 'crests of foam' include the massacres perpetrated by the allies' warplanes during the Gulf War, ethnic cleansing in Bosnia and Croatia, and the murder of Turkish women by German neo-Nazis? It was against a Hegelian theodicy which sought to explain away 'events' of this kind that Adorno sought to vindicate 'nonconceptuality, individuality, and particularity' as 'the matters of real philosophical interest at this point in history'.[6] Similarly, Lyotard's objection to '[t]he "philosophies of history" that inspired the nineteenth and twentieth centuries' is precisely that they 'claim to assure passages over the abyss of heterogeneity or of the event. The names which are those of "our history" oppose counter-examples to their claim' – names like 'Auschwitz', which refuted Hegel, 'Budapest 1956', which refuted Marxism, 'May 1968', which refuted liberalism.[7]

It is in large part just because, in defiance of such claims, Fukuyama seeks to rehabilitate the tradition of grand narratives that he enjoyed a remarkably sympathetic reception from a number of leading British left intellectuals – notably Perry Anderson, Gregory Elliott, Fred Halliday and Joseph McCarney.[8] They responded, that is, to what they saw as the presence, which various of Fukuyama's critics on the right also claimed to have detected, of what Anderson calls 'an inverted Marxism' in his theory.[9] The ineffable Bernard-Henri Levy, prince of the Parisian *nouveaux Philosophes*, even denounced Fukuyama as the 'Last Marxist'; similar charges were made by various British commentators.[10] Thus, as Elliott puts it, Fukuyama is, as Blake said of Milton, 'of the Devil's party without knowing it' – that is, he is engaged in the same kind of intellectual project as Marxists, namely the formulation of a comprehensive account of history as a process of development.[11] From this perspective the defect of Fukuyama's theory is not that it seeks to construct a grand narrative but the idealist account it offers of the sources of historical change. Thus, Halliday concludes, '[t]he problem with Fukuyama's theory, and his account of history, is fundamentally the same as that of Hegel himself. There is, of course, a classical solution to this problem: to do to Fukuyama what Feuerbach did to Hegel, namely to turn him on his head.'[12]

There is, moreover, another reason why Anderson, Elliott and Halliday all responded so sympathetically to Fukuyama: they agreed with him on the key empirical issue. That is, they accepted his claim that capitalism has successfully taken on and beaten socialism. (McCarney's position, as we shall see in section 1.3 below, is considerably more complex, since he disputes that this is Fukuyama's claim.) Thus Halliday praises Fukuyama for understanding that, contrary to 'much left and liberal discourse in the West', the Cold War was 'an intersystemic conflict'.[13] Behind this assertion lies Isaac Deutscher's analysis – taken over by *New Left Review* (which Anderson edited for over twenty years) and developed especially by Halliday – of the Cold War as a 'Great Contest' between rival modes of production, capitalism and 'historical Communism', in which the Western left should give critical support to the Soviet bloc. The inference to be drawn from 1989 and 1991 on this view is that capitalism has won the Great Contest.

It is from a similar standpoint that Anderson dismisses Fuku-yama's Johnsonian critics: 'No reply to Fukuyama is of any avail, ... if it contents itself with pointing out problems that remain within the world he predicts. An effective critique must be able to show that there are powerful systemic alternatives he has dis-counted.'[14] And Anderson makes it clear in what follows that he believes it to be a moot point whether socialism, traditionally the most important of these alternatives, has any future. Elliott is more explicit:

> With the destruction of actually existing socialism – the eradication of the Second World and its ongoing integration into the First – we are witnessing the elimination, possibly only temporary, of socialism as a world-historical move-ment ... relative to the projections of classical Marxism, socialism is utopian once again: a desirable future con-fronting an unamenable present.[15]

Now, I believe that both the reasons behind these left-wing intel-lectuals' favourable response to Fukuyama – that he is practis-ing (if this isn't an oxymoron) an idealist version of historical materialism, and that he is right to see in 1989/91 the triumph of capitalism – are highly disputable. The bulk of this chapter is devoted to considering Fukuyama's alleged Hegelianism, but first I wish briefly to dispose of the second of the reasons just men-tioned. I offer, in partial excuse for this brevity, the fact that this is a subject I have discussed at much greater length elsewhere.[16]

The fundamental difficulty here is that to equate the collapse of Stalinism with the triumph of capitalism is to presume that the former embodied a social system other than capitalism. Such, surely, is the burden of formulations like 'actually existing socialism' and 'historical Communism': imperfect in many respects though they were, these phrases seem to imply, the Soviet Union and its counterparts did represent a major and at least temporarily successful attempt to transcend the defects Marx long ago identified as inherent in capitalism – above all, class inequality and economic anarchy. The trouble is that the falsehood of this claim is all too demonstrable empirically. Not only did the Stalinist societies fail, over the full sixty-year span of their existence, to meet the criterion of historical progress specified by Marxism (a distorted and vulgarized version of which was, of course, these societies' ruling ideology) – that is, they were unable to develop the productive forces faster than their Western rivals – but their internal relations took the opposite form to that envisaged by Marx when he sought to imagine the lineaments of a socialist society; far from basing itself on the direct exercise of power by the masses through a network of institutions of democratic self-government, 'existing socialism' involved an unprecedented centralization of power – economic, political and cultural – in the hands of the *nomenklatura*, as the ruling class of top bureaucrats and managers was known.

The conclusion that the Soviet Union and its like constituted no kind of socialism but some sort of class society seems unavoidable. But what sort of class society? Some contemporary Marxists, such as Robert Brenner and Eero Loone, claim that it was 'a new formation', 'the bureaucratic mode of production'.[17] Their main grounds for doing so are the failure of the Stalinist states to develop the productive forces as intensively as Western capitalism has. But this involves a strained reading of the empirical evidence: the Soviet Union's ultimate economic collapse should not obscure the fact that between the 1930s and the 1960s it attained rates of growth which allowed it to build up a military establishment comparable to that of the far larger and stronger US economy, and to increase living standards through much of the Brezhnevite 'era of stagnation' (1964–82). A better interpretation of the phenomenon of Stalinism than one which in effect places it in the category of the precapitalist modes of production (whose distinguishing feature, according to Brenner, is that they are unable intensively to increase the productive forces) is to see it as an instance of a particular variant of capitalism, what Tony Cliff calls bureaucratic state capitalism. Here it is the *nomenklatura* which through its collective control of the means of production assumes the function of capital, exploiting wage labour in a particularly stark and brutal fashion; the pressure to accumulate which Marx identified as the driving force of capitalism is provided by competition, not in the domestic market, but on a world scale, in the shape of the military rivalries between the Soviet Union and the Western bloc, which compelled the *nomenklatura* to give priority in the allocation of resources to the heavy industries directly or indirectly supplying the armed forces.[18]

One virtue of this way of thinking about Stalinism is that it sets it in a context broader than that of the contingencies of the October Revolution and its outcome and more historical than that implied by the ineluctable logic of totalitarianism at the centre of most Western (and now Russian) analyses. For the 1930s – the decisive period of the construction of Stalinism as a social system characterized by the centralization of power in the hands of the *nomenklatura* and the consolidation of a bureaucratic command economy – saw a general trend in the advanced economies towards militarized state capitalism. The emergence under National Socialism of a substantial state-controlled sector of the economy, centred on the Four-Year Plan and the *Reichswerke* and directed by the priorities of military expansion, is the clearest example of this trend outside the Soviet Union.[19] The fragmentation of the world market into rival protectionist blocs during the Great Depression, however, encouraged all the Great Powers to exert greater control over their economies: the New Deal in the United States and even the National Government in Britain are witnesses to this process. Against this background, the formation of Stalinism seems much less a totalitarian aberration, or an idiosyncratic Russian lapse into primitivism, and much more an extreme case of a universal tendency. Correlatively, the collapse of the Stalinist regimes sixty years later becomes much easier to understand from this perspective. By the 1980s the norm of international capitalism had become not national autarky but global integration through trade and investment; the Soviet Union and its allies had by this stage truly become a backwater of the world economy, unable because of their high degree of national organization to achieve the increases in labour productivity which now depended on participation in global markets.[20]

However well or ill this argument may stand up as historical interpretation and economic analysis, it does at least have the advantage of avoiding the kind of apologetics for Stalinism into which Fukuyama's left-wing sympathizers risk lapsing. It is Elliott who seems least resistant to this danger. He praises 'historical Communism' for three crucial achievements: 'the resistance to, and defeat of, European fascism', 'the subsequent emergence of the Third World and its protection thereafter' from a Western imperialism restrained by the support given by the Soviet bloc to national liberation movements; and 'the meliorist reconstruction of Europe – counter-cyclical economic regulation, full employment, welfare services, universal suffrage, etc. – after Liberation' under pressure from the Soviet Union and its Communist sympathizers in the West.[21] These claims raise historical issues which cannot properly be addressed here. Suffice it to say that Elliott's is a very strained reading of the facts: one which treats the Second World War as a conflict in which traditional Great Power interests in military security and territorial and economic expansion apparently did not prevail in a regime which in August 1939 was prepared to sign a non-aggression pact with Berlin; one which ignores the manner in which these interests led Moscow to support Third World nationalism highly selectively after 1945, cautiously backing China and Vietnam, for example, but underwriting Ethiopia's military rulers in their efforts to deny Eritrea independence; and one which seems to discount the role of domestic working-class movements (in which, in northern Europe, Communist influence was at best limited, and often marginal) in forcing the concession of the social reforms which came to be known as the postwar settlement. Elliott suggests that the proper attitude to adopt to the world since 1989 is that recommended by Isaac Deutscher in 1950 to 'the intellectual ex-Communist' – 'to rise *au-dessus de la mêlée*', to 'withdraw into a *watchtower*', and 'watch with detachment and alertness this heaving chaos of a world'.[22] But, in the absence even of what Deutscher regarded as the main force for progress amid this chaos – the Stalinist societies – it is hard to see how this stance differs from the elitist pessimism which, as we shall see, is Fukuyama's real view on things.

The fact remains, however, that the interpretation of Stalinism set out above only partially meets the challenge Anderson offered to Fukuyama's Johnsonian critics. If successful, this interpretation shows that 'existing socialism' was, in Anderson's words, 'a particularly degenerate form of capitalism'.[23] Liberal capitalism therefore triumphed, not over 'historical Communism', but over one of its own, now backward, variants; but it may still be the case that the future belongs to capitalism. I do not believe this, for reasons which I, and others, have sought to offer at some length elsewhere.[24] The future of capitalism is not, however, the focus of this book, although I discuss matters relevant to this subject in chapters 3 and 4 below. For the present, however, I wish to concentrate on the presuppositions of Fukuyama's argument that the future is capitalism.

1.2   KOJÈVE: FROM HEGEL TO STALIN

Fukuyama is claimed by Elliott for 'the Devil's party'. Elliot has in mind, presumably, a dialectical demon, Goethe's Mephistopheles, 'The spirit I, that endlessly denies. / And rightly too; for all that comes to birth / Is fit for overthrow, as nothing worth', the 'power that would / Alone work evil, but engenders good.'[25] In other words, Fukuyama's theory must be seen as a reprise of Hegel's philosophy of history. Yet it is easy to demonstrate that his Hegelianism is of a peculiarly diluted – indeed, distorted – character.

Fukuyama's Hegelianism is in fact derived not directly from Hegel himself, but via Alexandre Kojève. Indeed, at one point he explicitly acknowledges that his references to Hegel are actually to 'Hegel–Kojève'.[26] Kojève's *Introduction to the Reading of Hegel* (1947), a collection of lectures he gave in Paris during the 1930s, is the masterwork of what one might call the third wave of left Hegelianism (the first came, of course, in Germany in the 1840s; the second was produced by the impact between the wars of Lukács's *History and Class Consciousness*), which swept Paris in mid-century. Among its luminaries were Lacan, whose analysis of desire is profoundly influenced by Kojève's version of the dialectic of Master and Slave, Sartre and, it now appears, the young Althusser.[27]

Kojève's interpretation of Hegel is distinguished by the interplay it introduces between *Being and Time* and the *Phenomenology of Spirit*. Kojève says that Heidegger's 'phenomenological anthropology ... adds, fundamentally, nothing new to the anthropology of the *Phenomenology* (which, by the way, would probably never have been understood if Heidegger had not published his book).'[28] This rather paradoxical assertion does at least have the merit of underlining Heidegger's influence on Kojève. The *Introduction* emerged, however, from a more complex theoretico-political field than that involved merely in rereading Hegel through a Heideggerian grid, as we shall see. Lutz Niethammer observes:

if he [Kojève] fascinated his listeners so deeply with his austere material, it was because he brought to Hegel's text a version of Marxism, an anthropological reduction drawn from Heidegger, and an updating of history, the final interpretation being as bold as it was elegant.[29]

The shadow of Heideggerian Being-towards-death undoubtedly hangs over Kojève's version of the historical process. This assumes the form of the dialectic of Master and Slave in chapter IV of the *Phenomenology* (or, perhaps better, of Kojève's reconstruction of this dialectic).[30] Brutally summarized, this is based on the thesis that self-consciousness requires intersubjective recognition, which is only fully achieved if won at the risk of one's own life. History thus starts with the 'fight to death for pure prestige'. The Master is he who emerges from the fight victorious, the Slave he for whom his life proved more important than recognition. (The masculine pronouns here accord perfectly with Kojève's view of history.) Here, however, immediately emerge the limits of the Master's victory, since he has triumphed over someone whose 'human dignity and reality' he does not acknowledge. 'Hence he is recognized by someone he does not recognize.' Moreover, the Master depends on the Slave's work to live. But it is through labour that the Slave transforms both the world and himself. 'Laborious slavery' thus 'is the source of all human, social, historical progress'. The culmination of this progress is the abolition of the very distinction between Master and Slave in a suitably Hegelian *Aufhebung*: 'History will be completed at the moment when the synthesis of the Master and the Slave is realized, that synthesis that is the whole Man, the citizen of the universal and homogeneous State created by Napoleon.'[31]

Now, there are three ways in which one may register the distance separating Kojève from Hegel. First, as Jean Hyppolite pointed out at the time, Kojève offers an anthropological version of the dialectic.[32] That is, like all left Hegelians, he gives a reading of Hegel which privileges the *Phenomenology* (David Strauss called it 'the alpha and omega of Hegel's works'), the major text most easily assimilable to an interpretation of the dialectic as the process through which forms of human consciousness succeed one another, and plays down, or seeks to read metaphorically, Hegel's Platonism, his insistence on understanding the historical process as the embodiment of a concept – or, rather, *the* Concept, the Absolute Idea – whose meaning transcends and explains it.[33]

This anthropological misreading of Hegel has one effect of immediate relevance to the subject under discussion: it obscures the fact that Hegel shows no interest in the idea of the End of History, at least as it is understood by Kojève and Fukuyama. The Absolute does not achieve self-realization in history, which is part of the sphere of Objective Spirit, of human social life, but beyond it, in the realm of Absolute Spirit, whose culmination is in philosophy. Thus historical knowledge is a form of applied knowledge, which rests on the '*presupposition*' that 'reason governs the world, and that world history is therefore a rational process', a presupposition that has been '*proved* in philosophy by speculative cognition':

> That world history is governed by an ultimate design, that it is a rational process – whose rationality is not that of a particular subject, but a divine and absolute reason – this is a proposition whose truth we must assume; its proof lies in the study of world history itself, which is the image and enactment of reason. The real proof, however, comes from a knowledge of reason itself; for reason appears in world history only in a mediate form.[34]

Philosophy itself, whose results we must presuppose in interpreting world history, only renders explicit what was already the case, implicit in the structures of Logic, 'the Realm of Pure Thought', whose content '*shows forth God as he is in his eternal essence before the creation of Nature and of a Finite Spirit*'.[35] Hegel draws out a corollary of his overall conception of the dialectic when discussing the category of End in the *Lesser Logic*:

> Within the range of the finite we can never see or experience that the End has been secured. The consummation of the infinite End, therefore, consists merely in removing the illusion which makes it seem yet unaccomplished. The Good, the absolutely Good, is eternally accomplishing itself in the world: and the result is that it need not wait upon us, but is already by implication, as well as in full actuality, accomplished.[36]

This is a hard saying, because it appears to conflict with Hegel's insistence that the Absolute only becomes fully actual through a process of development which brings to articulated consciousness what has been implicit from the start. As Hyppolite puts it, '[i]t is one of the originalities of Hegel's *Phenomenology* to justify idealism by history.'[37] And indeed Hegel makes it clear that the emergence and development of philosophy, the form of consciousness proper to Absolute Knowledge, have historical preconditions. Thus '[p]hilosophy only appears in History where and in as far as free institutions are formed,' since it is only where human beings become aware of their essential freedom that thought can acquire the autonomy required to focus on its proper object, itself; philosophy, 'the thinking of thinking', therefore originates in the Greek city-states.[38]

But if the Absolute comes to self-consciousness in time, this process is one of liberation *from* time:

> Spirit necessarily appears in Time, and it appears in Time just so long as it has not *grasped* its pure Notion, i.e. has not annulled Time. It is the *outer*, intuited pure Self which is *not grasped* by the Self, the merely intuited Notion; ... Time, therefore, appears as the destiny and necessity of Spirit that is not yet complete within itself, the necessity to enrich the share which self-consciousness has in consciousness, to set in motion the *immediacy of the in-itself*, which is the form in which substance is present in consciousness; or, conversely, to realize and reveal what is at first only *inward* (the in-itself taken as what is *inward*), i.e. to vindicate it for Spirit's certainty of itself.[39]

Gérard Lebrun comments on this passage:

> Thus the presence of time measures the long error which Spirit committed on itself, even while it realized itself: the condition of its effectual development was also the symptom of its lack of self-consciousness. From which one understands that Spirit only becomes a historian [*se fait historien*] to obtain the guarantee of no longer having to be one; if it recuperates lost time, it is because it no longer confuses itself with representative consciousness ... and because the Concept as 'the power over time' (*Encyclopaedia*, §258) has suppressed the envelope which dissimulated it.[40]

Therefore Alan Ryan goes badly astray when he asserts: 'For Hegel, as for Kant before him and Marx after him, History was a finite process, preceded and followed by a condition that was not strictly part of history as well.'[41] Putting it like this suggests that the attainment of Absolute Knowledge brings history to a halt. But history for Hegel, as a succession of events in time, can only be a case of what he calls 'bad infinity', an endless series of presents. These events are only of significance inasmuch as they participate in 'the progress of the consciousness of freedom', which, in turn, as we have seen, is of interest chiefly because it provides the historical presuppositions for the development of Absolute Knowledge in philosophy. The philosopher, therefore, need only 'take up history at that point where rationality begins to manifest itself in worldly existence – i.e. not where it is still a potentiality *in itself* but when it is in a position to express itself in consciousness, volition, and action', a condition which for Hegel commences with the articulation and co-ordination of individual wills in the institutional structure of the state. Societies without a state are therefore outside history. Thus 'history is in fact out of the question' in sub-Saharan Africa, where human existence is but 'a succession of contingent happenings and surprises'.[42] Is this what history will revert back to once the Absolute attains self-consciousness? The question is an irrelevant one for Hegel, since Absolute Knowledge itself consists in thought's liberation from the 'picture-thinking' or 'representational consciousness' which conceives of reality as 'a succession of contingent happenings' undergone by finite beings, and its comprehension of these events and entities as manifestations of an Absolute which, Hegel says, 'transcends time'.[43]

The End of History for Hegel therefore lies beyond history. Just because he has bigger fish to fry he can afford to be rather vague about the outcome of the historical process whose inner meaning he claims to have deciphered. Anderson makes the same point more elegantly: 'Because Hegel's system closes itself beyond the empirical world, although the course of history is subject to the movement of the spirit, its upshot need not to be as conclusive – the drop in the level of vision allows for less resolution in the image.'[44] Anderson illustrates the point by highlighting the uncertainties and hesitations in Hegel's treatment of the modern state and civil society in *The Philosophy of Right*. There are other examples. One is the extraordinarily casual way in which Hegel introduces America in *The Philosophy of History* as 'the country of the future', which will 'abandon the ground on which world history has hitherto been enacted', without giving any indication of the implications this might have for his conception of world history, with its three main stages – Asiatic despotism, Graeco-Roman antiquity, and the modern Germanic state-system.[45]

The underlying theme of this conception of world history constitutes the second respect in which Hegel differs from Kojève. As McCarney points out, '[f]or Hegel history is emphatically not to be characterized as a struggle for recognition. It is rather "the progress of the consciousness of freedom".'[46] But then, freedom doesn't figure much in Kojève's version of the dialectic of history. This lack of interest in freedom must be seen in relation to Kojève's Stalinist politics, which he was prepared sometimes openly to avow. Roger Callois reports a celebrated lecture Kojève gave in Paris in December 1937: 'Kojève told us that day that Hegel had seen something correct but had miscalculated by a century: the man of the end of history was not Napoleon but Stalin.'[47]

After the Second World War Kojève did not cease to view Stalin as Hegel had seen Napoleon, as the World Spirit on horseback (or perhaps better, as Yann Moulier Boutang suggests, mounted on a tank).[48] Indeed, he sought to provide a stronger theoretical rationale for his position. In his celebrated critique of Leo Strauss's *On Tyranny* Kojève asks 'whether, in certain cases, renouncing "tyranny" would not be tantamount to renouncing government altogether, and whether that would not entail either the ruin of the State, or abandoning any real prospect of progress in a particular State or for the whole of mankind (at least in a given historical moment)'.[49]

Kojève goes on to refer to 'the tyrant who here initiates the *real* political movement towards universal homogeneity by consciously following the teaching of the intellectual who deliberately transformed the idea of the philosopher so that it might cease to be a "utopian" ideal'. Any doubt that the 'progressive tyrant' Kojève has in mind here is Stalin is removed when he says: 'Thus, while recognizing that the tyrant has "falsified" the philosophical idea, we know that he has done so only to "transpose" it from the realm of abstraction to that of reality.'[50] Kojève's disparaging reference in the *Introduction* to 'the Revolutionary who dreams of a "permanent revolution"' gives a clear idea of who he thinks might accuse the tyrant of having 'falsified' Marx's 'philosophical idea'.[51] The differences in their attitudes to Trotsky aside, Kojève is here remarkably close to Deutscher, who at much the same time, at the end of the Second World War, was developing an interpretation of Stalin as one of the 'great revolutionary despots', like Cromwell, Robespierre and Napoeleon an unconscious instrument of historical progress.[52]

Here at any rate Kojève is thoroughly Hegelian: his treatment
of Stalin recalls Hegel's conception of 'the great individuals of
history' as 'the instruments of the substantial spirit', and implies
a view of history as an objective process which, thanks to 'the
cunning of reason' realizes its aims through human actors un-
aware that their subjective schemes are fulfilling deeper purposes.[53]
Thus Kojève saw the cunning of reason at work in the Cold War:

> Historical action necessarily leads to a specific result ...,
> but the ways that lead to this result are varied (all roads
> lead to Rome!) ... For example, if the Westerners remain
> capitalist (that is also to say nationalist), they will be de-
> feated by Russia, and *that* is how the End-State will come
> about. If, however, they 'integrate' their economies and
> policies (they are in the way to doing so) then *they* can
> defeat Russia. And *that* is how the End-State will be reached
> (the *same* universal and homogeneous State).[54]

This helps to explain why Kojève turned from philosophy
to bureaucracy after the war, and helped to found the European
Economic Community; by doing so he was promoting the onward
march of world history towards its conclusion. His belief that
'all roads lead to Rome' – that different paths lead 'necessarily'
to the same 'End-State' – also throws light on the famous Note
to the second edition of the *Introduction*, added in 1960, where
Kojève asserts that, 'from a certain point of view, the United
States has already attained the final stage of Marxist "communism".'[55] If the End of History is going to happen anyway,
why worry too much about the precise socio-political form it
will take?

Kojève's relative indifference to political forms highlights the
third respect in which he differs from Hegel, one which Fukuyama
himself notices. Hegel conceives the political state as an articulated and differentiated structure that provides a framework in
which the conflicts endemic to civil society can be contained and
reconciled. By contrast, Fukuyama observes, 'Kojève's universal
and homogeneous state makes no room for "mediating" bodies
like corporations or *Stande* [Estates]; the very adjectives Kojève
uses to describe his end state suggest a more Marxist version of a
society where there is nothing between free, equal, and atomized
individuals and the state.'[56]

This is a travesty of Marx's conception of communist society,
one of whose main characteristics is the *abolition* of the state,

not the subjection of 'atomized individuals' to it.[57] It is nevertheless true that Kojève is interested less in the political structures of the 'universal and homogeneous State' than in its social
content. Thus he says at one point: ' "homogeneous" here means
free from internal contradictions: free from class strife and so
on.'[58] For Hegel, however, the political state arises from, but
does not abolish, a civil society whose rule by particularity, by
the pursuit of private interest, is intrinsically liable to generate
poverty, crises and class conflict:

> The essence of the modern state is that the universal should
> be linked with the complete freedom of particularity and
> the well-being of individuals, and hence that the interests of
> the family and of civil society must become focused on the
> state: but the universality of the end cannot make further
> progress without the personal knowledge and volition of the
> particular individuals, who must retain their rights. Thus,
> the universal must be activated, but subjectivity on the other
> hand must be developed as a living whole. Only when both
> moments are present in full measure can the state be re-
> garded as fully organized.[59]

Elliott is therefore wrong to say that 'Hegel, let alone Kojève,
was – dialectically – *anti-liberal*, rejecting the social contrac-
tarianism and individualist pluralism of the classical liberal tradition.'[60] This description may be true of Kojève, but Hegel was
concerned rather to find a place for what he regarded as the
rational basis of the liberal tradition – 'the complete freedom of
particularity and the well-being of individuals' – within a state
whose control by a disinterested bureaucracy would prevent it
from becoming the tool of rival classes. Hegel's friend Victor
Cousin called him 'profoundly liberal without being the least
bit republican'.[61] This characterization seems just about right,
placing Hegel as it does in the camp of moderate liberalism,
midway between those of Legitimist reaction and Jacobin revolution. In this respect, at least, Fukuyama is closer than Kojève
to Hegel when he claims that liberal capitalism will conclude
the historical process by according to all the universal recognition institutionalized in the formal equalities of representative
democracy. He makes clear that this universal recognition is
consistent with social inequality, though this 'will increasingly be
attributable to the natural inequality of talents, the economically
necessary division of labour and to culture'.[62]

1.3 FUKUYAMA: FROM SPENGLER TO REAGAN

Nevertheless, Fukuyama's philosophy of history is even further removed from Hegel's than is Kojève's. The distance is made most obvious when Fukuyama seeks to ground his version of the historical dialectic in a theory of human nature. He claims: 'It would appear impossible to talk about "history", much less a "Universal History", without reference to a permanent, trans-historical standard, i.e., without reference to nature.' Thus he seeks to derive the Kojèvian struggle for recognition from Plato's concept of *thymos*, or spiritedness, that portion of the soul inter-mediate between the appetites and reason, which he calls 'the psychological seat of Hegel's desire for recognition'. Recognition, in turn, is 'the central problem of politics because it is the origin of tyranny, imperialism, and the desire to dominate'.[63]

Plainly this appeal to a psychology of faculties is very different from Kojève's treatment of the struggle for recognition as a kind of transcendental presupposition of self-consciousness. Using Plato's theory of the soul to found a 'Universal History' is, moreover, a world away from Hegel, who accords the concept of human nature only a subordinate place in his system. It is only when he comes to consider civil society, the 'system of needs' analysed by the classical economists, that Hegel introduces the concept of '*the human being*', but he is quick to make it clear that this is a 'concretum of *representative thought*', of the kind of picture thinking transcended by genuinely speculative reason, and that the pursuit by self-seeking individuals of particular ends provides 'the first, and in fact the only occasion when we shall refer to the *human being* in this sense'.[64] Kojève exceeds Hegel in his hostility to the idea of 'a "given" or "innate" human nature'. Arguably he is inconsistent here. Hegel's anti-humanism follows from his conception of reality as a dialectical process whose subject, the Absolute, is not a person but a relationship somehow identical to the process itself. But Kojève, as we have seen, anthropologizes the dialectic, so that it becomes a historical drama whose subject is Man. It is hard to see how one can sustain this kind of theory without making some generalizations about human beings (as Marx does when he develops a quasi-Hegelian anthropology in the Paris *Manuscripts*). The tensions in Kojève's appropriation of Hegel are indicated elsewhere as well: for example, consistent with his project of anthropologizing the dialectic, he repudiates any attempt to see the categories of

Hegel's *Logic* at work in nature, but at the same time he sticks to one of that book's most speculative themes – namely, the account Hegel gives there of the dialectic as describing a circle, so that the ultimate development of the process returns to, and vindicates (and is vindicated by) its starting point.[65]

Whatever the inconsistencies in Kojève's Hegelianism, he does conceive the dialectic (albeit confined to history) as a unitary process: 'We know that the *real* Dialectic (History) progresses by the negation which is implied by Man's Fighting and Work.'[66] Fukuyama's resort to an account of human nature, by contrast, produces a dualistic theory of history in which the motor of change is provided by two forces: need-driven instrumental rationality, embodied in the logic of 'modern natural science', and 'the struggle for recognition'. 'Fighting and Work' – wars, revolutions, and other forms of political conflict, on the one hand, and the transformation of nature, on the other – are separated out and essentialized into two distinct, potentially conflicting factors, the latter leading to the economic triumph of capitalism, the former (though more equivocally) to the universalization of liberal democracy.[67]

This dualistic theory of history must be set in the context of Kojève's debate with Strauss – not only publicly, over the latter's *On Tyranny*, but in a lengthy private correspondence spanning more than thirty years. It might seem odd that a left-Hegelian Stalinist should have engaged so continuously with one of the century's principal conservative philosophers, but their regard for each other is unquestionable. Strauss, for example, assured Kojève that he was 'one of the three people who will have a full understanding of what I am driving at'.[68] They seem to have shared, despite their profound political and intellectual differences, a conception of philosophical knowledge as an esoteric form of wisdom. In 1967 Kojève told leading student radicals in Berlin to learn Greek and then went to see one of the key intellectual figures of the twentieth-century German right, the legal and political theorist Carl Schmitt, 'the only person in Germany with whom he considered it worthwhile to enter into dialogue'.[69]

The debate between Strauss and Kojève undeniably played a formative role in shaping the intellectual context of Fukuyama's book. Joe McCarney has highlighted the importance in this regard of Harold Bloom, Strauss's pupil, Kojève's acquaintance (and the editor of the English translation of the *Introduction*) and Fukuyama's teacher. 'Indeed,' McCarney suggests, 'Fukuyama's book can plausibly be read as the record of a struggle for his

soul between Kojève and Strauss.'[70] One could go further and argue
that the outcome of this struggle is an attempted fusion of two
very different philosophical perspectives. Such an interpretation –
Fukuyama's theory as an uneasy synthesis of Kojève and Strauss
– may help to explain the dualistic character of his account of
the dynamics of historical change.

McCarney indeed detects in Fukuyama's book a Straussian
'esoteric meaning': its 'true meaning' is that liberal democracy 'is
itself a transitory historical form, the process of whose dissolution is already well advanced'. The evidence for this conclusion,
'inescapably grounded in the logic of the argument', is provided,
for example, in Fukuyama's worry that advanced capitalism may
turn out still to depend on *thymos* in ways which liberal democracy is unable to achieve – hence the threat he sees presented to
the United States and Western Europe by the more authoritarian,
less atomized capitalisms in East Asia – and his prediction that
the main internal threat to the Western bourgeois democracies
is likely to come from their incapacity to contain *megalothymia*,
the desire to be recognized as a superior rather than an equal.[71]

McCarney's interpretation is an ingenious and carefully argued
example of internal critique, that is, of exploiting the inconsistencies in a theorist's discourse to draw conclusions directly
opposed to those at which she wishes to arrive. Thus he praises
Fukuyama's acknowledgement of these strains within liberal
capitalism:

> His retreat may be seen from one point of view as a tribute
> to his realism and sensitivity to a range of conflicting con-
> siderations. Yet it shows also his curious tendency to register
> them by simply incorporating the alternatives into the text,
> so that they lie down side by side without any movement
> of integration or mediation. Thus the thin consistency of
> Kojève is replaced by a richer incoherence.[72]

It is not clear, however, that we need to explain this incoherence
by making Fukuyama a secret dialectical critic of capitalism:
thus the absence of 'any movement of integration or mediation'
between 'conflicting considerations' which McCarney notes seems
closely related to the more general dualism which structures
Fukuyama's theory of history. This is an undoubted weakness in
Fukuyama's overall argument, since he gives no account of the
relative importance of the two driving forces he identifies –
instrumental rationality and recognition – or of their principal

forms of interaction. The work of criticism does not have to go any further than this: so strategic a weakness may simply be regarded as a sign of an inherently defective theory. If we do want to go further, and trace the tensions in Fukuyama's theory to the presence of two souls – Strauss's and Kojève's – within his breast, then the kind of critique of capitalism we discover is one very different from that issuing from the Hegelian–Marxist tradition for which McCarney, dialectic in hand, wishes to claim him.

Thus consider Fukuyama on the threat posed to liberal capitalism by *megalothymia*:

> does the granting of liberal rights by itself constitute the fulfilment of that great desire that leads the aristocratic master to risk death? And even if many people were satisfied by this humblest sort of recognition [i.e. liberal equality], would it be more satisfying for the few who have more ambitious natures? If everyone was *fully content* merely by virtue of having rights in a democratic society, with no further aspirations beyond citizenship, would we not find them worthy of contempt?[73]

By treating these considerations as a 'more powerful criticism of [liberal] universal recognition' than the Marxist critique of capitalism, Fukuyama places himself (as he acknowledges) within the tradition of the aristocratic critique of modernity whose greatest figure is Nietzsche. Indeed, the theme of the 'Last Man' highlighted in the title of Fukuyama's book derives directly from the Prologue to *Thus Spoke Zarathustra*:

> 'The earth has become small and upon it hops the Last Man, who makes everything small ...
>
> ' "We have discovered happiness," say the Last Men and blink ...
>
> 'They still work, for work is entertainment. But they take care the entertainment does not exhaust them.
>
> 'Nobody grows rich or poor any more: both are too much of a burden. Who still wants to rule? Who obey? Both are too much of a burden.
>
> 'No herdsman and one herd. Everyone wants the same thing, everyone is the same: whoever thinks otherwise goes voluntarily to the madhouse.'[74]

Fukuyama does not, however, acknowledge that it was Strauss who first linked the Nietzschean theme of the Last Man to the left-Hegelian idea of the End of History. Strauss wrote to Kojève: 'I am not convinced that the End of History as you describe it can be either the rational or the merely-factual satisfaction of human beings. For the sake of simplicity today I refer to Nietzsche's "last men".' In their public debate Strauss goes further, arguing that the End-State is 'the state in which the basis of man's humanity withers away, or in which man loses his humanity. It is the state of Nietzsche's "last man".' He predicts a 'nihilistic revolution' in which the men who desire to be Masters 'revolt against a state which is destructive of humanity or in which there is no longer a possibility of noble action and of great deeds'.[75]

Kojève lays himself open to this line of attack by the way in which he transforms the Hegelian dialectic into 'an *existential* dialectic in the modern sense of the word', where *Being and Time* provides the benchmark of modernity. The place of Heideggerian *Dasein* in Kojève's version of the dialectic is occupied by Man, whose essence is defined (contrary to Kojève's pronouncements against the concept of human nature but as required by his anthropology) as 'Freedom which realizes itself as Action negating the given'. The main form of this negation is Work, but the Fight that leads to the struggle between Master and Slave is also part of the same process, functioning as a catalyst. But

> after the End of History Man no longer negates, properly speaking (that is, *actively*). However, Man does not become an animal, since he continues to speak ... But posthistorical Man, omniscient, all-powerful, and satisfied Man (the Wise Man) is not a Man in the strict sense of the word either: he is a 'god' (a mortal god, admittedly).[76]

Kojève does not believe that Work ceases at the End of History because human beings can now live on air, but rather that it loses its distinctive characteristic feature – namely, that of acting on 'the given real to make true a human error'. This dialectic of truth and error now comes to a close because at the end of History we arrive at the Truth, a total comprehension of reality which, because it is fully satisfying, quiets the unrest which drives human beings to seek to transform reality. Kojève later formed a less sanguine view of the 'disappearance of Man at the end of History'.[77] But this way of conceptualizing the overthrow of capitalism is, of its very nature, open to a process of displacement, in which the issue is no longer the left-Hegelian conception of communist revolution as the solution to the riddle of human existence (as the young Marx put it) and instead becomes the question of modernity's chronic failure to find a place for the aristocratic virtues.

Thus Lutz Niethammer, in a study first published in German in 1989, more or less simultaneously with Fukuyama's original article, has traced the genealogy of the concept of *Posthistoire*. He shows how it was developed in West Germany during the immediate postwar years by conservativist cultural theorists such as Arnold Gehlen as part of their critique of modern 'mass society'. The term – a German neologism despite its French sound – refers, Niethammer argues, to 'a mortal life lived without seriousness or struggle, in the regulated boredom of a perpetual reproduction of modernity on a world scale. The problematic of posthistory is not the end of the world but the end of meaning.' It thus articulates with some of the central themes explored by such key figures in the twentieth-century German intellectual right as Heidegger, Schmitt and Jünger.[78]

Although Niethammer does not express the thought explicitly, he seems to regard the concept of posthistory as part of the theoretical corpus used by conservative German intellectuals to come to terms with the failure of National Socialism (with which all four writers mentioned in the previous paragraph were more or less equivocally associated) and with the apparent triumph of liberal capitalism after 1945. The concept is, however, present in the work of a somewhat earlier theorist, though one very much part of the same intellectual and political milieu. Oswald Spengler's *The Decline of the West*, published in two volumes in 1918 and 1922 respectively, was one of the main texts of the German right between the wars (Ernst Jünger dedicated *Der Arbeiter* (1932), an important influence on Heidegger during his Nazi period, to Spengler, 'who forged the first new weapons after Germany's disarmament').[79] Spengler argues that the plight of the West, dramatized by the Great War, represented a particular stage in the cycle of birth, development, maturity and decline undergone by all complex cultures. The turning point in this process, which is to be understood as 'a strict and necessary *organic succession*', is the transition from Culture *stricto sensu*, characterized by an organic unity which imparts to every aspect and event a distinctive and shared meaning, to Civilization, where a kind of rigidification sets in, 'the progressive exhaustion of forms that have become inorganic or dead' – a stage reached by the West in the nineteenth century.[80]

Spengler's philosophy of history is in large part a variant of the vitalist critique of modernity commonplace on the German right of his day: the opposition of *Kultur*, where social life forms a harmonious yet dynamic totality, and *Zivilisation*, the empty formalism of modernity, is one of the standard topoi of the German conservative-revolutionary tradition which provided National Socialism with its intellectual foundations, and in which Heidegger, Jünger and Schmitt were central figures.[81] But what is of interest here is that Spengler claims that Civilization, once it is fully entrenched, gives rise to posthistory. Thus he argues that

> man is historyless not only before the birth of the Culture, but again becomes so as soon as a Civilization has worked itself out fully in the definitive form which betokens the end of the living development of the Culture and the exhaustion of the last potentialities of its significant existence.[82]

It follows that history and the existence of the human species do not occupy coextensive spans of time. The characteristic features of history mark it off from the times before it opens and after it closes:

> In the history, the genuine history, of higher men the stake fought for and the basis of the animal struggle to prevail is ever – even when driver and driven are completely unconscious of the symbolic force of the doings, purposes and fortunes – the actualization of something that is essentially spiritual, the translation of an idea into a living historical form. This applies equally to the struggle of big style-tendencies in art, of philosophy, of political ideals and of economic forms. But the post-history is void of this. All that remains is the struggle for mere power, for animal advantage *per se*. Whereas previously power, even when to all appearance destitute of any inspiration, was always serving the Idea somehow or other, in the late Civilization, even the most convincing illusion of an idea is only the mask for purely zoological strivings.[83]

This 'non-historical state in which time-periods cease to mean anything', Spengler assures us, lies 'many generations' ahead for the West, which is still at a comparatively early phase of the development of Civilization.[84] Posthistory nevertheless awaits modernity as its unavoidable fate. It is remarkable how Spengler here anticipates later discussions of the End of History. As we have seen, Kojève believes that, with the End of History, '[w]hat disappears is Man properly so-called – that is, Action negating the given'. The drama of Master and Slave closes, and with it, Kojève initially thought, humanity enters Marx's realm of freedom, where it can enjoy 'art, love, play, etc.; in short, everything that makes Man happy'. Later, in his 1960 Note to the second edition of the *Introduction*, Kojève distances himself from this utopian view of posthistory. Since self-consciousness arises from the struggle for recognition, that struggle's conclusion would do away with 'human Discourse (*Logos*) in the strict sense. Animals of the species *Homo sapiens* would react by conditioned reflexes to vocal signals or sign "language", and thus their so-called "discourses" would be like what is supposed to be the "language" of bees.' The result would be a condition to which terms such as 'happiness' would no longer apply:

If Man becomes an animal again, his arts, his loves and his play must also become 'natural' again. Hence it would have to be admitted that after the end of History, men would construct their edifices and works of arts as birds build their nests and spiders spin their webs, would perform musical concerts after the fashion of frogs and cicadas, would play like young animals, and would indulge in love like adult beasts.[85]

In a famous passage in his original article, Fukuyama expresses 'the most ambivalent feelings for the civilization that has been created in Europe since 1945, with its north Atlantic and Asian offshoots', and, like Spengler and Kojève before him, depicts posthistory as a 'zoological' condition:

The end of history will be a very sad time. The struggle for recognition, the willingness to risk one's life for a purely abstract goal, the worldwide ideological struggle that called forth daring, courage, imagination, and idealism, will be replaced by economic calculation, the endless solving of technical problems, environmental concerns, and the satisfaction of sophisticated consumer demands. In the post-historical period there will be neither art nor philosophy, just the perpetual caretaking of the museum of the human spirit.[86]

This portrayal of posthistory is a legitimate inference from a view of history which, like Kojève's, is liable to reduce it to the struggle for recognition. But there is more to Fukuyama's confessed ambivalence towards liberal capitalism than that. He begins his book by confronting 'our pessimism', claiming that '[t]he twentieth century has made all of us deep historical pessimists', and going on to argue that the victories won by liberal capitalism in the past few decades show that 'the pessimistic lessons about our history that our century supposedly taught us need to be rethought from the beginning'.[87] McCarney shows how this note of Reaganite triumphalism fades as the book's argument progresses and the difficulties of liberal capitalism (above all, the East Asian challenge and *megalothymia*) come to occupy centre stage.[88] But these uncertainties are, in my view, the symptoms of a deeper pessimism, whose ultimate source can be traced to the German intellectual right's obsession with the spiritlessness of capitalist modernity. This influence, filtered through the cultural criticism of the Chicago coterie of neo-conservative intellectuals – Harold Bloom, Saul Bellow, et al. – who, through Strauss, link Fukuyama to Kojève, inhabits the grand synthesis of neo-Hegelian philosophy of history and liberal economics which Fukuyama offers us. Far from belonging to 'the Devil's party', he turns out to be practising a version of the conservative *Kulturkritik* that has become all too familiar since the French Revolution.

1.4   HISTORY AND REASON

Probably the most tempting conclusion to draw from this survey of the theme of the End of History is that it demonstrates, yet again, the inherently defective character of the philosophy of history as a form of theoretical inquiry. That is, far from re-habilitating the practice of seeking to make our circumstances intelligible by constructing a grand narrative, Fukuyama has provided a definitive proof, if one were still needed, that this practice should once and for all be abandoned. His crude and reductive account of the mechanisms of historical change, and highly ambivalent treatment of the End of History itself, offer a valuable reminder of the grounds on which philosophers, social theorists and historians rejected his twentieth-century predecessors, Spengler and Toynbee, as well as his far greater nineteenth-century precursors, Hegel and Marx.

Joe McCarney resists such a conclusion, however much it may accord with the intellectual temper of the times. He argues that Fukuyama should be turned on his head:

> The case for Fukuyama from the Left rests on the assumption that his project and some of his methodology can be adapted in the service of quite different conclusions. From this standpoint it appears that the Right show a sound instinct in being suspicious of him. The philosophy of history is *our* subject and, now that Fukuyama has helped put it back on the agenda, we have to take it over and revivify it.[89]

There are two chief difficulties with this kind of attempt to appropriate Fukuyama for Marxism. In the first place, to what extent is the problematic of the End of History part of the classical Marxist tradition? We saw above (section 1.2) that it does not play a significant role in Hegel's thought. Moreover, as Althusser points out in an important early text that must be seen as a response to the debate initiated in mid-century Paris by Kojève, Marx doesn't describe the overthrow of capitalism as marking the End of History but rather the end of the '*prehistory* of human society'.[90] Hegel and Marx have directly opposing reasons for refusing to bring the historical process to a close. If for Hegel history matters too little to find a site within it for the moment at which Absolute Knowledge is attained, for Marx history matters too much for him to conceive of its having a terminus other than that of the human species itself. Marx still distinguishes between forms of human social life as more or less authentic, but – in radical opposition to the German conservative tradition which lies behind Fukuyama's treatment of the End of History, for example when he declares: 'I can feel in myself and see in others around me, a powerful nostalgia for the time when history existed' – authenticity is to be found in the future rather than the past: in Saint-Simon's words, '[t]he golden age is not behind us, but in front of us.'[91] Marx conceptualizes the historical process as the development of distinctively human powers over nature (the productive forces) within the framework offered by a succession of social forms (the relations of production). The attainment of a mode of production no longer based on the needs of exploitation – i.e. communism – doesn't end this process but rather subordinates the further development and use of human productive powers to conscious, democratically organized collective regulation. It is this – the entry into the 'realm of freedom' – which confers on history after the transcendence of class society an authenticity it has hitherto lacked.[92]

The second obstacle facing McCarney's attempt to turn Fukuyama on his head concerns the difficulties inherent in such a theoretical enterprise. Althusser demonstrated how, when Marx sought to perform the same operation on Hegel, what was in fact involved was not the application of the same method to a different object, but the transformation of one theoretical discourse into another.[93] The problem is an even more acute one in Fukuyama's case, since his theory of history is dialectical only in the fairly weak sense that it allows for the possibility of conflict between the two driving forces it identifies, instrumental rationality and the struggle for recognition. By contrast, not simply is the development of systemic contradictions between the forces and relations of production the principal mechanism treated by historical materialism as a cause of social change, but the forces and relations themselves are not discrete 'factors' arbitrarily counterposed to one another, but rather aspects of the same fundamental process of social production. Indeed, G. A. Cohen in his influential explication of Marx's concepts defines the production relations as relations of control over the productive forces.[94] But if Marx conceptualizes social contradictions as strains generated within a unitary process, Fukuyama treats his two mechanisms of historical change as in effect heterogeneous to one another, and offers no account of their relationship.

The foregoing amounts to a restatement of the main theme of the previous two sections, namely that Fukuyama's claim to have formulated a dialectical theory of history cannot be sustained. There is, however, a further conceptual difficulty. The End of History plays, for Fukuyama, a formal as well as a substantive role. As we saw above (section 1.1), he believes that historical explanation is necessarily teleological: the End of History is what makes the entire process retrospectively intelligible. Now, it would be pushing it to say that historical materialism is free of teleology. As one would expect, teleological explanations are generally associated in Marx's writing with his resort to Hegelian forms of reasoning: Hegel's system involves a very strong form of objective teleology, undergirded by his conception of the dialectical method as describing a circle in which the beginning and end of the process mutually justify one another. There is, however, nothing inherently teleological about the kind of explanations central to historical materialism, which appeal to the contradiction between the forces and relations of production and to the class struggle which arises on the basis of that contradiction.[95]

These considerations suggest that there might be some merit in distinguishing between different kinds of theorizing about the historical process in its entirety. Take, for example, this fairly representative account by one analytical philosopher, Maurice Mandelbaum, of the differences between ordinary historical writing and the philosophy of history – by which he means 'speculative' or 'metaphysical' philosophy of history, not the real stuff (analysing the truth-conditions of narrative sentences and so on). First, 'every historical inquiry is limited in scope, dealing with what is recognized to be only one segment or aspect of human history. Most philosophers of history, on the other hand, have traditionally embarked on sweeping surveys of what they have regarded as the whole of the significant past.' Secondly, 'every philosopher of history seeks to find a principle of explanation, or of interpretation, which illuminates every significant aspect of the historical process.' Thirdly, the philosopher of history displays an 'absolute commitment to the view that there is some discernible lesson, or "meaning", in history'.[96]

Now, there is no reason why these three features should always go together. One might distinguish *theories* of history from *philosophies* of history. Both share the first of the three features listed by Mandelbaum: that is, they differ from straightforward historical accounts of some event, episode or phenomenon in that they range over the whole of the historical process. But theories of history, unlike philosophies of history, possess the second, but not the third, feature: they offer universal mechanisms responsible for historical change, but do not seek to discover the meaning of the historical process, if by that is meant providing some judgement of its overall moral significance. In philosophies of history, by contrast, accounting for historical developments and subsuming them under ethical principles are part of the same intellectual enterprise; typically, teleological explanations are used, so that the discovery of objective purposes at work in the historical process provides the key to understanding its course. The classic example of this form of reflection is provided, of course, by Hegel. He describes his philosophy of history as 'a theodicy' which 'should enable us to comprehend all the ills of the world including the existence of evil, so that the thinking spirit may be reconciled with the negative aspects of existence'.[97]

Two points of clarification may be in order here. First, the distinction just drawn between theories and philosophies of history should not be taken to imply that those forms of historical inquiry which meet Mandelbaum's three conditions should be consigned to the flames as so much metaphysical rubbish. Reflection on the moral significance of the course of human history is a perfectly legitimate, and indeed valuable form of intellectual activity. Consider, among recent examples of this theoretical genre, Walter Benjamin's enormously influential 'Theses on the Philosophy of History'. The difficulty comes, however, when the distinction between moral judgement and causal explanation is effaced: Benjamin's text is, in part, a protest against precisely this confusion – the assumption, shared by Hegel and the German historical school, that, in Schiller's words, 'die Weltgeschichte ist das Weltgericht,' 'world history is the world's court of law.'[98] This brings me to my second point: it is never possible or indeed desirable completely to separate explanation and judgement. Some of the connections between ethics and historical theory are explored in section 4.1 below, where I begin to confront the problem of progress, with which Benjamin grapples in his 'Theses'. Nevertheless, there seems to be no good reason why one cannot postulate the existence of mechanisms responsible for historical change across the whole range of human societies without falling into the trap of teleology. The crucial difference here from philosophies of history is that the theories specifying these mechanisms rely on straightforward causal and intentional explanations not requiring appeal to objective purposes and the like (see sections 3.1 and 4.2 below).

Distinguishing in this way between theories and philosophies of history seems a worthwhile effort if only because there are a number of candidates which seem to have a plausible claim to belong to the first category. Historical materialism is one. Indeed, the distinction was first suggested to me by a passage where G. A. Cohen declares: 'we may attribute to Marx, as we cannot to Hegel, not only a *philosophy* of history, but also what deserves to be called a *theory* of history, which is not a reflective construal, from a distance, but a contribution to understanding its inner dynamic.'[99]

Marx's concepts, Cohen goes on to argue, 'do not serve only to express a vision. They also assert their candidacy as the leading concepts in a theory of history, a *theory* to the extent that history admits of theoretical treatment, which is neither entirely nor not at all.' This version of the difference, which treats philosophies of history as 'lacking the degree of articulation suggested by the term "theory"', is not identical to mine, which focuses rather on the explanatory principles embodied in two kinds of theoretical discourse – teleological in philosophies of history, causal and intentional in theories of history.[100] Nevertheless, the substantive point made by Cohen remains: Marx offers a theoretical account of the 'inner dynamic' of history. So too do the neo-Weberian historical sociologies developed recently by Ernest Gellner, Anthony Giddens, Michael Mann and W. G. Runciman. Chapters 3 and 4 examine in more detail the nature of such theories and some of the difficulties facing them. First, however, let us confront the claim that all forms of theorizing about history are illegitimate.

2
HISTORY AS NARRATIVE

Herodotus of Halicarnassus, his *Researches* are here set down to preserve the memory of the past by putting on record the astonishing achievements both of our own and of other peoples; and more particularly, to show how they came into conflict.

Herodotus

2.1   THE CLAIMS OF NARRATIVE

Controversy over the relationship between history and narrative is an old story. At the beginning of the twentieth century, G. M. Trevelyan launched a polemic against J. B. Bury's famous declaration that history had become 'a science, no less and no more', in which he insisted that 'the art of history remains always the art of narrative. That is the bedrock.'[1] Lucien Febvre and Marc Bloch founded the *Annales* school between the wars on a very different rock. One of their heirs, Jacques Le Goff, describes them as engaged in

> the struggle against political history, ... which is, on the one hand, a narrative story and, on the other, a history of events, a *histoire événementielle*, a theatre of appearances masking the real play of history, which takes place behind the scenes and in the hidden structures where it is necessary to go to detect, analyse, and explain it.[2]

Le Goff here links the refusal of narrative to an attempt to uncover underlying structures: it is as if a shift away from the traditional object of historiography – the doings of the men in command of great states – requires the adoption of different techniques with which to organize the historian's researches and to present their results. Probably the outstanding twentieth-century example of this kind of 'structural' or 'analytic' history is Fernand Braudel's great book *The Mediterranean and the Mediterranean World in the Age of Philip II*, which relegates political narrative (focusing primarily on the struggle for dominance of the Mediterranean between Habsburg Spain and the Ottoman Empire in the late sixteenth century) to part three – 'Events, Politics and People' – and accords priority in parts one and two to, respectively, 'The Role of the Environment' and 'Collective Destinies and General Trends'. In justifying his decision to give the objective context of human actions precedence over *l'histoire événementielle* Braudel claims, 'against Ranke or Karl Brandi, that the historical narrative is not a method, or even the objective method *par excellence*, but simply a philosophy of history like any other'.[3]

More recently, Lawrence Stone has detected a reaction against the kind of structural history practised so well by Braudel, and a 'revival of narrative' among scholars associated with the 'new history' which was pioneered by the *Annales* school. Stone defines narrative to mean 'the organization of material in a chrono-logically sequential order and the focusing of the content into a single coherent story, albeit with sub-plots'. But it soon becomes clear that the historians under discussion – Stone mentions Norbert Elias, Theodore Zeldin, Peter Brown, Georges Duby, Carlo Ginzburg, Emmanuel Le Roy Ladurie, Carlo Cipolla, Eric Hobsbawm, Edward Thompson, Robert Darnton, Natalie Davis and Keith Thomas – rarely, if ever, organize their writing in the form of narrative thus defined. Stone in effect concedes the point in this discussion of Brown's *The World of Late Antiquity*:

> Brown builds up a portrait of an age in the manner of a post-Impressionist artist, daubing in rough blotches of colour here and there which, if one stands far enough back, create a stunning picture of reality, but which if examined up close, dissolve into a meaningless blur. The deliberate vagueness, the pictorial approach, the intimate juxtaposition of history, literature, religion and art, the concern for what was going on inside people's heads, are all characteristic of a fresh way of looking at history. The method is not narrative but rather a *pointilliste* way of writing history.[4]

The forms of historical writing which Stone discusses are thus better seen as attempts to address what Hobsbawm calls the 'technical problems of presentation' which arise when historians study society as a whole, 'everything from changes in human physique to symbol and ritual, and above all ... the lives of *all* people from beggars to emperors'. Since from Febvre and Bloch onwards the 'new history' preoccupied itself with society as a totality, Stone's 'revival of narrative' can largely be accounted for, in Hobsbawm's words, 'as a continuation of past historical enterprises by other means'.[5] This discussion does, however, serve to draw attention to the different kinds of claim that can be made for the role of narrative – in the strict sense of a chronologically sequential form, as Stone puts it – in the writing of history. I shall consider three such claims here.

The first one might call technical: the thought here is that a narrative form provides the best way of handling the material with which the historian is dealing. Thus James McPherson explains that the choice of a 'narrative framework' for his outstanding recent study of the American Civil War reflected

> my own convictions about how to write the history of these years of successive crises, rapid changes, dramatic events, and dynamic transformations. A topical or thematic approach could not do justice to this dynamism, this complex relationship of cause and effect, this intensity of experience, especially during the four years of war when developments in several spheres occurred almost simultaneously and impinged on each other so powerfully and immediately as to give the participants the sense of living a lifetime in a year.

So a narrative history of the Civil War can capture both how the participants experienced it and the objective interconnection of events. McPherson goes on later to make the further claim that 'a narrative format' is best designed to present 'the dimension of *contingency* – the recognition that at numerous critical points during the war things might have gone altogether differently'.[6] Though this last assertion obviously raises other issues, the general point is the same: narrative is the best form in which to organize certain material.

The second claim made for narrative carries with it much more openly substantial ideological and philosophical baggage. This is what one might call the traditional humanist defence of narrative historiography. Trevelyan's attack on Bury is an example. More recently, John Clive has argued that Gibbon, Macaulay and the other past masters of historical narrative should still be read on much the same basis as that on which Matthew Arnold offered culture to the Victorian aristocracy and middle class: both provide access to 'the best that has been known and said in the world'.[7] Clive recommends the great historians because they offer 'amusement and instruction' and can provide working historians with practical tips on how to solve problems of presentation.[8] Here the significance of narrative lies in its effect on the reader: reading Gibbon or Macaulay is good for us. Thus Trevelyan calls traditional English historiography 'the means of spreading far and wide throughout all the reading classes a love and knowledge of history, an elevated and critical patriotism and certain qualities of mind and heart'. The role which narrative historiography thus conceived may play in helping to constitute and sustain particular national identities is made plain in the next sentence, where Trevelyan attacks proponents of 'scientific history' modelled on the work of Ranke and his pupils for trying 'to drill us into so many Potsdam Guards of learning'.[9]

Whatever may be said for or against these claims, both assume the existence of several different genres of historical writing, of which narrative is merely one. Proponents of the second claim may believe narrative historiography to be superior to the other genres (or, in Trevelyan's case, argue that the version of narrative made in England is to be preferred to that produced in German seminar rooms), but this does not require them to deny the existence of these others. The third claim goes much further, and amounts to the assertion that narrative is not just a particular historiographical genre, but rather is constitutive of historical writing *tout court*. The work of Paul Ricoeur and (more equivocally) that of Hayden White provides examples of this third claim.

Ricoeur's discussion of historical writing occurs in his major study *Time and Narrative*. Narrative, he argues, offers a practical solution to the aporias inherent in the subjective experience of time. Augustine provides a paradigmatic account of these aporias when he suggests that time is 'an extension of the mind itself': rather than past, present and future constituting ontologically distinct regions of reality, they form the 'threefold present' of consciousness, where memory perceives 'the present of the past', attention 'the present of the present', and expectation 'the present of the future'.[10] The effect, Ricoeur contends, is to introduce 'discordance' (in the first instance, between the three presents) into the soul itself. But the concept of emplotment (*muthos*) developed by Aristotle in the *Poetics* gives 'the apposite reply' to Augustine, since 'Aristotle discerns in the poetic act par excellence – the composition of the tragic poem – the triumph of concordance over discordance'. His account of tragedy – which indeed 'is not purely a model of concordance, but rather of discordant concordance', since the typical plot involves a reversal of fortune – reveals the core structure of narrative, and allows us to understand its central function as the articulation of the human experience of temporality analysed by Augustine.[11]

Ricoeur devotes the bulk of his book to seeking to demonstrate in great detail that this general model captures the specific features of the two main forms of narrative, history and fiction. He does not, it should be said at once, seek to efface the differences between historical and fictional narratives: thus he takes White to task for 'covering over' the 'referential intention' which, in historical writing, 'runs across the "tropics of discourse" in the direction of past events'. His main aim with respect to historiography is to demonstrate *'the ultimately narrative character of history'*, which, he insists, *'is in no way to be confused with a defence of narrative history'*. That is, Ricoeur seeks to show that works belonging to genres of historical writing other than that of narrative possess the underlying structure revealed in Aristotle's account of emplotment.[12]

The heart of Ricoeur's argument is revealed when he asks: 'Does not every narrated story finally have to do with reversals of fortune, whether for better or worse?' But in Aristotelian tragedy such reversals are undergone by individual persons, by Oedipus or Agamemnon. How can this model be extended to the kind of structural history practised by the *Annales* school, for example, which disdains the study of persons and the events they experience? Ricoeur is too careful and catholic a thinker to take the easy way out offered by methodological individualism and simply ban any reference to structures and other relationships and entities which cannot be reduced to individuals and the consequences of their actions. Instead he establishes a series of 'relay stations' which indirectly link the various forms of historical writing to narratives straightforwardly conforming to the Aristotelian model. Perhaps the most important of these relay stations consists of 'the first-order entities of historical knowledge, that is, those societal entities that, while they are indecomposable into a dust of individuals, nevertheless do refer, in their constitution and in their definition, to individuals capable of being considered as the characters in a narrative'. It is by virtue of this 'oblique reference' to individual persons that first-order entities can be treated as characters (or rather 'quasi-characters') in a narrative. Similarly, the accounts given by historians of what is undergone by these entities are best understood as 'quasi-plots' in which 'quasi-events' occur, namely 'the life and death of the structures themselves'. Ricoeur's most extended attempt to justify this claim takes the form of an analysis of Braudel's *Mediterranean*:

> What frames the plot of the Mediterranean? We may say without hesitation: the decline of the Mediterranean as a collective hero on the stage of world history. The end of the plot, in this regard, is not the death of Philip II. It is the end of the conflict between the two political leviathans and the shift of history toward the Atlantic.[13]

For Ricoeur, then, narrative is one of the chief ways in which human beings cope with the experience of temporality. History is one form of narrative; even the most austere structural histories dramatize the changes in fortune undergone by the entities of which they give accounts:

> the emergence of a new event-like quality ... reminds us that something happens even to the most stable structures. Something happens to them – in particular, they die out. That is why, despite his reticence, Braudel was unable to avoid ending his magnificent work with the description of a death, not, of course, the death of the Mediterranean, but the death of Philip II.[14]

Ricoeur's discussion of historical writing is part of a much more extended philosophical analysis of the significance of the experience of time for human beings – an analysis which, naturally enough, embraces a detailed account of fictional narrative, and a sustained engagement with Husserl's and Heidegger's reflections on time.[15] White's focus is, by contrast, much narrower, concentrating as it does on the rhetoric of historical writing. He may be thought of as offering three main claims. First, historical writing must be understood as a poetic act, whose critical moment comes when the historian seeks to represent to herself the events of which she intends to give an account: 'In order to figure out "what *really* happened" in the past, ... the historian must first *prefigure* as a possible object of knowledge the whole set of events reported in the documents.' As a process of representation, this 'prefigurative act' is best understood in terms of the four tropes of figurative language: Metaphor, where things are depicted in terms of their similarities and differences; Metonymy, the substitution of a part of a thing for the whole; Synecdoche, in which a part-stands for a quality, presumably of the whole; and Irony, where what is affirmed literally is negated figuratively. To these tropes correspond the four 'modes of emplotment', which give 'the "meaning" of a story by identifying the *kind of story* that has been told': Romance, Tragedy, Comedy and Satire.[16]

White insists, secondly, that this narrative organization of historical writing cannot be understood as merely a neutral form. The adoption of a particular mode of emplotment is not a simple technical decision, nor is it one that is somehow imposed by the nature of the material with which the historian is dealing: 'narrative, far from being merely a form of discourse that can be filled with different contents, real or imaginary as the case may be, already possesses a content prior to any actualization of it in speech or writing.' Modes of emplotment involve 'ontological and epistemic choices with distinct ideological and even specifically political implications'.[17] These choices are in no sense dictated by the empirical evidence available to the historian:

> In my view, 'history', as a plenum of documents that attest to the occurrence of events, can be put together in a number of different and equally plausible narrative accounts of 'what happened in the past', accounts from which the reader, or the historian himself, may draw different conclusions about 'what must be done' in the present.[18]

Rhetoric is concerned particularly with a discourse's effects on its audience. White's analysis thus displaces attention from the question of how well historians succeed in representing the past to that of the nature and role of historical narratives. He gives, thirdly, an account of them which stresses their quality of closure:

> The historical narrative ... reveals to us a world that is putatively 'finished', done with, over, and yet not dissolved, not falling apart. In this world, reality wears the mask of a meaning, the completeness and fullness of which we can only imagine, never experience. In so far as historical stories

can be completed, can be given narrative closure, can be shown to have had a plot all along, they give to reality the odour of the ideal.

In so doing, historical narratives perform a social function. Borrowing from Althusser's theory of ideology, White argues that by allowing their audience to imagine a reality that is whole and complete, they contribute to 'the production of the "law-abiding" citizen'. Historical writing must thus be understood primarily as a form of ideology.[19]

White's work is undoubtedly the decisive influence on contemporary discussion of history as narrative. Yet it is not wholly clear whether he is committed to what Ricoeur calls 'the ultimately narrative character of history'. White acknowledges that some historians – he mentions Tocqueville, Burckhardt, Huizinga and Braudel – have used 'nonnarrative, even antinarrative modes of representation'.[20] Yet it is clear that he believes that all forms of historical writing, including those which refuse to employ the straightforward narrative form, involve modes of emplotment. Thus *Metahistory* includes extended discussions of Tocqueville and Burckhardt who are depicted as writing in the genres of, respectively, Tragedy and Satire. This apparent tension – White focuses on narrative yet employs a formal framework which provides space for non-narrative historiography – is to some extent relieved when one notes how he privileges the trope of Irony and its corresponding mode of emplotment, Satire.

White thus tells us that

Irony is in one sense metatropological, for it is deployed in the self-conscious awareness of the possible misuse of figurative language ... Irony thus represents a stage of consciousness in which the problematical nature of language has been recognized. It points to the potential foolishness of all linguistic characterizations of reality as much as to the absurdity of the beliefs it parodies.

White detects a movement in nineteenth-century European historiography towards 'an Ironic apprehension of the irreducible relativism of all knowledge'. The key figure here is Burckhardt, who subverts Ranke's realism, which depicts history as a Comic drama culminating in a moment of ultimate reconciliation. In Burckhardt's Ironic imagination the world is 'a literal "satura", stew or medley, fragments of objects detached from their original contexts or whose contexts are unknowable, capable of being put together in a number of different ways, of figuring a host of different possible, and equally valid, meanings'. White thus sees Ironic historiography as a kind of immanent critique of historical narrative, and in particular of its claim to represent reality in its 'completeness and fullness' – one that involves modes of emplotment and the rest of the rhetorical apparatus analysed by White, but which differs from historical writing employing the other tropes in that it openly displays these devices and thereby gives discursive embodiment to 'a mode of thought which is radically self-critical'. [21]

There is therefore less paradox than might first seem to be present in F. R. Ankersmit's attempt to dissociate the term 'narrativism' from any connotation of story-telling. ' "Narrativism" ', he tells us, 'should rather be associated with (historical) interpretation.'[22] For what White offers us is a pragmatics of historical writing. Historical narratives, by virtue of their tropological organization, will always fail in their attempt to represent reality. This attempt, realized by that very organization, in fact plays a very different role: by depicting, through the device of narrative closure, a world that is whole, historical narrative helps to turn out good citizens. The Ironic historian, in refusing to offer a complete story, is not trying to give a better representation of reality than practitioners of narrative historiography, but is seeking to subvert the whole practice of historical representation. In cultivating a reflexive awareness of the rhetorical devices through which an imaginary totalization of reality is sought, she merges with the metahistorian describing the process through which this awareness emerged. Both seek to demonstrate the limits of historical representation. No wonder that White, at the end of *Metahistory*, denies that there is any fundamental distinction between 'proper history and speculative philosophy of history'.[23]

One is inclined to ask what the political upshot of all this is. After all, White's pragmatics of historical writing does seek to identify the social role played by historical narrative as a form of ideology. It was probably inevitable that in the intensely politicized atmosphere currently pervading the American academy he should become a target of neo-conservative red-baiters. In a particularly inept example of the flourishing genre of conservative *Kulturkampf* Gertrude Himmelfarb denounces White as a closet Marxist, engaged, along with Foucault and Derrida, in a postmodernist conspiracy 'to subvert the structure of society together with the structure of language'.[24] But consider these remarks in one of White's most important essays. 'The Politics of Historical Interpretation', which Himmelfarb cites, but does not seem to have understood:

> In my view, relativism is the moral equivalent of epistemological skepticism; moreover, I conceive relativism to be the basis of social tolerance, not a licence to 'do as you please'. As for revolution, it always misfires. In any event, political revolution, in advanced industrial states at least, is likely to result in the further consolidation of repressive powers rather than in the dissolution thereof. After all, those who control the military-industrial-economic complex hold all the cards. In such a situation, the socially responsible interpreter can do two things: (1) expose the fictitious nature of any political programme based on an appeal to what 'history' supposedly teaches and (2) remain adamantly 'utopian' in any criticism of political 'realism'.[25]

The Ironic metahistorian thus floats midway between left and right, disdaining Marxism's claim to ground its political project in the nature of the historical process but also offering a utopian critique of conservative reconciliations with reality. The philosophical underpinning of this political stance is provided by its anti-realism: the inadequacy of left and right alike lies in the appeal both make to particular representations of reality. The metahistorian, by contrast, understands the fictive character of all such representations. The figure he cuts is a familiar enough one, that of the 'liberal ironist' depicted by Richard Rorty, 'the sort of person who faces up to the contingency of his or her own most central beliefs and desires – someone sufficiently historicist and nominalist enough to have abandoned the idea that those central beliefs and desires refer back to something beyond the reach of time and chance', but who at the same time hopes that 'suffering will be diminished', recognizing that this hope cannot be objectively justified.[26]

So White is not one of the professorial reds Himmelfarb is eager to hunt down, but rather, like Rorty, a 'postmodern North Atlantic bourgeois liberal'.[27] There is more to be said about the politics of narrativism than this, as we shall see in section 2.3 below. It is necessary first, however, to engage more closely with White's central claims concerning the fictive character of historical representation – though we shall do so via a detour.

2.2   THE SPECIFICITY OF MODERN
HISTORICAL DISCOURSE

Theorists who seek to reduce historical writing to narrative
typically offer some account of the nature of narrative itself.
Thus Ricoeur argues that narrative, through the order it imposes
in the form of emplotment, offers a response to the contradictions inherent in the human experience of time. Where Ricoeur
offers a metaphysics of temporality, White develops a social
pragmatics, depicting historical narratives as a form of ideology,
serving, through the closure they involve, as a means of subsuming individuals under prevailing social relations. Common
to both accounts is the relationship they posit between the formal
characteristics they attribute to narratives – what Ricoeur calls
'discordant concordance', the discovery of order in chaos – and
the resolution of an extradiscursive problem, in one case existential (the aporetic character of the experience of time), in the
other social (the reproduction of relations of domination). Other
theorists provide what one might call an anthropological account
of narrative, where the focus is less on the formal properties
of narratives than on the role they play in allowing human beings
to make sense of their own lives and their relations with others.
Alasdair MacIntyre offers quite a strong version of this kind
of theory. 'Narrative history of a certain kind turns out to be
the basic and essential genre for the characterization of human
actions,' he says. Every individual lives out narratives in her own
life; the narrative form therefore provides the basis on which
to understand both her own actions and those of others. Thus
'man is in his actions and practice, as well as in his fictions,
essentially a story-telling animal.' If correct, this claim has,
MacIntyre believes, the most radical implications for the philosophy of mind and of action. For example: 'Personal identity is
just that identity presupposed by the unity of the character which
the unity of a narrative requires. Without such a unity there
would not be subjects of whom stories could be told.'[28]
Some such anthropological account of narrative has, in my
view, many attractions. Not only would it help to make intelligible the ubiquity of story-telling in human societies, but it
could also contribute to articulating one fundamental feature
of the modern experience of the self, where, in Ricoeur's words,
'the subject ... appears both as a reader and the writer of its
own life, as Proust would have it.'[29] What else did Freud seek

to do but help his patients arrive at, not a complete narrative of their lives, since analysis is in principle interminable, but a fuller one that included, at least, those critical episodes occulted by repression? The example of psychoanalysis is significant, since it highlights the one-sidedness of White's theory of narrative. Narratives on this account are an inherently mystifying form of representation, binding the subject to the existing order through the sense of wholeness they convey. But the kind of narrative analysis helps the patient to develop involves an act of liberation, since the reconstruction she develops of her personal history allows her to break out of the neurotic compulsions whose roots lie in a hitherto unmastered past. This way of looking at psychoanalysis does, of course, take its claims at face value; this defect is, however, outweighed by the fact that we have here a model of narrative as a potential source of *enlightenment* rather than as necessarily mystifying.

Whatever account of narrative we may choose to adopt does not settle the claim of narrativism. This claim typically takes the form of the subsumption of historical writing under some account of narrative – say, Ricoeur's extension of the Aristotelian *muthos* into a narrative configuration always centring on a change of fortune, or White's employment of the rhetorical tropes and narrative genres to identify the mode of emplotment at work in every instance of historical writing. But surely this way of proceeding carries with it the danger that it fails to capture features of historical writing which simply do not figure in any general theory of narrative because they are specific to this kind of discourse. These features may be considered at two distinct levels.

In the first place, the reduction of history to narrative occludes the typical aim of historical writing, namely to give an explanation of some event or episode or phenomenon in the past. Maurice Mandelbaum made much the same point when he responded to the first wave of narrativism, represented by analytical philosophers such as Arthur Danto and W. B. Gallie, in the 1960s: 'The task of the historian is not one of tracing a series of links in a chain; rather, it is his task to analyse a complex pattern of change into the factors which served to make it precisely what it was.'[30] This explanatory objective is arguably constitutive of Western historiograpy; certainly it can be traced back to its very origins in the *Histories* of Herodotus. It is customary to regard Herodotus as a teller of stories, some of them pretty tall. Dilthey expresses this conventional judgement

when he contrasts the '[j]oyful narrative art' of Herodotus with
the 'penetrating explanation' offered by Thucydides and the
'application of systematic knowledge' made by Polybius.[31] But
Herodotus begins the *Histories* with a sentence forming the epigraph to this chapter which makes plain that his objective is
explanatory – to discover the causes of the wars between the
Persian Great King and the Greek city-states. His book is an
investigation – *historiē* after all means inquiry or research. As
A. R. Burn notes, 'Herodotus deliberately introduces digressions,
"that notable achievements may not be forgotten"; but never
loses sight of his theme: Greece and the East, "and especially the
causes of their conflict".'[32]

To insist that the objective of historical writing is to give an
explanation is not to require that the explanations offered by
historians take only one form. There may indeed be many cases
where constructing a narrative is a perfectly valid form of historical explanation. Consider, for example, some of the arguments offered by Danto. He attacks the distinction, drawn by
W. H. Walsh, between 'a plain narrative of past events', where
'the historian confines himself ... to an exact description of
what happened', and 'a significant narrative', where the historian
'aims not merely at saying what happened but also at (in some
sense) explaining it'.[33] Danto argues, first, that all narratives
are significant; the construction of a plain narrative is an un-
attainable ideal, since even if everything could be exactly described
the result would be not a narrative but an unstructured chaos:
'any narrative is a structure imposed upon events, grouping some
of them together with others, and ruling out some as lacking
relevance.' Secondly, the criterion of relevance according to which
events are selected for inclusion in a narrative is their contribution to explaining some other event. 'A narrative describes
and explains at once.' It does so in history by identifying some
occurrence responsible for a change undergone by the subject of
the narrative.[34]

Now, one may readily accept this analysis of historical narratives, conducted as it is with great subtlety and rigour: we shall
return to some of its implications in the next section. Danto's
account does not, however, license the reduction of history to
narrative. On the contrary, by seeking to show that narratives
explain, he helps establish how they contribute to the previously
defined explanatory objective of historical writing. It may be
that historical narratives have effects other than that of providing
explanations – they may, for example, play at least some of the

roles identified by theorists of narrative, for example, allowing subjects to form a conception of themselves as coherent selves relating to other such selves. But it is not these functions which pick out what is distinctive to these narratives in as much as they figure in history as a particular form of discourse.

The point is reinforced when we consider this discourse close up. More specifically: what are the distinctive features not so much of historiography in the Western tradition generally, but of the particular form it has taken since the end of the eighteenth century, when, as is generally accepted, modern historical discourse took shape? Danto, as we have seen, argues that the 'role of narratives in history' is 'to explain changes'.[35] And it is customary to treat the emergence of modern historiography as a response to what Eric Hobsbawm calls 'the "dual revolution" – the French Revolution of 1789 and the contemporaneous (British) Industrial Revolution'.[36] Thus Lord Acton writes: 'History issues from the Romantic School. Piecing together what the Rev[olution] snapped.'[37] But putting it like this, as if the formation of modern historiography were a reaction to an external upheaval – what Acton calls 'the shock of the Revolution' – is wholly inadequate.[38] The great Greek historians were, after all, concerned to account for great changes: Herodotus the defeat of Persia at the hands of the Greek city-states, Thucydides the overthrow of Athenian hegemony in Greece in the Peloponnesian war, Polybius the emergence of Rome as the dominant power in the Mediterranean. Nevertheless, they offered their explanations within a conceptual framework that was, in certain respects, radically opposed to that implicit in modern historical writing.

Three crucial assumptions are implied by the practice of Greek historiography. First, human nature is constant. Thucydides hopes that his book will be 'judged useful by those who want to understand clearly the events which happened in the past and which (human nature being what it is) will, at some time or other and in much the same ways, be repeated in the future'.[39] This theme of recurrence finds its source not only in the belief that human beings, sharing the same nature, will respond uniformly to similar circumstances, and so produce the same effects, but also in a second major assumption, that the rise and fall of polities, which provides Greek historiography with its main theme, must be understood as episodes in a cyclical movement. Polybius discerns a 'cycle of political revolution, the law of nature according to which constitutions change, are transformed, and finally revert to their original form'. The movement is from good to bad

forms of government, from monarchy to tyranny, from aristocracy to oligarchy, from democracy to ochlocracy and 'a state
of bestiality' from which the whole cycle commences again. The
cycle is thus one of decline and degeneration, powered by the
infirmities of human nature: each good form of government
becomes corrupted when a generation unfamiliar with the circumstances which led to its introduction takes the helm.[40] It is
the tendency of history to repeat itself which underlies a third
assumption, namely that the function of historiography is primarily what Benedetto Croce called the pragmatic one of offering lessons capable of guiding the conduct of statesmen. Cicero
expressed the thought when he called history *magistra vitae*, the
teacher of life, but Lucian traces it back to Thucydides:

> He introduces the concept of usefulness and the purpose
> (*telos*) which a sensible man would attribute to history:
> according to him, it is that if men ever again encounter
> similar circumstances, they should be able, by paying atten-
> tion to what has been recorded of the past, to deal properly
> with the situation that confronts them.[41]

It would be going much too far to treat these assumptions as
evidence of the fundamentally unhistorical character of Greek
thought. R. G. Collingwood's attack on Thucydides as an 'anti-
historical' thinker 'whose mind cannot be fully concentrated on
the events themselves, but is constantly being drawn away from
the events to ... some unchanging and eternal truth' behind
them simply casts doubt on his own judgement.[42] Far from being
the proto-Platonist depicted by Collingwood, Thucydides seems
to have been heavily influenced by the naturalistic and empirical
conception of scientific knowledge developed by the Hippocratic
school of medicine.[43] The fact remains, however, that the constitution of modern historiography required, for reasons that will
become apparent, a break with the Greek conception of history.
Set in its context, in his 1824 Preface to the *Histories of the Latin
and Germanic Nations*, Ranke's injunction to depict the past
wie es eigentlich gewesen turns out to be, not, as is sometimes
claimed, a naive commitment to the impossible goal of constructing a plain narrative, but rather a repudiation of the slogan
historia magistra vitae: 'To history has been given the function
of judging the past, of instructing men for the profit of future
years. The present attempt does not aspire to such a lofty under-
taking. It merely wants to show how things actually happened.'[44]

What, then, are the distinguishing features of modern historical discourse? Once again, we may identify three main characteristics. First, historical writing is based on what Eero Loone calls 'the *presumption of qualitative difference*', that is, on 'a presupposition which asserts that, in the past ..., the way people lived was different "in principle", "qualitatively" from the way people live now'.[45] It was perhaps Herder who first clearly articulated this thought when he developed his theory of the irreducible diversity of human societies. 'Each age is different,' Herder declared, 'and each has its centre of happiness within itself.'[46] The effect was radically to undercut the Greek assumption of the constancy of human nature and the pragmatic conception of history as a guide to life. Machiavelli demonstrates the extent to which Renaissance historians still moved within the classical framework when he complains that people enjoy reading about the deeds of the ancients, 'but never think of imitating them, since they hold them to be not merely difficult but impossible of imitation, as if heaven, the sun, the elements and man had in their motion, their order, and their potency, become different from what they used to be'.[47] Compare Ranke's famous declaration that 'every epoch is immediate to God, and its worth is not at all based on what derives from it but rests in its own existence, in its own self.' Every society and period is a singularity, worthy of study for its own sake, and not as a source of models and warnings: 'In this way the contemplation of history, that is to say of *individual life in history* acquires its own particular attraction, since now every epoch must be seen as something valid in itself and appears highly worthy of consideration.'[48]

The entire expanse of human societies was thus opened up to historical inquiry. But to realize this project required, in the second place, a methodological revolution. Western historiography up to the Enlightenment relied on eye-witnesses as its main source of evidence. Thucydides, the first historian to reflect on his method, assures us that 'either I was present myself at the events which I have described or else I heard of them from eyewitnesses whose reports I have checked with as much thoroughness as possible.'[49] The critical work comes in the careful crossquestioning of eye-witnesses, no doubt on the model provided by the practice of the law courts in Athens and other city-states. As Collingwood observes, this method 'inevitably imposed on its users a shortness of historical perspective ... Their method tied them to a tether whose length was the length of living memory: the only source they could criticize was an eyewitness with whom they could converse face-to-face.'[50] The great historians of antiquity – Herodotus, Thucydides, Polybius, Tacitus, Ammianus Marcellinus – generally practise what Reinhart Koselleck calls 'the historical writing of the present or the recent past'.[51] Hence the decisive importance of the development of the new method of *Quellenkritik*, the critical examination of primarily documentary sources, which, taking shape in various forms in early modern Europe, notably in classical philology, biblical criticism and legal scholarship, reached maturity during the eighteenth century in the Göttingen school of historians (J. G. Schlözer, J. C. Gatterer, Johann von Müller and their followers). The resulting transformation of the scope of historical scholarship is underlined by Niebuhr, whose *History of Rome* is often regarded as the first fruit of *Quellenkritik*. He calls philology 'the transmitter of eternity, thus affording us the enjoyment of unbroken identity, across thousands of years, with the noblest and greatest peoples of antiquity; to make us as familiar with their spiritual creations and their history as if no gulf separated us'.[52] Thus, as Koselleck puts it, '[t]he past was henceforth no longer to be preserved in memory by an oral or written tradition, but was to be reconstructed through the process of criticism.'[53]

Paradoxically, then, modern historical discourse affirmed both the qualitative difference between past and present, and the possibility of rigorous critical inquiry gaining access to the totality of the past. These apparently contradictory propositions were reconciled through a third distinctive characteristic of modern historical discourse, namely the assumption of the unity of human history. Typically this presupposition was sustained, not by appeal to the constancy of human nature, as in ancient and Renaissance historiography, but by resort to the claim that the differences between periods could be understood as corresponding to the existence of distinct *kinds* of society, all of which were, however, interrelated through their common participation in the progressive movement of human history. This claim was, of course, first fully articulated in the Enlightenment. The decisive development here is the formulation, first made by Turgot and taken up and developed by Smith, Ferguson and other members of the Scottish historical school, of what Andrew Skinner calls 'an economic interpretation of history', in which society progresses through four stages, each characterized by a distinctive 'mode of subsistence' – hunting, pasturage, farming and commerce.[54]

This conception of history as a process of development from one socio-economic system to another is, to some extent at least, a philosophical elaboration of discoveries that predate the Enlightenment. Thus even so complacent an exponent of unreflecting historical empiricism as John Kenyon is able to register the intellectual significance of Sir Henry Spelman establishing in 1641 for the first time 'the relationship between military services, or labour services, and land tenure, which has ever afterwards been acknowledged to be the framework of feudalism, bolted together by the feudal oath'. By thus identifying the *sui generis* characteristics of feudalism as a distinct social order, Spelman introduced a discontinuity into English history. 'The result was to impose on mediaeval history a concept of "progression",' Kenyon observes. 'Spelman's demonstration that feudalism was a Norman import ... implied a three-stage scenario: a pre-feudal age, a feudal age, ending about 1485, and a post-feudal age.'[55] If Smith's and Turgot's four stages theory of history could claim such developments as anticipations of its more general claims, it was rapidly to be embodied in what is still one of the greatest works of narrative historiography, Gibbon's *Decline and Fall of the Roman Empire*. Hugh Trevor-Roper has recently called Gibbon 'the first modern European historian'. His modernity is to be attributed directly to the respects in which the *Decline and Fall* emerged in the context of the Enlightenment. Deeply influenced by Montesquieu and the Scottish historians, Gibbon sought, by examining the collapse of classical antiquity, to discover whether, as many of the *philosophes* feared, the progress of European society in their own day would be followed by a new Dark Age. Methodologically, however, he advanced beyond his predecessors. Thus, Trevor-Roper contends, in his famous treatment of Christianity Gibbon 'saw it less as true or false, but as the ideology of a new world order', to be studied in the context of 'the objective condition of the society within which it worked, and which it transformed: secular institutions, economic movements, questions of population, defence, culture, and the arts'.[56]

It is thus misleading to regard modern historiography as emerging from what Acton calls '[t]he romantic reaction' to the French Revolution, and taking the form of a Burkean 'revolt of outraged history' against the Jacobins' violation of hallowed tradition.[57] Not simply were the three main elements of this discourse – conceiving historical periods as qualitatively different, employing the methods of philological criticism to acquire

knowledge of even the remotest past and theorizing the differences revealed by these inquiries as the progressive movement
of one stage of society to another – in place before 1789, but
they are best seen as a synthesis of the Enlightenment and
Romanticism, though one characterized by the tensions between
the two: between, that is, the characteristically Romantic celebration of the irreducible diversity of human forms of life, and
their equally valid claims to represent the good, on the one hand,
and the Enlightenment attempt to integrate these forms into a
unified account of the development of humankind, on the other.[58]

Three points arise from this account of the main features of
modern historical discourse. First, it is possible to identify certain
transitional figures between ancient and modern conceptions of
history. The most important of such figures are perhaps Ibn
Khaldûn and Vico. Both offer accounts of history as a succession
of different social forms. Ibn Khaldûn indeed makes some strikingly modern formulations. Thus 'man is a child of the customs
and the things he has become used to. He is not a product of
his natural dispositions and temperament.' Historians often fail
to take into account the changes in conditions undergone by
human societies, and 'differences in condition among people are
the result of the different ways in which they live.' Yet this
proto-materialist conception of history is integrated into a version
of the classical cyclical theory of constitutions. '*Dynasties have
a natural life span like individuals,*' and this life-span is regulated
by the differences between the two main forms of civilization,
Bedouin and sedentary culture. The group feeling ('*asabîyah*)
developed by nomads in desert conditions allows them to conquer the cities. But the luxuries of sedentary civilization gradually
erode the group feeling which brought the Bedouin dynasty to
power, until some new band of nomads emerges from the desert
to replace them, and undergo the same process of corruption and
decline.[59]

Vico distinguishes between the ages of gods, heroes and men,
each of which is characterized by its peculiar customs, institutions, language and legal system; he also takes a decisive step
towards the formulation of the critical historical method when
he proposes that the beliefs and traditions of past societies should
be treated as evidence of the nature of these societies. But the
'constant and uninterrupted course of events present in every
nation' makes of the course of history a *ricorso*, a recurrence
produced by the descent of society into 'the perfect tyranny of
anarchy' which reigns when private interests are given free rein;

providence then comes to our rescue, replacing 'the barbarism of reflection' with barbarism *tout court*, and allowing the survivors to return to 'the primitive simplicity of the first world of peoples', and start the whole cycle again.[60]

In retrospect, then, the theories of Ibn Khaldûn and Vico can be seen as compromise formations, combining as they do elements of a characteristically modern conception of history with the classical assumption that, in Polybius's words, '[e]very organism, every state and every activity passess through a natural cycle, first of growth, then of maturity, finally of decline.'[61] This raises, secondly, the question of how it became possible to formulate the thought that history, rather than describing this cyclical movement, is a process of innovation, the generation of *new* social forms. There are, broadly speaking, two answers to this question. One is that offered by Koselleck, who argues that the eighteenth century saw a change in the experience of historical time. More precisely, the relationship between experience and expectation – orientations respectively to past and future – underwent a decisive modification. Hitherto, there had been an 'almost seamless transference of earlier expectations into coming expectations'; what had happened in the past provided the horizon of the future. With the Enlightenment, however, 'no longer can expectation be satisfactorily deduced from previous experience.'[62] Thinking of the future as open made possible a new way of conceiving the past, in which it ceased to be a cycle of decline, and became instead a forward movement, reaching towards that future. On this account, therefore, the formulation of a new conception of history was part of the process through which European societies, as a result both of their internal transformation with the onset of industrial capitalism and of their incorporation through colonial conquest of other societies, began to conceive themselves as breaking radically with the past. As Habermas puts it, '[m]odernity can and will no longer borrow the criteria by which it takes its orientation from the models supplied by another epoch: *it has to create its own normativity out of itself.*'[63]

The other explanation treats this belief in the novelty both of modernity and of the conception of history that arises at the end of the eighteenth century as an illusion. For, after all, the cyclical theory of history had come under attack long before the Enlightenment. In seeking to vindicate the idea of a divine Providence that governs, along with everything else, the fate of kingdoms and empires, Augustine attacks the pagan concept of

eternal recurrence, counterposing to it Christ's death and resur-
rection as unique and unrepeatable events.[64] As Karl Löwith
says, for Augustine 'history itself is an interim between the
past disclosure of its sacred meaning and its future fulfilment.'
Löwith argues that the modern conception of history takes over
and transcribes into secular terms this distinctively Christian
orientation on the future: 'the moderns elaborate a philosophy
of history by secularizing theological principles and applying
them to an ever increasing number of empirical facts.' Thus,
'[h]istorical materialism is essentially, though secretly, a history
of fulfilment and salvation in terms of social economy.'[65] Modern
historical discourse, on this account, is nothing but a secularized
theology, its projection of a forward movement into the future
having the same status as the Christian eschatology of salvation.
We shall return to this interpretation when we come to consider
the question of historical progress in chapter 4 below.

Löwith's reduction of Marxism to theology leads us to a third
point: the place occupied by Marxism in historical discourse.
Professional historians tend to oscillate in their treatment of
Marx between the denunciatory and the dismissive. On the one
hand, the inherent defects they discover in his thinking are held
up to ridicule and patronage – a move nicely captured in Sir
Geoffrey Elton's description of Marxism as 'in its day a truly
remarkable achievement of scientific insight and ill-controlled
speculation'.[66] On the other hand, what is conceded to have
been valid in Marxism is held to have long ago been incorporated into the practice of historical scholarship. Thus Tony
Judt declares: 'The central tenets of Marxism ... are so much
a part of modern historical writing that it is hard to say what
is and what is not "Marxist".' Judt goes on to suggest that 'it
is not clear what it is that remains distinctive about Marxist
historiography.'[67] But one might draw the opposite conclusion;
one might argue, that is, that the absorption of many of the
propositions of historical materialism into professional practice
has been made possible by the particularly privileged position
that Marxism occupies within modern historical discourse. For it
is Marxism that gives articulated and systematic expression to
the third of the assumptions I have identified as distinctive to
this discourse, namely the differentiation of human history into
a multiplicity of social forms each possessing its own idiosyncratic
internal logic but bound together through their participation in
the common movement of humankind through successive phases
of development. Of course, if Löwith is right, then all that this

establishes is that Marxism and modern historiography will hang together, having been exposed as secret theologies concealing within their apparently secular explanations a suprahistorical drama of salvation.

Another way of putting what has come to be known as Löwith's secularization thesis is to describe the kind of interpretations issuing from modern historical discourse as metanarratives, which, according to Lyotard, seek to weave together a diversity of events into the story of humankind's approximation to some goal – Absolute Knowledge, communism, or whatever. Metanarratives thus possess the kind of closure which White claims is a characteristic of all narratives: the sense of wholeness and completeness generated by narratives is in this case achieved by the treatment of all events as somehow tending towards whatever goal the grand narrative assigns to the historical process. Whether this kind of narrative closure is indeed a necessary feature of historical writing in general and of Marxism in particular is something I take up in chapter 4. I wish now, however, to confront the challenge presented by narrativism and postmodernism alike to historical discourse's claim to give explanations and thereby to provide *knowledge*.

2.3 FACING THE FACTS

Historians seek to reconstruct the past by studying its traces. These traces largely – but not exclusively, since they include, for example, the artefacts sought by archaeologists – consist in documents, some intentionally produced to record certain events (chronicles, newspaper reports), the bulk acting as an involuntary witness to the past. The historian's practice thus takes the form, in Edward Thompson's felicitous formulation, of 'the close interrogation of texts and contexts'.[68] The historian's evidence comprises primarily texts; hence the strategic significance, in the formation of modern historical discourse, of *Quellenkritik*, the critical examination of documentary sources. It is hardly surprising, given the tendency of twentieth-century intellectual culture (articulated most powerfully by some poststructuralist philosophers) to conceive language as a reflexive, self-referential activity, that contemporary scepticism about historical knowledge should focus on the fact that historians work on texts to produce other texts.

Carlo Ginzburg captures the nature of this scepticism when he contrasts what he believes to be two mistaken attitudes towards historical evidence. On the one hand, in positivism, 'the evidence is not regarded as a historical document in itself, but as a transparent medium that gives us direct access to reality.' On the other hand, 'contemporary sceptics regard it as a wall, which by definition precludes any access to reality.'[69] The effect, as we have seen, is to displace attention on to the process of historical representation itself; the question of whether or not there is anything to which that representation might or might not correspond, a reality to which the documents might give us access, is dismissed as *vieux jeu*, the kind of naive realism we ought all to have grown out of long ago. There are other versions of scepticism about historical knowledge: the celebrated debate among American historians between the wars was provoked by Charles Beard's and Carl Becker's claim that the historian interprets the past from within a frame of reference informed by value judgements and therefore cannot attain objective knowledge.[70] Contemporary discussion, however, foregrounds the discursive character of historical inquiry. From this perspective, the significance of Hayden White's version of narrativism lies less in his rather evasive treatment of historical writing as a form of narrative than in the fact that this treatment highlights its character as *writing*, and in the more or less explicitly sceptical conclusions he draws from this treatment, most notably when he privileges those forms of historiography which involve 'an Ironic apprehension of the irreducible relativism of all knowledge' (see section 2.1 above).

If the historian's evidence is a wall, then what's on the other side of the wall ceases to be an issue; it becomes beside the point to ask what referents her own discourse has, when she uses this evidence to reconstruct the past. Once the referents of historical writing have been occluded, the boundary separating it from fiction is inevitably blurred – a process reinforced by the stress White lays on that aspect of historiography, the employment of rhetorical tropes and narrative genres, which it shares with fiction. But here a pressing problem emerges to confront the historical sceptic. For surely there are events which it would be simply outrageous to treat as constructs of the historical imaginary. The most obvious example is that of the Holocaust. As Saul Friedlander observes, '[t]he extermination of the Jews of Europe, as the most extreme case of mass criminality, must challenge theoreticians of historical relativism to face up to the corollaries of positions otherwise too easily dealt with on an abstract level.'[71]

Paradoxically, the further the Holocaust slips back in time, the greater an object of controversy it has become. The debates surrounding it in recent years have focused on three issues. First, that of existence: the development – closely associated with the revival of the far right in Europe – of 'revisionist' historians who either deny that the Nazis exterminated the European Jews or claim that the number and significance of Jewish deaths have been greatly exaggerated (the French fascist leader Jean-Marie Le Pen called the Holocaust a mere 'detail of history'). The second question is that of representation: many hold that the unique horror of the Holocaust sets limits to how it may be treated in art, and certainly forbids the kind of cinematic treatments which, from *The Night Porter* to *The Winds of War*, have aestheticized barbarism and trivialized the unspeakable. The final issue is that of explanation: do not attempts to set Auschwitz in a larger social and historical context – for example, those from the left by Arno Mayer, and from the right by Ernst Nolte, to treat what the former calls the 'Judeocide' as an episode in the more general crisis produced by the breakdown of the old European order in 1914 – tend to relativize and obscure the particularity of a crime without parallel?[72]

The embarrassment these controversies pose for the historical sceptic is evident enough. No decent person would throw her lot in with the Holocaust revisionists: but how is one to avoid association with them without conceding that it is possible to discriminate between historical representations on the basis of their relative success in capturing what really happened? The problem is one with which both Lyotard and White have grappled. Lyotard indeed embraces it eagerly in order to illustrate the pluralist philosophy of language he avows. All we can be sure exists, he claims, are phrases (which is how Lyotard's translator chooses to render *phrase*, the French word meaning 'sentence'). Phrases are subject to different regimens – reasoning, knowing, describing and so on. A phrase belonging to one regimen cannot be translated into another; at best heterogeneous phrases can be linked together in a genre of discourse, for some particular purpose. This state of affairs gives rise to conflicts between different genres and regimens, but since there is no translation between them, there can be no 'universal genre of discourse to regulate them'. Lyotard calls such a conflict a 'differend'. He gives the example of the court case involving the French Holocaust revisionist Robert Faurisson, whose argument he summarizes as follows:

in order that a place be identified as a gas-chamber, the only witness I will accept would be a victim of this gas-chamber: now, according to my opponent, there is no victim that is not dead; otherwise, this gas-chamber would not be what he or she claims it to be. There is, therefore, no gas-chamber. [73]

Of course, Lyotard doesn't accept this conclusion. Indeed, he loads enormous significance on to the Holocaust, greatly extending Adorno's famous declaration that '[t]o write poetry after Auschwitz is barbaric.' [74] Thus he claims: 'The "Auschwitz" model would designate an "experience" of language that brings speculative discourse to a halt. The latter can no longer be pursued "after Auschwitz".' But Lyotard seems to believe that the revisionist argument is irrefutable so long as we remain within the cognitive phrase-regimen:

The 'revisionist' historians understand as applicable to this name [Auschwitz] only the cognitive rules for the establishment of historical reality and for the validation of its sense. If justice consisted solely in respecting these rules, and if history gave rise only to historical inquiry, they could not be accused of a denial of justice. [75]

Lyotard thus offers a challenge to his critics. As long as you seek to establish the truth of historical assertions, for example, about the Holocaust, he says, you are engaged in a game which the revisionist is bound to win. The only way of properly acknowledging the reality of the Holocaust is to recognize the existence of a plurality of mutually irreducible phrase-regimens and discursive genres, and to refuse any attempt to subsume them under a comprehensive grand narrative of the kind that has already produced the catastrophes of the Holocaust and the Gulag Archipelago.

Lyotard presumably intends us to take this argument seriously, but it is hard to see how we can. Let us leave aside the highly speculative claim that fascism and Stalinism were the children of grand narratives, a thesis which very quickly reduces to the Cold War theories of totalitarianism which sought to deduce all the foes of liberal capitalism from a common essence. More to the point at issue here, how on earth can Lyotard justify conceding the historical case to the revisionists? The cultural historian Stephen Greenblatt – as one of the founders of the 'New Historicism' hardly himself a fact-grubbing empiricist – has definitively disposed of the 'differend' that is supposed to have been generated by disputes over the existence of the Holocaust:

> The Faurisson affair is at bottom not an epistemological dilemma, as Lyotard claims, but an attempt to wish away evidence that is both substantial and verifiable. The issue is not an Epicurean paradox – 'if death is there, you are not there; if you are there, death is not there; hence it is impossible for you to prove that death is there' – but a historical problem: what is the evidence of mass-murder? How reliable is this evidence? Are there convincing grounds for denying or doubting the documented events? And if there are not such grounds, how may we interpret the motives of those who seek to cast doubt on the historical record?[76]

Notice that it is not open to Lyotard to dismiss this criticism by claiming that it begs the question of whether or not historical discourse can be understood as a representation of events external to it. For his argument was that the Holocaust revisionist cannot be refuted within the phrase-regimen defined by 'the cognitive rules for the definition of historical reality'. The revisionist, in other words, will win the historian's game. But, as Greenblatt implies, this is nonsense. That Lyotard can simply ignore the vast effort aimed at reconstructing and rendering intelligible the Holocaust – the recovery of eye-witness accounts (from perpetrators as well as victims) by Claude Lanzmann in his film *Shoah* and by historians such as Christopher Browning, the memoirs of survivors such as Primo Levi, Raul Hilburg's great synthetic account of the Nazi machinery of destruction, essays in interpretation by Arno Mayer, Zygmunt Bauman and others – is a symptom of the kind of belle-lettrism, with its love of superficial paradox, into which French philosophy in the dog days of poststructuralism is all too apt to degenerate.

White struggles with the same problem with little more success in two essays which at least serve to highlight the systematic uncertainties which pervade his philosophy of history. The first, 'The Politics of Historical Interpretation', we have already touched on (see section 2.1 above). Here White's discussion of the Holocaust occurs in the context of an account of what he calls 'the disciplinization of history', whose aim is 'to make realism effectively identical with antiutopianism'. He seeks to explicate how this happens by appealing to the contrast between the beautiful and the sublime so central to eighteenth-century aesthetics. Disciplinized history – of which Marxists as well as conservatives are practitioners – represents its object under the category of the beautiful: it 'impute[s] a meaning to history that renders its manifest confusion comprehensible to either reason, understanding, or sensibility'. The effect is to deprive historical writing of any utopian impulse, which can only be articulated through the 'apperception of history's meaninglessness', expressed particularly in Schiller's account of the sublime:

> It seems to me that the kind of politics that is based on the vision of a perfected society can compel devotion to it only by virtue of the contrast it offers to a past that is understood the way Schiller conceived it, that is, as a 'spectacle' of 'confusion', 'uncertainty', and 'moral anarchy'.[77]

Are there are any examples of this kind of utopian 'vision'? Yes, says White: 'Something like Schiller's notion of the historical sublime or Nietzsche's version of it is certainly present in the thought of such philosophers as Heidegger and Gentile and in the intuitions of Hitler and Mussolini.' Though, of course, '[f]ascist social and political policies are undeniably horrible,' we should not cave into 'sentimentalism' and 'write off such a conception of history simply because it has been associated with fascist ideologies'. It is an interesting choice of words to call revulsion at anything tainted by Nazism 'sentimentalism'. Let us leave this aside. White's willingness to toy with what one might call the fascist sublime forces him directly to confront the issue of the Holocaust. He does so by way of a discussion of Pierre Vidal-Naquet's response to Faurisson's revisionism. Vidal-Naquet draws a distinction between a 'total lie' – the far right's attempt to deny that the extermination of the Jews took place – and what he calls an 'untruth', of which he gives the example of the political uses of the Holocaust made by Zionists, for whom 'Auschwitz was the ineluctable, logical outcome of life lived in the Diaspora, and all the victims of the death camps were destined to become Israeli citizens'. White is quick to spring to the defence of the Zionist interpretation: 'its truth, as a historical interpretation, consists precisely of its effectiveness in justifying a wide range of current Israeli political policies [*sic*] that, from the standpoint of those who articulate them, are crucial to the security and indeed the very existence of the Jewish people.' Indeed, the Zionist account of the Holocaust is a version of the historical sublime White has discovered at work in fascist ideology:

> It is, in fact, fully comprehensible as a morally responsible response to the meaninglessness of a certain history, that spectacle of 'moral anarchy' that Schiller perceived in 'world history' and specified as a 'sublime object'. The Israeli political response to this spectacle is fully consonant with the aspiration to human freedom and dignity that Schiller took to be the necessary consequence of sustained reflection on it.[78]

One wonders how pleased Zionists would be to have their interpretation of the Holocaust defended on the grounds that it involves the same conception of history as the Nazis'. It is hardly surprising that this extraordinary essay has come under strong attack, notably from Carlo Ginzburg, who argues that White's treatment of history can be traced back to the influence on him of Italian neo-Hegelianism – not merely the liberal Croce but the fascist Gentile. Ginzburg concentrates his fire especially on the equation of truth with effectiveness that we find in White's defence of Zionism: 'White's argument concerning truth and effectiveness inevitably reminds us not of tolerance but of its opposite – Gentile's evaluation of a blackjack as a moral force.'[79]

Ginzburg isn't calling White a fascist – he is in fact careful to stress the theoretical and political differences that separate him from Gentile – and Perry Anderson is no doubt right to stress that contemporary historical scepticism has a variety of sources, notably American liberal pragmatism – a judgement whose validity is strengthened if one takes a broad view of this tradition, so that it embraces historians such as Beard and Becker as well as philosophers such as Peirce, James and Dewey.[80] Nevertheless, White's relativism deprives him of any means by which to maintain a critical distance from nationalist historical mythologies. For it is these – even when not in the virulent form of fascism – which form the principal examples of what he calls the 'historical sublime'. What is more typical of the construction of what Benedict Anderson calls the imagined community of the nation than the invention of a history based on the contrast between the sufferings undergone by the people of this would-be nation and their redemption in the state which is the nation's destiny?[81] Sometimes these sufferings are real enough (too real for the imagination to comprehend, in the case of the Jewish people); frequently they are inflated or invented with that tone of self-pity all too typical of the nationalist political entrepreneur bent on state-building at others' expense. Yet by identifying the truth of nationalist histories with their effectiveness in promoting the power of a particular nation-state, White removes any basis on which the crimes committed in the name of such projects can be criticized. 'The Politics of Historical Interpretation' was published in 1982. That year the Israeli Defence Force invaded Lebanon, besieged Beirut, bombarded the city indiscriminately with phosphorus shells and other vicious munitions and, after the Palestinian forces had been withdrawn, allowed its Christian fascist allies to massacre the inhabitants of the refugee camps at Sabra and Chatila. Are these acts really 'consonant with the aspiration to human dignity and freedom' expressed by Schiller?[82]

If you're in a hole, stop digging, runs a sound piece of practical wisdom. White, however, returned to the issue of the Holocaust in a second essay. 'Historical Emplotment and the Problem of Truth'. Here he focuses on the question of the representation of the Holocaust. After reaffirming that '[t]here is an inexpungeable relativity in every representation of historical phenomena,' he goes on ask: 'do the natures of Nazism and the Final Solution set absolute limits on what can be truthfully said about them?' The answer seems to be that they do not. 'We can confidently presume that the facts of the matter set limits on the *kinds* of stories that can be *properly* (in the sense of both veraciously and appropriately) told about them only if we believe that the events themselves possess a "story" kind of form and a "plot" kind of meaning.' Now, White's whole treatment of historiography as a form of rhetoric implies that what kind of story the historian tells is a matter of her choice, expressed above all in the mode of emplotment adopted. But he then goes on to say that, under certain conditions, there are limits on the kind of stories we may tell about Nazism. Representing the Holocaust as a Comedy, for example, would be ruled out, but 'only if (1) it were presented as a *literal* (rather than a *figurative*) representation of the events, and (2) the plot-type used to transform the facts into a specific kind of story were presented as inherent in (rather than imposed upon) the facts'. If, on the other hand, 'a story of this kind had been set forth in a pointedly ironic way and in the interest of making a metacritical comment', that would be all right. As usual, the ironic metahistorian wins out. This is, however, all very confusing, since the central theme of

White's earlier work was that historical writing is inherently figurative: whence, then, the contrast between figurative and literal representations of the Third Reich? The confusion is compounded when White goes on to argue for a break with 'a realism that is inadequate to the representation of events, such as the Holocaust, which are themselves "modernist" in nature', and to recommend modernism as a higher form of realism, one that is capable of representing 'the totalitarian form that Western society assumed in the twentieth century'. So the events, at least in the case of the Holocaust, do come ready-formed, since they are ' "modernist" in nature'.[83]

No wonder that Ginzburg says this essay 'suggests a milder (though somewhat self-contradictory) form of scepticism' than is to be found in White's 'previously published work'.[84] There are, I think, two sources of this – to speak plainly – hopeless muddle. One is the moral impossibility for anyone who isn't a fascist of adopting a relativist stance towards the Holocaust which would tolerate either the denial of Nazi crimes or their representation as Comedy or Romance. White twists and turns between this impossibility and philosophical views that would underwrite the relativism it rules out. As Peter Haidu points out, the case of the Holocaust shows that there are ethical and political as well as epistemological reasons for insisting that historical discourse has referents:

> Our grasp of the Event [the Holocaust] must inevitably be mediated by representations, with their baggage of indeterminacy. But this is a context in which theory is forced to reckon with reference – as unsatisfactory as contemporary accounts of reference may be – as a necessary function of language and all forms of representation. There are other arguments for reference: this is the argument of an ethics and politics of history.[85]

The second source of White's confusion lies within his philosophy of history itself. Despite the impression he sometimes gives to the contrary, White does not espouse an idealist version of Derrida's textualism, according to which there really is nothing outside the text. On the contrary, as Martin Jay observes, he distinguishes between 'the facts or events of history' and 'their narrative representation'.[86] Thus White takes over Croce's distinction between history and chronicle:

First the elements in the historical field are organized into
a chronicle by the arrangement of the events to be dealt
with in the temporal order of their occurrence; then the
chronicle is organized into a story by the further arrangement
of the events into components of a 'spectacle' or process
of happening, which is thought to possess a discernible beginning, middle, and end.[87]

Historical writing is constituted, White claims, by the organization of the events recorded in chronicle into a narrative belonging to one of the genres of Romance, Comedy, Tragedy, and
Satire. Putting it like this poses the question of the relationship
between the events and the narrative. White tends to think of
the narrative giving form to the events, as when (in his discussion quoted above of the representation of the Holocaust) he
talks of 'the plot-type' being 'imposed upon ... the facts'. This
suggests that, prior to their narrative representation, events are
a shapeless chaos, rather in the way Kant argues that sense impressions would be 'a blind play of representations', were they
not subsumed under the categories of the understanding.[88] But
Kant believes that we only become aware of these impressions as
organized by the categories. White, by contrast, identifies a stage
prior to the imposition on to events of a narrative form, where
they are recorded in the temporal sequence of a chronicle. Is
the chronicle the site of an unmediated encounter with the events
themselves? White's most extended discussion of the matter is
characteristically ambivalent. Here he distinguishes from full-
blown historical narratives annals, which 'represent historical
reality as if real events did not display the form of a story', and
chronicle, which represents events 'in the form of unfinished
stories'. White says the three forms are 'particular products of
possible conceptions of historical reality', which implies that
annals and chronicle are not innocent transcriptions of reality,
but embody some theory about the world. But then he declares:
'It is surely much more "universalistic" simply to record events
as they come to notice,' as the annalists do. But what does
'universalistic' mean here – neutral relative to different conceptions of the world embodied in particular cultures? And are
annalists supposed to record *everything*? Or does noticing (as it
surely must) involve a process of selection relative to the beliefs
and interests of the annalist?[89]
White thus oscillates between treating events as the chaotic raw
material of history, nothing without the form-giving intervention

of narrative, and positing a prenarrative discourse, chronicle, which offers unmediated access to these events. After this, what Jay calls White's 'failure of nerve' in his second Holocaust essay should come as no surprise, since it takes the form of conceding that there are, after all, some events which come with their form ready-made: the Holocaust was ' "modernist" *in nature*'.[90] The distinction White draws between chronicle and historical narrative recalls that made by W. H. Walsh between plain narratives, which offer exact descriptions of events, and significant narratives, which try to explain what happened – not by accident, since Walsh is trying to reformulate Croce's original contrast between chronicle and history proper.[91] All versions of the distinction are vulnerable to Arthur Danto's critique, which rests on the truth that any account must select what it reports, and thereby imposes a structure on events (see section 2.2 above). In this sense, all narratives are significant, and chronicles and annals are narratives, even if they end *in medias res*.

Danto draws one conclusion from his critique of Walsh which is highly relevant to the question of historical scepticism: 'narratives may be regarded as kinds of theories, capable of support, and introducing, by grouping them together in certain ways, a kind of order and structure into events.' Moreover, in using narratives, historians are, 'since a narrative itself is a way of organizing things, and so "goes beyond" what is given, involved in something one might call "giving an interpretation" '.[92] Though couched in the analytical idiom and explicitly opposed to Beard's version of historical relativism, Danto's position is in one respect more radical than White's, since it dispenses with the apparent security offered by the idea of an undiscriminating record of events from which the authors of historical narratives can choose for their plots. Philosophers and historians in other traditions have been equally robust in refusing the crutch offered by the idea of a layer of facts unmediated by any discursive process of selection. F. H. Bradley, for example, established a starting point for one of the richest twentieth-century meditations on history, pursued by later British neo-Hegelians such as Collingwood and Oakeshott, when he bluntly asserted that 'in every case that which is called a fact is in reality a theory'.[93] Or take these remarks on the historical fact by Lucien Febvre in his inaugural lecture at the Collège de France in 1933: 'Given? No, created by the historian, so many times. Invented and fabricated, with the aid of hypotheses and conjectures, by a delicate and fascinating labour.'[94]

2.4 THEORY AND INTERPRETATION

History, in other words, is theory all the way down. The facts in which historians deal are themselves discursive constructs, and not items in the real world which are first collected and then assembled into stories. If Danto, Bradley and Febvre are right, then the problem with White is not his radicalism, but rather the timidity which holds him back from recognizing the discursive character of historical facts.[95] But doesn't this leave us adrift in a sea of relativism? If facts are theories, then what is to stop the Holocaust revisionist adjusting them so that Auschwitz vanishes from the historical record? But the debates over the Holocaust have already highlighted that even reporting events is not a matter of neutrally transcribing what actually happened: as we have seen, whether or not descriptions of Nazi crimes succeed in referring is an issue loaded with ethical and political implications. Indeed, many – perhaps most – people's moral intuitions would probably tell them that even to express a willingness to consider whether the Holocaust took place, as if it could be an open question, is just repugnant, an unacceptable stand to take. But if there is anything to these intuitions (as there surely is), then the idea of a neutral domain of facts is seriously compromised by those who will have no truck with Holocaust revisionism.

To establish where this leaves us requires taking a closer look at what is implied in acknowledging the discursive character of historical facts. One line of thought moves from the recognition that all reporting is selective to the conclusion that, since the principle on which the historian selects will embody a partial perspective on the world, the account she gives will be inherently subjective. E. H. Carr, for example, argues that, since 'the facts of history ... are always refracted through the mind of the recorder,' 'when we take up a work of history, our first concern should not be with the facts it contains, but with the historian who wrote it.'[96] The problem then is one of the inherent limitations of the historian's subjectivity confronted with an infinite array of events. Although very common (it is, for example, essentially the starting point of Charles Beard's version of historical relativism), this is not a very interesting way of thinking about the status of historical facts. The truism that any attempt to record events is selective offers no guidance about how to identify the position occupied by empirical evidence in the process of historical inquiry itself.

Here Collingwood's treatment of the issue, which draws on the work of Bradley and Oakeshott, seems to me definitive. *The Idea of History* is, among other things, a sustained polemic against 'scissors-and-paste history', the construction of accounts by bringing together and seeking to render compatible the available evidence. Collingwood does not pursue this course in order to arrive, as Carr suggests, at 'total scepticism' ('history is what the historian makes'[97]); rather, he seeks to understand the historian's practice as conforming to what he calls 'a logic of question and answer'. Eero Loone puts his views on the matter very well:

> The distinguishing feature of scientific historiography, according to Collingwood, is the putting by the historian of his own questions on the subject of his research, and not mere acceptance of the questions implicit in his manuscript sources, as with 'scissors-and-paste' historiography. The historian then draws conclusions from his answers to these questions (and not from the sources), these answers being based on facts for which the sources provide evidence.[98]

Historical facts are thus not the starting point of the process of inquiry but its result. 'The fact that in the second century the legions began to be recruited wholly outside Italy is not immediately given. It is arrived at inferentially by a process of interpreting data according to a complicated system of rules and assumptions.'[99] Conceiving the historian's practice in this way, as the interplay of question and answer, in which the autonomy of the process is established when the historian poses her own questions, rather than taking them ready-made from the sources, displaces the attempt to reduce historiography to narrative. Collingwood acknowledges that viewing historical inquiry as a process of question and answer is a development of Lord Acton's famous injunction, in his 1895 Inaugural Lecture at Cambridge, to 'study problems in preference to periods'.[100] Precisely the same conception of historiography is to be found at work in the *Annales* school. As Peter Schöttler points out, for Febvre 'the science of history' is 'a history of problems which does not start from facts encountered, but which must on each occasion construct its research object'.[101] Narrative on this view is at best one way of answering a particular question, but there is no reason why in principle it is to be preferred to either the kind of *pointilliste* historiography with which Lawrence Stone confuses narrative proper (see section 2.1 above) or the structural history with which both Marxism and the *Annales* school are identified.

Accepting Collingwood's account of the process of historical inquiry does not, of itself, settle the question of whether or not this process, when it is well conducted, issues in knowledge. This question is best addressed at two levels: that of the relationship between theory and evidence, and that of interpretation. The first of these issues is in no sense unique to historiography, or indeed to the humanities or the social sciences more generally. Richard Lewontin observes:

> The social structure of scholarly work and its rhetorical practices have given rise to the belief, even among the most sophisticated, that there is a fundamental difference between the concept and role of 'facts' in science and in history. It is by no means clear that such a fundamental difference exists.[102]

Indeed, the theory-ladenness of facts, as the jargon has it, is almost a basic postulate of contemporary philosophy of science; it can be traced back to the writings of the American pragmatists and to Karl Popper's path-breaking *Logic of Scientific Discovery* (1935). One way of putting the point is to say that basic statements, which report observations, have an irreducibly conjectural character. It follows that, should some observation appear to refute a well-established theory, it is logically permissible to save the theory by rejecting the basic statement reporting this inconvenient observation, perhaps by adjusting the observational theory by means of which experimental results are interpreted. So instead of theory confronting – and being put to the test of – independently established facts, we have a clash between two theories – the one which is apparently refuted by the observation, the other the observational theory. If we explain away the observation, we are preferring the first theory to the second (which we alter in order to get rid of the observation); if we uphold the observation, we have chosen the second over the first. There seem to be no objective criteria governing these decisions. It may come down, as W. V. Quine argues, to how well entrenched the theories are within the overall system of our beliefs; or, if Richard Rorty is right, it is a matter of aesthetic preference, no more a matter of rational adjudication than my liking one painting better than another.[103]

There is, however, a way of avoiding this kind of subjectivism. It is provided by Imre Lakatos. He accepts that there is no way, in principle, of determining how the scientist should respond to an experimental result which appears to refute some well-loved theory. It is open to the scientist to accept the theory's refutation or to explain away the observation: Lakatos notes that scientists as great as Newton have done the latter. He proposes, however, that we acknowledge any theoretical adjustments as constituting progress over the previous state of scientific research only if two constraints are observed. First, these changes must be consistent with what Lakatos calls the 'heuristic' employed by the scientist. Rather than operating with discrete hypotheses, scientists work within larger-scale research programmes, series of theories unified by the heuristic, which defines both the problems to be addressed and the methods by which they are to be resolved: like Collingwood, Lakatos believes that new knowledge emerges from a logic of question and answer. Scientists may, of course, choose to desert an unsuccessful research programme, but to make this more than a confession of despair they must come up with a new one. Secondly, a new version of a programme must open itself up to potential refutation by predicting some novel facts. It is not good enough that the scientist respond to some recalcitrant observation by reformulating her theories till they are consistent with this observation; the reformulated theories must entail observational statements other than those used in constructing them. If these statements are experimentally upheld, then the new version of the research programme has had its claim to make progress over its predecessor vindicated. If they are not – if the predictions of novel facts do not stand up to testing – then it is open to researchers to come up with yet another version; but if it (or yet more successors) fails to predict or have its predictions refuted, then the programme, Lakatos contends, must be regarded as degenerating.[104]

But why worry in the first place over whether scientific research programmes are progressive or degenerating? The only satisfactory answer to this question, Lakatos concludes, is that the criteria he formulates, and which, he believes, articulate the best scientific practice, offer some guidance in establishing which of our theories are true and which are false. The indications these criteria give are only approximate, since the best-established theory may turn out to be false, but this does not alter the fact that the sciences represent a search for the truth, and the consequent need to appraise our theories by their relative degree of success in attaining this objective. Lakatos understands truth in

classical terms, according to what is sometimes called the correspondence theory, by which sentences are true or false in
virtue of the nature of the world. The fact that a research programme is progressive – especially if it is 'empirically progressive',
that is, if its predictions turn out to be experimentally confirmed
– is a marker of its truth, or at least indicates that this programme is the best available approximation to the truth.[105]

The correspondence theory of truth is related to, even if it
does not entail, and is not entailed by, the metaphysical doctrine
of realism, according to which the world exists independently
of the mental.[106] Truth and realism have provoked enormously
wide-ranging and complex debates among analytical philosophers.
It is no part of my plans to engage with these debates in any
depth here. Nevertheless I cannot ignore them completely, since
some very influential philosophers have poured scorn on the idea
that our theories are to be appraised on the basis of how well
or badly they represent the world. Consider, first, these remarks
of Rorty's:

> We need to make a distinction between the claim that the
> world is out there and the claim that truth is out there. To
> say that the world is out there, that it is not our creation,
> is to say, with common sense, that most things in space and
> time are the effects of causes that do not include human
> mental states. To say that truth is not out there is simply
> to say that where there are no sentences there is no truth,
> that sentences are elements of human languages, and that
> human languages are human creations.
>
> Truth cannot be out there – cannot exist independently
> of the human mind – because sentences cannot so exist, or
> be out there. The world is out there, but descriptions of the
> world are not. Only descriptions of the world can be true
> or false. The world on its own – unaided by the describing
> activities of human beings – cannot.[107]

Although Rorty would undoubtedly resist being labelled a
realist, he seems here to be accepting realism – the proposition
that the world exists independently of thought – but rejecting
the correspondence theory of truth. But does the correspondence
theory really say that truth is 'out there'? It asserts, as we have
seen, that sentences are true or false in virtue of the nature of
the world. Truth is thus a property of sentences, and sentences
are linguistic entities. So the correspondence theory asserts, just

as Rorty does, that 'where there are no sentences there is no truth'. Truth, according to the correspondence theory, in this sense depends on language and its users, human beings. Does it follow, as Rorty would like us to infer, that human beings 'make' truth? No. Even if truth would not exist without human beings and their language, what makes a sentence true is the nature of the world. The correspondence theory posits a relationship between language and the world. Rorty's argument amounts to claiming that the correspondence theory makes truth somehow inhere in the world, and then appealing to the fact, common to any theory of truth, that it is sentences which are true or false. He thus misrepresents the correspondence theory; nevertheless, we can be grateful to Rorty, since correcting this misrepresentation serves to underline that, for the correspondence theory, truth relates language and the world.

One major problem concerns how to characterize this relationship. P. F. Strawson showed some decades ago that pseudo-entities like 'the facts' and 'states of affairs' which are supposed to make statements true or false are in reality part of the same discourse as concepts such as 'truth' itself.[108] Much more recently, Donald Davidson has made a more direct and comprehensive attack on correspondence theories of truth, declaring that 'there is nothing interesting or instructive to which true sentences might correspond.' This move by Davidson is significant, since he has sought to develop a philosophy of language and of mind which makes great use of Alfred Tarski's semantic conception of truth, according to which, where s is a sentence, 's' is true if and only if s. Davidson, like others (for example Popper), used to think that Tarski's concept of truth was a correspondence theory. He has now changed his mind, in part under Rorty's influence. Yet he still rejects anti-realist accounts which identify truth with, say, what the established scientific standards of the day justify us in asserting, because these 'deprive ... truth of its role as an intersubjective standard'. This role is important to Davidson because of his theory of radical interpretation. When we are confronted with an alien speaker whose utterances we do not understand we engage in radical interpretation. Proceeding according to the Principle of Charity, we assume that what the alien says is true. By then comparing the alien's utterances with what is going on around us, we are able progressively to assign a content to these utterances, taking what *we* hold to be true in the circumstances as the benchmark. Interpretation thus proceeds on the basis

that there is a ground level on which speakers share views,
but also that what they share is a largely correct picture
of a common world. The ultimate source of both objectivity
and communication is the triangle that, by relating speaker,
interpreter, and the world, determines the contents of thought
and speech. Given this source, there is no room for a rela-
tivized concept of truth.[109]

So Davidson wants a non-relativistic concept of truth, which is
concerned with the relationship between speakers and the world,
but rejects the correspondence theory. There seem, to say the
very least, to be tensions in this position. Part of the difficulty
lies in the fact that the correspondence theory relates language
and the world, but we can never, as it were, get out of language
to compare the two terms of the relationship. Hence the absurdity, highlighted by Strawson, of saying that sentences 'correspond' to facts which can only be identified by means of the
very sentences they are supposed to verify. We can then only
relate language and the world from inside language itself. But
this does not in any way remove the necessity of thinking about
that relationship. That necessity would only vanish if the world
did (in which case so would we, and a distinctly odd relationship would come to an end). The point of the correspondence
theory is that it defines what happens when our utterances capture the way the world is. As to Davidson's charge that 'there
is nothing interesting or instructive to which true sentences might
correspond', what about the world itself? The correspondence
theory doesn't require that we pick out particular segments to
which true sentences correspond, nor that we postulate some kind
of isomorphism between language and the world (as, for example,
does Wittgenstein's picture theory of meaning in the *Tractatus*).
It is the nature of the world which makes sentences true or
false. This does not mean that the world and sentences resemble
one another – though, of course, sentences are produced by
human beings, themselves a natural species that is itself part of
the world.

This line of thought serves to underline the connection between the correspondence theory of truth, which is part of the
philosophy of language, and the metaphysical doctrine of realism.
Realism asserts that the world is independent of the mental;
the correspondence theory gives an account of one way in which
the mental is itself related to the world. That account in turn
needs supplementation by, for example, a full-blown theory of

how utterances succeed in referring to items in the world, and an epistemology which shows how human beings as a particular kind of living organism are able to arrive at beliefs, and more especially at true beliefs.[110] Lakatos's methodology of scientific research programmes represents yet another supplement, in that it gives an account of how those very complex systems of beliefs called scientific theories can be appraised by their relative degree of success in approximating to the truth. It does so in a way that has the merit, from the point of view of our discussion of historiography, of conceiving scientific inquiry as a dialogue between theory and evidence. It is open to the theorist, Lakatos suggests, to criticize and indeed to reinterpret the evidence, provided that the outcome predicts novel facts, thereby widening the theory's coverage of the evidence. Plainly this account requires modification before it can be satisfactorily extended to the process of historical inquiry. Historians, who seek to reconstruct the past, cannot in general be expected to predict the future. But, on the face of it, there seems no reason why Lakatos's criteria of scientific progress cannot be suitably modified. We might, for example, say that a historical account will be regarded as representing progress over other accounts of the same phenomena if, directly or by implication, it covers a wider range of evidence than it was originally constructed to explain.[111]

These criteria do not, however, simply concern the relationship of theory to evidence. They also imply an account of the nature of scientific theories which claims that they form large-scale research programmes each unified by the heuristic which defines a set of problems and sets down guidelines for resolving them. But many philosophers and historians would deny the existence, or at any rate the desirability, of such complexes of theories in historiography. Their grounds for doing so typically include the claim that history differs from the physical sciences because it involves the interpretation of human action. Collingwood, for example, dismisses the construction of 'systems of pigeon-holes' in which to arrange the available evidence – philosophies of history, in other words – as scientifically worthless. The authors of such systems are misled by the idea that the physical sciences constitute a model for other forms of inquiry, and therefore fail to grasp what is distinctive to historical knowledge, namely that it consists in the reenactment by the historian of past thoughts.[112] This is, of course, a version of Dilthey's claim that history, like the human sciences more generally, is constituted by the practice of understanding, which perceives the social world as the creation of human minds, and which, in its highest form as empathy, consists in the historian re-experiencing a situation from the standpoint of the actor forming the object under investigation.[113]

While even those broadly sympathetic to Dilthey's and Collingwood's general approaches have tended to distance themselves from their precise formulations because they seem to make historical knowledge depend on an act of subjective projection unamenable to critical examination, the problem they pose is unavoidable. It would be too narrow simply to equate the object of historical inquiry with human action; nevertheless, historical accounts unavoidably deal with human beings and their actions, and therefore must find ways of identifying the beliefs and desires lying behind these actions. If historiography of necessity involves interpretation, however, it does not follow that it consists in interpretation alone; nor does it follow that the practice of interpretation by historians is inconsistent with the use of large-scale theories of history. I have discussed the philosophical issues involved at some length elsewhere.[114] Here I wish, by considering two accounts of interpretation, simply to establish that making sense of human actions does not rule out, but in fact requires, theorizing.

The first of these accounts is Gadamer's. He seeks to overcome Dilthey's subjectivism by drawing on Heidegger's analysis of human *Dasein* (There-being) in *Being and Time*. The 'throwness' characteristic of human existence – the fact that we live in a particular time, loaded down with the contingencies of our own personal circumstances and the practices of the society to which we belong – is not, as relativists like Beard and Carr think, a barrier to understanding, but rather its prerequisite. 'Understanding is not to be thought so much as an action of one's subjectivity, but of the placing oneself within a process of tradition, in which past and present are constantly fused.' Therefore, 'a person seeking to understand something has a relation to the object that comes into language in the transmitted text and has, or acquires, a connection with the tradition out of which the text speaks.' This connection is not, however, one of identity. There is rather a tension between the horizon of the present, the range of vision we have in our own situation, constituted by the specific set of historically formed circumstances in which we find ourselves, and the horizon of the past, that of the text we are trying to understand, itself formed within a different set of circumstances. We succeed when we are able to place ourselves in the position of the other – of the author of that text – and thereby to recognize the difference that separates us. This allows us to achieve 'a higher universality', one that transcends our own particularity and that of the other by placing both within the same tradition:

> The horizon of the present is continually formed, in that we have continually to test all our prejudices. An important part of this testing is the encounter with the past and the understanding of the tradition from which we come. The horizon of the present cannot be formed without the past. There is no more an isolated horizon of the present than there are historical horizons. Understanding, rather, is always the fusion of those horizons we imagine to exist by themselves. [115]

Gadamer's definition of historical understanding as the fusion of horizons, with the dialectic of identity and difference it implies, is undoubtedly immensely attractive. The difficulty is that Gadamer conceives understanding as something that occurs within a single tradition. It is true that he says, in a passage cited above, that the interpreter 'has, *or acquires*, a connection with the tradition out of which the text speaks'. But more typically the stress is on a fusion of horizons that takes place within the same tradition – or, perhaps better, which establishes the identity of that tradition. Thus, '[t]ime is no longer primarily a gulf to be bridged,' but 'a positive and productive possibility of understanding. It is not a yawning abyss, but is filled with the continuity of custom and tradition, in the light of which all that is handed down presents itself to us.'[116] But what happens when we seek to understand texts produced by those with whom we share no such continuity of tradition? The problem is most obvious in the case of Western historians seeking to reconstruct the past of other parts of the world, where Gadamer's conception of historical understanding would seem to condemn us to a kind of cultural solipsism. But a version of the problem presents itself even when we are studying the past of our own society. For who is to say that in a given society a particular set of beliefs and practices is sufficiently widespread to justify treating all members as participating in the same tradition? The work of a historian such as Carlo Ginzburg, who in a remarkable series of studies has sought to reconstruct the beliefs of the subordinate classes in early modern Europe, has been based, in part, on a rejection of the idea that these beliefs were a version of those

held by the dominant class.[117] But once we have admitted the
possibility of such discontinuities of belief within a society, it
becomes much harder to rest much weight on the notion of a
continuity of tradition stretching across time.

These difficulties with the idea of understanding as occurring
within a single tradition are obvious enough, and it is therefore
worth asking why Gadamer does not pay more attention to
them. Two possible reasons are worth mentioning. First, Gadamer
sees himself as continuing Dilthey's project of providing the
philosophical underpinnings of the work of the German historical
school. But Ranke, for example, defines as his object world
history, which is more or less explicitly identified with the evolution of the European state-system (see section 4.3 below) –
a conception of historiography easily worked up into the idea
that historical understanding unfolds within a single, unbroken
tradition. Secondly, Gadamer's conception of understanding is
deeply influenced by Hegel's concept of Spirit, which attains
full self-consciousness when it recognizes its complete identity
with its apparently alien object. Thus Gadamer argues that the
starting point for the human sciences is the concept of *Bildung*
(cultivation), and in particular Hegel's analysis of the concept,
which he endorses because it captures 'the basic tendency of the
historical spirit: to recognize oneself in other being'.[118] What is
historical understanding conceived as the transcendence of the
difference between past and present within the unity of a single
tradition but a version – toned down, no doubt, and shorn of
Hegel's absolute idealism – of this discovery of self in the other?

Gadamer is nevertheless right, I believe, to suggest that interpretation presumes the existence of something in common between
interpreter and interpreted. In what can it consist if not in the
continuity of shared tradition or participation in the movement
of Absolute Spirit? The obvious answer is surely that interpreter
and interpreted are both human beings, and therefore have a
common nature. It is this fact which lies behind the second theory
of interpretation, which explains human actions on the assumption
that those performing them acted *rationally*. Usually rationality
is understood in instrumental terms, so that an agent acts rationally where she selects the means appropriate to attaining a
given end. This conception of rationality is derived in its theoretically articulated form from neo-classical economics, but in
recent years, in the shape of rational choice theory, it has been
extended to the whole gamut of the social sciences. There have
also been attempts to make the concept of instrumental rationality

the basis of an account of historical explanation. Thus William Dray, a critical follower of Collingwood's, argues that the use of rational explanations 'gives a real point to the "projection" metaphors used by empathy theorists'.[119]

Now, historians undoubtedly do appeal, at least tacitly, to the concept of what it would be appropriate for a particular actor to do in a given situation. Take, for example, Steven Runciman's discussion of Pope Honorius IV's decision in September 1285 to issue, as suzerain of Sicily, two bulls reforming the government of the island, which was then in rebellion: 'Honorius doubtless thought that by admitting that there had been misgovernment and by guaranteeing a better future he removed from the Sicilians and the Calabrians their only reasons for continuing in rebellion.'[120] The adverb 'doubtless' tells us that Runciman lacks direct documentary proof for this attribution of motive. His explanation of Honorius's decision is a hypothesis, involving the claim that issuing the bulls was an appropriate means of achieving the goal of bringing the Sicilian rebellion to an end.

The fact that historians resort to explanations resting on the assumption that human beings act rationally does not, however, settle how this assumption can be justified and how the concept of rationality should be given content. Davidson's Principle of Charity, according to which we should proceed on the basis that those utterances of an alien speaker which she holds true are true, offers answers to these questions. Davidson makes it clear that the Principle of Charity is an assumption of rationality: 'If we cannot find a way to interpret the utterances and other behaviour of a creature as revealing a set of beliefs largely consistent and true by our own standards, we have no reason to count that creature as rational, as having beliefs, or as saying anything.'[121] This is a very strong condition and even, some commentators have argued, an ethnocentric one, since it makes the interpreter's beliefs the benchmark of truth. So an alternative to the Principle of Charity was developed: the Principle of Humanity. This states, according to Graeme Macdonald and Philip Pettit,

> that the interpreter should not so much maximize agreement, whatever the cost, as minimize a certain sort of disagreement which we find unintelligible. Where charity would have us recoil from the ascription of any disagreement or, as we are going see it, error, humanity would only have us do so when we cannot explain how such disagreement or error could have come about.[122]

Ascribing the beliefs and desires which give rise to action on the basis of what we think it intelligible that the actors believe and desire in the circumstances under study, however, only shifts the problem. For what principles will guide our judgements of intelligibility? David Wiggins, I think, gives the answer when he says that radical interpretation can only get going because 'we think we know more than nothing not only about the world but also about men in general.'[123] In other words, we can interpret the actions of others – and in particular of those human beings with whom we do not share the tradition whose existence is for Gadamer a condition of the possibility of understanding – because we draw on the knowledge that we already have of human beings in general and in the different kinds of society with which we are already acquainted. Bradley expresses a somewhat similar thought when he proposes the following criterion on which 'critical history' must base itself: 'every man's standpoint ought to determine his belief in respect to *all* past events.' This 'canon of history' is directed against Christian histories which by offering instances of divine intervention in human affairs – miracles and the like – require us 'to affirm the existence in history of causes such as we can find nothing analogous to now in our present experience'. Nevertheless, Bradley's claim that 'it is only from our knowledge of what is that we can conclude to that which has been' is capable of wider application.[124]

For historical criticism often proceeds by using the knowledge currently available to the historian in order to assess the validity of the factual claims made in the sources. The great Prussian military historian Hans Delbrück is a case in point. His *History of the Art of War* makes copious use of what he calls *Sachkritik*, the critical reappraisal of the historical record in the light of geographical information, comparisons with analogous situations in other periods and the rules of logic. Thus he appeals to the current practice of the German Imperial Army to cast doubt on some of Herodotus's figures, pointing out, for example, that, if Xerxes' army really had numbered 4,200,000 men, then, given that an army corps of 30,000 covered about 14 miles in the German march order, '[t]he march column of the Persians would ... have been 2,000 miles long, and when the head of the column was arriving before Thermopylae, the end of the column might have been just marching out of Susa, on the far side of the Tigris.' Delbrück offers the following justification of his method:

the farther the art of historical interpretation proceeds, the more it has become convinced that even contemporary reports are often falsified and clouded by fantasies of every type, and that in cases where the available material is not sufficient to permit checking one source against the other, objective-type interpretation remains the last resort. It is only a matter of following through and of acquiring so much special knowledge of the subject that one can be certain of not being led astray by a simple false analogy.[125]

There is an obvious danger with this way of proceeding, namely that 'objective-type interpretation' may turn out in fact to be highly subjective, allowing the historian to reconstruct the past to suit contemporary prejudices. Martin Bernal indeed believes that this was exactly what happened when nineteenth-century classical scholars rejected what he calls the 'Ancient Model' found, for example, in Herodotus, according to which Greek civilization was the result of colonization by more advanced societies in Asia and Africa, and replaced it with the 'Aryan Model', in which classical Greece developed endogenously from northern barbarian invasions, rather in the same way as modern Europe was supposed to have done. The assumption basic to *Quellenkritik*, that the sources cannot be taken at face value but must be subjected to rigorous examination, 'gave the – mainly German – scholars the confidence both to dismiss ancient descriptions of early Greek history and to invent new ones of their own without any regard to the Ancients'. Bernal notes that Niebuhr, the first major historian to make full use of *Quellenkritik*, was also 'the first to challenge the great ancient historians on their own turf'. The effect was that the history of classical antiquity was rewritten to conform to the racist ideology increasingly well entrenched as the nineteenth century wore on, and thus to rule out the possibility that the Greeks, exemplar to modern European civilization, could owe anything to the ancestors of the African and Asian peoples then in the process of being subjected to that civilization.[126]

The danger that historical criticism may degenerate into the kind of ideology-driven subjectivism described by Bernal is undeniable. It does not follow that the historian can abjure resort to currently available knowledge when she seeks critically to interpret the traces from which she aims to reconstruct the past. For how could she, without giving up her identity as a human being existing in a particular set of circumstances and

transforming herself into a disembodied Cartesian ego? Two
aspects of Gadamer's theory of understanding are relevant here.
First, the historian exists thick with all the characteristics that
have come to inhere in her as a result of the time and the place
in which she lives. These characteristics are not obstacles to
knowing the past, but rather resources on which the historian can
draw. The Rankean ideal of impartiality, in which the historian
seeks to approximate to God, whom he imagines 'as seeing the
whole of historical humanity (since no time is before the deity),
and finding it all equally valuable', is a dream and a delusion.
The historian must use her circumstances – including the currently available knowledge – in order to comprehend the past.[127]
Secondly, Gadamer's conception of understanding as the fusion
of horizons affirms at once the existence of a distance separating
past and present and the possibility of overcoming them. But this
fusion should not be thought of as merely the assimilation and
incorporation into our knowledge of some new description of past
events. On the contrary, reconstructing the past may require the
revision of existing beliefs in order properly to take account of
phenomena which perhaps cast new light on societies other than
that under study. Historical understanding, Gadamer suggests, is
a dialectic of identity and difference: this implies that the effort
to understand the past may change us, rather than historical
interpretation merely feeding our narcissistic self-importance.

Now, in so far as the knowledge on which the historian draws
is historical knowledge it includes theories. In one sense of the
word 'theory' the preceding sentence is a truism. For we have
seen that every narrative is a theory in that, by selecting only
certain events for inclusion, it imposes a structure on them (see
section 2.3 above). A large segment of the stock of knowledge
which the historian uses in critically examining her evidence
will consist in this kind of theory – that is, in those historical
accounts which, having passed the appropriate tests, are now accepted as true (perhaps for reasons best explicated using Lakatos's
methodology of scientific research programmes). I am, however,
interested here in theories in a strong sense – for example, those
about the nature and forms of human society. It is hard to see
how the historian can do without some kind of social theory.

For consider the act of interpretation itself. We have seen
that, as Wiggins suggests, it can proceed only because 'we think
we know more than nothing ... about men in general'. But
this knowledge cannot consist merely of, for example, the kind
of currently available information about military logistics that

Delbrück uses when he practises *Sachkritik*. It cannot, in fact, simply be knowledge of 'men in general'. As we have seen, modern historical discourse depends on an awareness of temporality, and of the radical differences it introduces between societies and epochs. Marc Bloch calls history '"the science ... of men in time". The historian does not think of the human in the abstract. His thoughts breathe freely the air of the climate of time.'[128] But if this is right, then historical inquiry requires some conception of how human beings relate to their variable social contexts, and of the nature of and the differences between these contexts. In other words, it requires a social theory.

The trouble is, of course, that so well entrenched is empiricism in the historical profession, in the English-speaking world at any rate, that most practising historians are likely to reject the line of reasoning set out in the preceding paragraph. This does not mean, however, that they can avoid reliance on a social theory. Take, for example, the following remarks by one of the central figures in twentieth-century British historiography, Lewis Namier:

> A dilettante is one who takes himself more seriously than his work; and doctrinaires enamoured of their theories or ingenious ideas are dilettanti in public affairs. On the contrary, the historical approach is intellectually humble; the aim is to comprehend situations, to study trends, to discover how things work: and the crowning attainment of historical study is a historical sense – an intuitive understanding of how things do not happen (how they did happen is a matter of specific knowledge).[129]

Like many professions of humility Namier's definition is most arrogantly expressed. The historian, abjuring theory, develops a sense of 'how things do not happen', of the constraints on human action. Presumably this 'intuitive understanding' is capable of being expressed in propositional form. But of what could these propositions consist except a number of generalizations, no doubt rather loose and vaguely formulated, about the conduct of human beings in society and the variations in societies? And what do these amount to except, once again, a social theory of some sort? Usually these generalizations can be elicited from historical texts of the traditional Anglophone empiricist mode only in the shape of the odd *obiter dictum* pronounced by the historian in passing, or through a careful analysis of the manner in which her narrative is constructed, the emphases and exclusions it effects.

Namier is a case in point, since his studies of both Hanoverian politics and European diplomacy imply a devaluation of the significance of abstract ideas and a stress on the role of irrational motivations in explaining political behaviour which he was, unusually, prepared on occasion to defend.[130]

The point is one that admits of generalization. It is well stated by Maurice Mandelbaum:

> Historical inquiries do not ever proceed without at least an implicit acceptance by the historian of one or other set of theoretical commitments – as Werner Sombart remarked, 'No theory, no history.' Among such commitments will be those that characterize the historian's view of the nature of societies and of the factors affecting social stability and change.[131]

This seems right: history is irreducibly theoretical. The only choice the historian has is between the self-conscious adoption of an articulated social theory and the tacit reliance on an unacknowledged theory. Taking the latter course means that the generalizations used by the historian escape precise formulation or critical scrutiny; in its own way this smacks of dilettantism just as much as the doctrinaire theorizing denounced by Namier. It does, however, have its ideological uses. Inevitably the historian's 'intuitive understanding of how things do not happen' is likely to draw on 'common sense', that is, on the repertoire of prevailing beliefs about human beings and the world which are treated as so well established as to require neither formal justification nor even explicit statement. Now, the hermeneutic tradition has highlighted the extent to which our understanding of and engagement with the world are dependent on the existence of such unexamined background beliefs, and of the practical skills with which these beliefs are interwoven: understanding, as Heidegger puts it, 'is grounded in *something we grasp in advance* – in a *fore-conception* [*Vorgriff*]'.[132] It is, however, one of the characteristic features of the intellectual tradition founded by the Enlightenment – of which, as we have seen, modern historiography is a chief glory – that the pre-understandings on which our explicit beliefs rest become the object of critical reflection. Is it asking too much to suggest that, as part of this process, the historian's tacit theoretical commitments should be acknowledged so that they can be given articulate shape and thereby subjected to the kind of scrutiny to which any claim to knowledge must submit?

Let me, in conclusion, attach two provisos to this argument. First, to say that every historical inquiry implies some social theory is not to reduce one to the other. Thus I do not claim that the kinds of theory of history discussed in the next chapter represent the only valid approach to understanding the past. The slightest acquaintance with historical literature soon makes one aware of the existence of a plurality of historiographic genres. Each of these genres, in the hands of skilful and imaginative practitioners, can give real insights.

The most one can ask is that, as I have already said, the dependence of historical inquiry on social theory be honestly recognized, and the implication accepted that consideration of rival theories may cast light on the nature of the object of historical inquiry as a whole, and therefore on the interrelationship of different historiographic genres.

These general considerations apply to the particular form of inquiry privileged by postmodernist historiography – the study of beliefs, symbols and other forms of representation. No one could doubt the great advances which have been made in this area over recent years – as is shown, for example, by the work of various historians on the iconography of the French Revolution, by Peter Brown's researches into late antiquity and by such brilliant individual studies as Georges Duby's *The Three Orders*, Simon Schama's *The Embarrassment of Riches* and Inga Clendinnen's *Aztecs*. None of this work, however, proceeds by treating representations as, to adapt Carlo Ginzburg's formulation, a wall of texts beyond which one cannot penetrate. Rather, as Gabrielle Spiegel puts it,

> it is by focusing on the social logic of the text, its location within a broader network of social and intertextual relations, that we best become attuned to the specific historical conditions whose presence and/or absence *in* the work alerts us to its own social character and function, its own combination of material and discursive realities that endow it with its own sense of historical purposiveness.[133]

Microhistory, the historiographic genre particularly associated with Ginzburg's name, has also been claimed as an exemplar of postmodernism. Its focus on the particular, the local, even the idiosyncratic, certainly might seem at odds with the tendency towards large-scale generalizations characteristic of both Marxism and Weberian historical sociology. But in fact on closer

examination the difference of principle between microhistory
and macrohistorical theories dissolves. Arguably one of the finest
instances of the genre, Edward Thompson's *Whigs and Hunters*,
is the work of a Marxist who is not afraid to use the outcome
of his investigations of localized struggles around Windsor in
the early eighteenth century to sketch out a damning portrait
of Hanoverian society as a whole. Ginzburg himself may lack
Thompson's well-known theoretical and political affiliations,
but is quite prepared, as *Ecstasies* shows, to extend (indeed,
arguably to overextend) his inquiries into the most wide-ranging
macrohistorical speculations, tracing early modern beliefs in
the Witches' Sabbath to the deep structure of Indo-European
myth; moreover, he has explicitly linked his distinctive historical
method, which he compares to that of the doctor, the detective,
and the modernist novelist, to 'an explicit rejection of the sceptical implications (postmodernist if you will) so largely present
in European and American historiography of the 1980s and early
1990s'.[134]

My second proviso is a corollary of the first. The empirical
studies undertaken by working historians – for example, those
referred to in the preceding paragraphs – provide an indispensable control on all species of social theory. The relationship
between theory and evidence, I have already said, is a dialogue.
Formulations such as this are common enough, and when used,
as now, to highlight the dependence of historical inquiry on
social theory, it is easy to lay the main stress on the first term
of the relationship. It is necessary, however, to insist on the irreducible role played by the second. Empirical evidence, even
when gathered in pursuit of a research programme and in order
to corroborate certain hypotheses, imposes inescapable limits on
all theorizing. This general principle, when applied to the case
of historical writing, may be thought to be a reflection of what
Spiegel calls 'the irreducible alterity of the past', which 'confers
on history its proper function, ... to recover that alterity in as
close an approximation of "how it actually was" as possible'.[135]
History may depend on social theory, but so too does social
theory on history. Let us turn, then, to those social theories which
embody a recognition of this truth.[136]

3
HISTORY AS THEORY

The inner meaning of history ... involves speculation and an attempt to get at the truth, subtle explanation of the causes and origins of existing things, and deep knowledge of the how and why of events. [History,] therefore, is firmly rooted in philosophy.

Ibn Khaldûn

3.1   WHAT IS A THEORY OF HISTORY?

Historians, in seeking to reconstruct the past, draw (albeit in most cases tacitly) on theories about the nature and transformation of human society. There is, however, an important distinction between this kind of unacknowledged reliance on theory – where the historian may quite sincerely deny that she is doing more than recount what happened – and the self-conscious pursuit of a research programme in history. In the latter case the historian is likely explicitly to articulate the theoretical basis of her research and may indeed be seeking to corroborate some hypotheses formulated within the programme. Marxist historiography is, of course, the most obvious instance of such self-consciously theoretically guided historical research. There are, however, other examples. One of the distinguishing features of the 'New History' developed by the *Annales* school was its resort to what in France tend to be called the 'human sciences' – anthropology, economics, sociology, psychoanalysis, and so on. The New Economic History – heavily reliant on sophisticated statistical techniques and on the concepts and propositions of neo-classical economics – is perhaps the closest counterpart of this approach to be found in the English-speaking world, but a variety of other historians have made much more individual uses of sociology and anthropology – for example, Keith Hopkins in his studies of the Roman state,

and Keith Thomas in his path-breaking exploration of popular
beliefs and practices in early modern England, *Religion and the
Decline of Magic*.

In many of the cases mentioned above the historian resorts,
often quite eclectically, to ideas derived from some social theory
or other, to clarify issues that have arisen in her research, or
even to define its objective. Though self-conscious enough, this
kind of theoretically guided historiography does not involve a
particularly tight relationship between a set of hypotheses which
bear on, *inter alia*, the nature of the historical process itself,
and the research being pursued by the historian. A much more
sustained dialogue between theory and evidence is, however,
attempted in other cases, for example, that of the historical
sociologies developed by various neo-Weberian theorists, which
are discussed at length below. Recent years, too, have seen an
efflorescence of historical research pursued by scholars influenced by poststructuralism, and particularly by Foucault's writings
– for example, the work of cultural historians, notably on the
English Renaissance, that achieved notoriety in the 1980s under
the label the 'New Historicism'.[1]

These examples suggest a heterogeneous collection of different
types of research. Indeed, one might argue that a consistent
Foucauldian should eschew historiography *tout court*: after all,
Foucault himself said that his books 'aren't treatises in philosophy
or studies of history: at most, they are philosophical fragments
put to work in a historical field of problems'.[2] Many historians
would in any case deny that historical sociology is 'proper' history,
since it lacks the research on primary sources – archival documents and the like – which is the defining characteristic of what
Sir Geoffrey Elton calls 'a reliable historiography'.[3] Matters are
not quite so simple, however. It is not clear, for example, how
in principle one could differentiate the kind of wide-ranging interpretive essay of which Hugh Trevor-Roper is the master – I
have in mind especially his two great essays on the gentry and
the crisis of the seventeenth century – from the outstanding work
of Weberian historical sociology, the first volume of Michael
Mann's *The Sources of Social Power*. It is true that Mann covers
a vastly greater sweep of history, as he traces the course of
Western state-building from Sargon to the Elder Pitt. But does
not Trevor-Roper cut himself loose from any firm anchorage
in the sources when he seeks to offer an account of the crisis
which gripped European society in its entirety in the seventeenth
century? Nor is historical sociology (as the caricatured versions

of it offered by some historians suggest) speculation uncontrolled by the discipline of empirical evidence: the culmination of Mann's narrative, where he recounts the rise of the modern European state-system, makes systematic use of a careful analysis of English state finances from the twelfth century onwards.[4]

The difference is, the sceptical historian might respond, that Trevor-Roper's large-scale interpretations are informed by an understanding of early modern European societies gained by a lengthy training in and practice of historical scholarship based on close study of the sources, while the historical sociologist is likely to treat particular historical cases as mere exemplifications of some general proposition derived from social theory, and therefore to efface the singularity of the phenomena under examination. Elton, for example, argues that the practice of the trained historian provides the only available guarantee of reliable knowledge of the past:

> The two uncertainties of the historian – lack of knowledge, and the need to select – have their cure in the proper practice of scholarship and research. The methods of the trained professional historian are designed to protect him against his human difficulties, and they very often do achieve their purpose.[5]

There is something to this. Their lengthy engagement with the sources seems to give some historians the ability to go beyond them in intuitive flashes. Consider, for example, this anecdote, told by A. J. P. Taylor to illustrate the difference between Lewis Namier and himself as historians:

> I often relied on intuition; Lewis believed in laborious research ... reviewing Weizsäcker's memoirs, I remarked that of course his criticisms of Hitler's policy were merely put in a drawer and not shown to anyone. Lewis said to me. 'How did you know that Weizsäcker's memoranda had no registration number on them? I worked in the archives for a fortnight to establish that point.' I said I felt it must be so. Lewis groaned: 'Ah, you have green fingers. I have not.'[6]

This is a good story. But, of course, having green fingers isn't enough to make a good historian – Namier managed to be a great one without them. At most, what Norman Stone calls

Taylor's 'inspired guesses' allowed him to formulate hypotheses which other scholars were able to corroborate by checking them against the sources.[7] Close acquaintance with the sources may let some historians take short cuts based on intuition, but the critical examination of the accounts they give using these inspired guesses cannot itself rely on intuition but must rather rest on intersubjectively acceptable standards – perhaps those criteria of scientific progress formulated by Imre Lakatos (see section 2.4 above). The scholarly practice of even the most experienced and inspired historian is thus accountable to a process of public ad-judication of the writing that issues from this practice. Once this is granted it is hard to draw a clear line of demarcation between a broad interpretive essay written by a historian and one produced by a historical sociologist: whatever their origins, whether only one has been sanctified by the chrism of direct contact with the sources, both are subject to the same process of critical appraisal. Unless legitimate historical inquiry is to be restricted to the research monograph – a step which even the most fuddled empiricist would hesitate at taking – then it seems hard to exclude from its domain interpretations generated by the kind of theories of history accepted by Marxists and Weberians.

But what is such a theory of history? A theory of history must, it seems to me, meet three conditions:[8]

(1) A theory of history includes a *theory of structure*. That is, it must give some account of the differences between various kinds of society, differences typically explained by appeal to the concept of social structure – of the fundamental relationships constitutive of a particular kind of society. These relationships have a number of important properties: their existence does not depend on the participation in them of particular named persons; they are sets of empty places, which can be filled by any suitably trained and motivated individuals. Moreover, structures exist independently of those occupying them being aware of their existence: the most important social relationships are those which, as Hegel put it, go on behind the backs of the human beings making up the society in question.[9]

A theory of structure seems to me a necessary condition of any theory of history, for two reasons. First, if all human soci-eties shared the same structure then what Eero Loone calls 'the *presumption of qualitative difference*' that is 'one of the most im-portant socio-theoretical presuppositions of historical knowledge' would fall away.[10] No theory can be a theory of *history* that does not include among its premises some account of the singularity of different human societies. Secondly, the concept of structure implies that the accounts given by participants in a given society cannot be taken at face value but must be subjected to critical examination if they are to provide evidence of the nature of that society. To borrow formulations used by Marx in *Capital*, how a society presents itself to those participating in it and how its inner structure actually functions do not correspond; hence the need for a *theory* of history, which is not content to register the surface appearances of social life but formulates explanatory concepts designed to uncover the underlying relationships which make that society what it is.[11] That the historian's concepts do not correspond with those she finds in the sources is, I think, a general feature of historical inquiry: otherwise, Marc Bloch observes, 'history would have little left to do'; he compares the historian who inherits terms such as 'feudal' and gives them new meanings to 'the physicist who, in disregard of Greek, persists in calling an "atom" something which he spends his time in dividing'.[12] This characteristic of historical inquiry is, however, given a systematic rationale in theories of history.

Historical materialism involves a theory of structure in the sense outlined above. This consists especially in the concept of mode of production. In contemporary usage (which does not correspond exactly to Marx's) this treats each social system as defined by a particular combination of the forces and relations of production – that is, of, on the one hand, the material elements of production (labour power and the means of production), the specific combination of which in the labour process represents a particular level of development of productive technique; and, on the other hand, a specific form of effective control of the productive forces, which, in class societies, gives rise to the appropriation of surplus labour by the controlling minority, and, on the basis of the definite form this exploitation takes, to the division of society into classes with antagonistic interests. Although the mode of production is constituted by the forces and relations of production, it is not exhausted by them: it comprises also law, politics and ideology, the superstructure whose movements are explained (in a manner whose precise character has been the subject of endless controversy among Marxist theorists) by the economic base. Finally, modes of production, basic types of human society such as slavery, feudalism and capitalism, are distinguished from social formations, actually existing societies

which may involve a combination of more than one mode of production, though one mode is always dominant over the others.[13]

The Weberian counterpart of this theory of structure is perhaps most perspicuously stated by W. G. Runciman when he
argues that social structure is defined by three 'dimensions of
power', 'access to or control of the *means of production, means
of persuasion* and *means of coercion*'. Consistent with a preoccupation with power that derives ultimately from Nietzsche
(see section 3.2 below), Weberian historical sociologists tend to
conceptualize societies as different forms of domination: thus
Runciman distinguishes between various 'modes of the distribution
of power'.[14] The most obvious difference between this style of
theory and historical materialism is that the Weberian theory of
structure is pluralist in the way it frames explanations. As Perry
Anderson puts it, 'there is no primacy of economic causation ...:
military-political and ideological-cultural determinations are of
equivalent significance.'[15]

(2) A *theory of transformation* is required to make a theory
properly historical. On its own a theory of structure would
merely issue in a typology of social forms, a theoretically informed
inventory of the differences between societies. To avoid being
merely a principle of societal classification, a theory of history
must contain some account of the mechanism or mechanisms
responsible both for the changes that take place within a particular society and, more importantly, for the transformation of
a society, that is, for the process through which it ceases to
embody one particular structure, and comes instead to embody
another.

Theories of history thus differ not simply in the accounts they
give of social structure but in the mechanism or mechanisms
they claim govern the transformation of societies. In principle,
each kind of society could have its own distinctive mechanism,
but I know of no theory of history representing this possibility:
its explanatory power would in any case be comparatively weak,
since a defining characteristic of a theory (as opposed to a description) is that it explains a wide range of phenomena on the basis
of a comparatively small number of propositions. The strongest
theory of history, therefore, is the one which claims that the
same mechanism is responsible for all historical transformations.
One example is provided by Arnold Toynbee, for whom the rise
and fall of civilizations are consequences of 'the interplay between
challenges and responses': this mechanism produces a universal

pattern, in which a civilization breaks down when it polarizes between a 'dominant minority' and 'internal and external proletariats' alienated from this ruling group; ultimately the proletariat, invigorated by a process of spiritual renewal, breaks away to found a new civilization.[16] But what *A Study of History* thereby gains in empirical range it loses in theoretical specificity, since the mechanism of challenge-and-response is characterized in such vague and loose terms that it is difficult to see what could constitute a counter-example to the explanatory claims made for it, so that the theory explains nothing and everything at the same time.[17]

The two most interesting theories of history occupy positions intermediate between the two extremes of allocating to each structure its own mechanism of change and explaining all social transformations by the same mechanism. Neo-Weberian theories are as pluralist in the accounts they give of change as in their conceptualizations of social structure. Each of the kinds of domination they identify is capable of effecting transformations in particular historical circumstances. As Anderson puts it, 'different societies and different epochs exhibit different dominants, which have to be established case by case.'[18] Thus if the same mechanisms are at work throughout history, the role they play varies from situation to situation. The thought is expressed with especial vigour by Mann (who differs from Runciman in treating as basic, not three dimensions, but four sources of power – ideological, economic, military, and political):

> there is no obvious, formulaic, general patterning of the interrelations of power sources. It will be evident by now, for example, that this volume cannot support a general 'historical materialism' ... Economic power relations, modes of production, and social classes come and go in the historical record. In occasional world-historical moments they decisively reorganize social life; usually they are important in conjunction with other power sources; occasionally they are decisively reorganized by them. The same can be said of all the power sources, coming and going, weaving in and out of the historical record.[19]

Historical materialism is, by comparison, strongly monist. Social transformation – the transition from one mode of production to another – is explained in terms of the same mechanism, the development of conflicts within the domain of social production.

These conflicts (or contradictions – a term which in the Marxist tradition is used to highlight the claim that they are inherent in the social form concerned) are of two kinds: the fettering of the productive forces by the relations of production (itself a consequence of the prior development of the productive forces) and the class struggle between exploiters and exploited. Although distinct, these two social contradictions are interrelated, since, generally speaking, the economic crises produced by fettering intensify class antagonisms. But though Marxism thus specifies a universal mechanism of change, albeit one conceptualized with far greater precision than Toynbee's, the forms taken by the two kinds of conflict vary significantly according to the nature of the prevailing mode of production. Each mode of production has its own 'laws of motion': this implies that the dynamics of economic crisis will differ significantly from one mode to another. Thus, whereas Marx's theory of capitalist crises conceives these as crises of *overproduction*, in which productive forces go to waste because it is unprofitable to use them, Marxist historians tend to treat the crisis of feudal society in the late Middle Ages as one characterized by scarcity, involving an imbalance between population and productive resources. Again, the forms taken by the class struggle differ significantly according to the manner in which the conflicting classes are constituted by the relations of exploitation. In these respects the Marxist theory of history is a compromise between accounting for all change by the same mechanism and identifying a mechanism for every different social structure.[20]

(3) Every theory of history has, finally, a *theory of directionality*, that is, it offers an account of the overall pattern described by the historical process. If the theory of transformation specifies the mechanism(s) responsible for the transition between one social form and another, the theory of directionality is concerned with the overall shape given to human history by the sum of these transitions. Three principal patterns have been identified. First, *progress*: each successive social form represents an increase in some property common to all kinds of society. Marxism conceives history as progress in this sense since it claims that there is a tendency for the productive forces to develop from one mode of production to another. Secondly, *regress*: the succession of social forms involves a cumulative decrease in the property in terms of which a pattern in the course of history is sought. Claims of this sort are common enough in Christian theologies in as much as,

following Augustine, they posit a radical disjunction between two polities, one heavenly and governed by divine providence, the other secular and subject to human wills suffering from the inherent flaw of original sin: thus, as Georges Duby puts it, European intellectuals around the year 1000 'thought human history in the grip of the forces of evil and consequently a history of decline'.[21] Modern theories which conceive history straightforwardly as a regress are comparatively rare: Rousseau's *Discourse on the Origins of Inequality* might be considered an example. It is more usual to explain what are thought to be periods of decline as the final stage in a historical cycle. For, thirdly, there are modern theories of history which revive the ancient idea that the course of history follows a *cycle* of progress and regression: Spengler and Toynbee represent the most important twentieth-century examples of this way of thinking.

It might be thought that giving an account of the directionality of history is not a necessary condition of a theory of history in the way that the first two are. After all, theories of structure and transformation serve to specify the explanatory objectives of a theory of history. By contrast, arriving at a judgement about the overall pattern described by the course of history might seem to be a superadded and dispensable element, a distinct intellectual operation from those closely linked explanatory activities laid down in the theories of structure and transformation, the ascription of a value to the process analysed by these theories. There are, I think, three reasons for resisting this line of thought. First, conditions (1) and (2) provide the conceptual means of giving an overall account of the historical process. Such an account would, however, surely be incomplete if it did not involve at least the attempt to discern some pattern emerging from the transformations of human societies. Secondly, this attempt need not be intrinsically evaluative in the sense of passing an ethical judgement on the course of history. All that is required for a theory of directionality is that it specify some property whose increase or decrease represents, respectively, progress or regress, and that it advances the claim that the historical process involves a tendency for progress or regression thus defined to occur (or, in the case of a cyclical theory, for progress and regress to alternate in some law-governed fashion). The theory need not involve the further claim that the increase of this property contributes to the good as defined by some ethical theory. Thirdly, and more pragmatically, the two most important theories of history, the Marxist and the Weberian, both involve theories of progress in the sense just specified.

This latter claim has been most effectively defended by Erik Olin Wright, Andrew Levine and Elliott Sober in a critical discussion of Anthony Giddens's theory of history. They give what amount to the necessary conditions of a theory of historical progress (which they call 'directionality', thus giving the latter term a narrower meaning than the sense in which it is used here):

> The probability of staying at the same point is greater than the probability of regressing ... In a proper theory of history, social forms must be 'sticky downward'.
> There must be some probability of moving from a given level to the next higher level.
> The probability of a 'progressive' change is greater than the probability of 'regression'. [22]

Plainly, historical materialism is a theory of progress in this sense, since it asserts that there is a tendency for the productive forces to develop (though there is, of course, considerable debate among Marxists about the precise character of this tendency and its implications for the nature of social transformation). [23] It is, however, much more controversial to claim that Weberian theories discern a progressive direction in history. Giddens, for example, sets his account of historical development explicitly in opposition to evolutionism (of which he counts Marxism an instance). [24] Nevertheless, as Wright, Levine and Sober point out, he does claim that successive social forms represent an increase in 'time–space distanciation', the processes through which societies gain access to larger expanses of space and time, thereby enhancing agents' control over economic and ideologico-military resources, and in this respect Giddens implicitly contradicts his explicit 'rejection of the idea that historical change has an epochal directionality'. [25]

Other Weberian theorists have been much less shy about acknowledging that they see history taking a progressive course. Runciman, who explicitly seeks to develop an evolutionary theory of society, declares: 'As in biological evolution, there has unquestionably been a progression towards more and more complex forms of social organization.' [26] And Mann, at the conclusion of his 'history of power to AD 1760', gives this retrospective judgement:

Social power has continued to develop, somewhat unsteadily perhaps, but nonetheless cumulatively throughout this volume ... Seen in the very long run, the infrastructure available to power holders and to societies at large has steadily increased. Many different societies have contributed to this. But, once invented, the major infrastructural techniques seem almost never to have disappeared from human practice. True, often powerful techniques have seemed inappropriate to the problems of a succeeding society and thus have declined. But, unless obsolete, their decline has proved temporary and they have been subsequently recovered.[27]

These remarks of Mann's are especially helpful since they serve to dramatize the logical gap separating the claim that history has a progressive direction from an ethical judgement which finds this movement good. The property which, according to Mann, increases over time is social power. Since this embraces more particularly the destructive capacities of states and their ability to penetrate and control the everyday existence of their subjects, this is a process of development which we may have good ethical and political reasons for condemning. Giddens is the contemporary theorist whose view of history is perhaps closest to Weber's when he described modernity as the confinement of humankind in an 'iron cage', but there is no reason why we should not draw a similar moral conclusion to Weber's from other accounts which conceptualize history as the growth of the resources of domination.[28] There is much more to be said about the question of historical progress, a subject to which I return in chapter 4. There is, however, a remaining issue to be clarified before I consider the differences between Marxist and Weberian theories of history more closely.

How do theories of history as defined by the three conditions given above differ from philosophies of history? In section 1.4 above I adopted Maurice Mandelbaum's definition of a philosophy of history as (1) covering the whole of the historical process, (2) offering a general principle of explanation of this process in all its aspects and (3) seeking out the meaning of history. I suggested that theories of history such as Marxism and Weberian historical sociologies met conditions (1) and (2) but not condition (3). It is time to say more about this. For it is undeniably the case that embedded within what are, on Mandelbaum's definition, philosophies of history are accounts which, on the face of it, meet the three conditions I have argued

are necessary features of the theory of history. Hegel's philosophy of history is a case in point: the social forms that make
up the subject matter of history have the constitution of a state
(structure); their succession is explained as a dialectical movement generated by internal contradictions (transformation); and
this movement represents the development of the consciousness
of freedom (directionality). Or take Toynbee's *Study*, which offers
an account of the nature of complex civilizations (structure),
of the mechanism – challenge-and-response – responsible for
their rise and fall (transformation) and of the pattern of historical
development, in which 'recurrence' is 'concurrent with progress'
(directionality).[29] There are, nevertheless, good reasons for regarding Hegel and Toynbee as philosophers rather than theorists
of history.

The overlap between philosophies and theories of history arises,
of course, from the fact that both seek to offer explanations
applicable to the whole of the historical process (Mandelbaum's
condition (2)). The differences separating these two forms of
theoretical discourse are best seen as consequences of the kinds
of explanation they offer. One might say that theories of history
are empirical whereas philosophies of history are not. This statement seems to me correct. One way of characterizing theories of
history is to say that they are research programmes subject to the
criteria of theoretical and empirical progress – respectively, the
prediction of novel facts and the corroboration of some of these
predictions – developed by Imre Lakatos (see section 2.4 above).
They are therefore empirical theories in a way that Hegel's
philosophy of history certainly is not. For Hegel the proposition
that history is governed by reason requires no empirical con-
firmation, since it derives from a 'real proof' which 'comes from
knowledge of reason itself' provided by philosophy, and more
particularly by a grasp of the self-movement of the categories of
Hegel's own speculative logic (see section 1.2 above).

Important though this difference is, it does not, however, seem
to me to cut to the core of what separates theories from philosophies of history. This is that philosophies of history are teleological – that is, the account they give of the meaning of the
historical process, and more particularly of the state of affairs in
which it culminates, explains the succession of social forms making
up the content of that process. Once again, Hegel provides a
good illustration of this pattern: the 'real proof' of reason's rule
over the world reveals a teleological structure in which the conclusion of the dialectical process justifies its starting point, so

that 'the science is seen to be a circle which returns upon itself'.[30]
Kant's critical philosophy seeks to avoid ontotheological speculation, but is no less teleological in its application to history:
'*The history of the human race can be regarded as the realization
of a hidden plan of nature to bring about an internally ...
perfect political constitution as the only possible state within
which all the natural capacities of mankind can be developed
completely.*' The mechanism through which nature's aim of fully
developing humankind's 'natural capacities' is to be realized is
'the *unsocial sociability* of man': in rather the same fashion as
Hegel's cunning of reason, human beings' 'self-seeking pretensions'
lead them to develop these capacities, a process that is likely
(but not certain) in the future to draw them into republican
government and a federation of peoples.[31]

Theories of history, by contrast, seek to give non-teleological
explanations of the historical process. Both Marxist and Weberian
theories discern a progressive directionality in the course of
history – respectively, the development of the productive forces
and the growth of social power. But the existence of such a
pattern does not provide the rationale for the explanations each
theory gives of specific social transformations. The nature of
every social form is to be understood, not in terms of the final
state of affairs towards which it is a step, but on the basis of
the powers and relations constituting it, which give that form its
identity but may threaten its survival.

This is not a particularly controversial claim to make of
Weberian theories of history, since positing a multiplicity of
mechanisms as the causes of historical change – in Runciman's
terminology, control over the means of production, coercion and
persuasion, or, as the title of Ernest Gellner's main work of
historical sociology has it, *Plough, Sword and Book* – would
sit ill with projecting a single path of historical development
predetermined by its outcome. Anderson ascribes to Weberian
theorists the claim that 'the procession of variant institutional
hierarchies that makes up the record of human development is
contingent – not a chapter, but an encyclopaedia of accidents.'[32]
This is perhaps to put it a bit strongly: Mann, for example,
does highlight the importance of historical accidents – 'the "might
have beens" and "almost weres" [that] could have led into fundamentally different historical tracks' from those which actually
unfolded – but his narrative of the growth of social power in
the West seems in fact to draw on an interplay of 'pattern' and
'accident' in which 'power struggles are the principal patterings

of history, but their outcomes have often been close-run.'[33]
What is undoubtedly true is that all Weberian theorists are
committed to giving an account of historical development which
makes no appeal, overt or tacit, to concepts of predetermination
or inevitability. Thus Runciman makes clear that his is a non-
teleological theory of social evolution:

> Evolution is more than qualitative change: it is change in a
> definite direction. But it must not be equated with progress
> in either of the two senses to which it was tied by nineteenth-
> century evolutionary sociologists who, for all their other
> differences, shared an unquestioned presupposition that evo-
> lution was not only change for the better but change in the
> direction of a predetermined goal.[34]

Runciman's and Mann's historical sociologies are instances
of what Wright, Levine and Sober call a 'theory of *historical
trajectories*', a theory, that is, that 'acknowledge[s] an overall
directionality to historical change' (directionality in the sense
given above, where it is equivalent to what I prefer to call progress, and involves a tendency for historical change to increase
some property), but rejects 'the view that directionality implies a
unique path and sequence of development'.[35] But Wright, Levine
and Sober argue that Marxism also is a theory of historical
trajectories – or, rather, that a non-teleological version of historical materialism would meet the conditions of such a theory.
The decisive move in any attempt to strip Marxism of teleology
comes with the rejection of what G. A. Cohen calls the Primacy
Thesis – the proposition defended by Second International Marxists
such as Kautsky and Plekhanov that '[t]he nature of the production relations of a society is explained by the level of development of its productive forces.'[36] While Cohen's own defence
of the Primacy Thesis does not depend, strictly speaking, on a
resort to teleological explanations (that is, explanations of an
event by the future events it brings about), his claim that the
production relations are functionally explained by their tendency
to promote the development of productive forces seems impossible
to sustain without the further claim that the replacement of
a mode of production that is less progressive (in the sense of
developing the productive forces) by one that is more progressive
is inevitable. The effect of dropping the Primacy Thesis is to
introduce an element of irreducible contingency into historical
materialism: the crisis of every mode of production may arise

from the fettering of the productive forces by the relations of production, but the outcome of that crisis – whether it leads to a social revolution inaugurating a new, more progressive mode of production, or whether instead prevailing production relations survive, giving rise to stagnation or even regression – is not predetermined. A space is thus created for Mann's 'might have beens' and 'almost weres' that articulates with the Marxist political project, with its stress on working-class self-emancipation and revolutionary subjectivity, far better than does Cohen's Primacy Thesis.[37]

There is much more to be said on the subject of Marxism and historical progress: I therefore return to this question in chapter 4 below. The upshot of this section has, I hope, been to establish the respects in which both historical materialism and Weberian historical sociology are similar kinds of social theory. Both meet the three conditions set out above for a theory of history; both – or, perhaps better, versions of both – further differ from philosophies of history in refusing to conceptualize the historical process as a sequence whose course is predetermined by its outcome. One implication of this latter feature is that it sets the limits any theory of history must respect. One way to deny the doctrine of historical inevitability is to say that the outcome of any major historical crisis, in which the survival of a particular social structure is in question, cannot be predicted on the basis of whatever general propositions a theory of history happens to assert. The interplay of factors which led to the actual outcome can only be reconstructed by careful empirical research. As we have seen (section 2.1 above), James McPherson justifies his use of a 'narrative format' in writing the history of the American Civil War by appeal to 'the dimension of *contingency* – the recognition that at numerous critical points during the war things might have gone altogether differently'. The contingencies inherent in historical situations do not render social theory otiose: on the contrary – to take the example of the American Civil War – it is indispensable to any understanding of the nature of the 'irrepressible conflict' between North and South, of the forces at work on both sides, and of the society which emerged from it. The point is, once again, that general theories of history and concrete historical inquiries are dependent on, and irreducible to, one another.

3.2   MARX OR WEBER?

It is almost a truism that the basic choice in social theory is that between Marx and Weber.[38] Weber – the 'bourgeois Marx' – is the only social theorist comparable to Marx in conceptual acuity and historical range (indeed, his writings on precapitalist societies are more extensive than Marx's). Their political stances represent a dramatic opposition, Weber's championship of the bourgeoisie and of German imperialism starkly confronting Marx's socialist internationalism. And their treatments of capitalism and modernity set the scene for a dialogue in which not merely rival social theories but radically different philosophical anthropologies – Marx's Promethean humanism in which people fulfil themselves through the active creation of their world, and Weber's *fin-de-siècle* pessimism deeply imbued with Nietzschean voluntarism and perspectivism – engage with each other.[39]

The sense in which the opposition between Marx and Weber is a fundamental one for social theory can, however, be brought into quite sharp focus in terms directly relevant to the understanding of history. Marx and Weber offer radically different accounts of domination – that is, of the existence in most societies of any complexity on the historical record of relationships in which one group of human beings, usually the majority, are subordinated to another, typically the minority. For Marx the existence of relations of domination is to be explained by the nature of the relations of production in a certain range of societies, what he calls class societies, where a minority (the ruling class) appropriates surplus labour from the direct producers (the exploited class). These modes of production – among them the slave, feudal and capitalist modes – correspond to a certain level of development of the productive forces, where productivity has reached the point where a minority of society can escape from the pressures of toil to meet their subsistence needs, but only at the expense of the majority, who must labour to support them. In other words, in class societies a surplus product exists, but so too does exploitation; in this they differ from their predecessors, what Marx calls primitive communism, where productivity has not advanced sufficiently to provide a surplus above basic subsistence and so exploitation is impossible, and from their successor, what one might call advanced communism, where the productive forces have advanced sufficiently to support all in conditions of relative abundance, and therefore, while a substantial surplus product exists, exploitation and the classes which arise from it can be abolished.[40] Relations of domination, according to Marx, spring from the requirements of class exploitation, and in particular the necessity of ensuring that surplus labour is regularly extracted from the direct producers and that they do not rebel against their lot. Domination, as a feature of class society, can therefore be abolished with it; it is not an unavoidable feature of human existence.

It is this conclusion that sets Marx in direct confrontation with Weber. For the latter follows Nietzsche in insisting that relations of domination are omnipresent and irreducibly multiple. Omnipresent: forms of domination are coextensive with the existence of the human species; a society without domination is a fantasy incapable of practical realization. Irreducibly multiple: no relation of domination has primacy over the others; in this sense the structure of society is inherently plural. The reason why I call Gellner, Giddens, Mann and Runciman *Weberian* historical sociologists is less because of their explicit adhesion to Weber's thought as a whole or their endorsement of any specific theses advanced by him – most, indeed, tend to present themselves as somehow transcending the Marx–Weber debate – than because they accept the proposition that relations of domination are universal and plural.[41]

What follows makes no pretence of being a comprehensive discussion of the relative merits of the Marxist and Weberian treatments of domination. For one thing, such a discussion would have to address the question of Stalinism. No historical development has lent more plausibility to the idea that relations of domination are inescapable and would survive the successful removal of capitalism as a socio-economic system than the fate of the October Revolution. As I indicated in section 1.1 above, a Marxist interpretation of Stalinism capable of refuting the claim that the Soviet experience rang the death-knell of historical materialism is available, but to outline and defend this interpretation in any detail falls outside the scope of this book.[42] Secondly, if we take seriously the idea that the Marxist and Weberian theories of history are scientific research programmes, then any definitive judgement of their relative merits can only rest on a detailed comparison of the success of each in generating interpretations which meet the canons of theoretical and empirical progress discussed in section 2.4 above. Once again, it is not my aim to undertake this task here.

Nevertheless some observations are in order on the claim, definitive of Weberian historical sociology, that relations of

domination are irreducibly multiple. One might see this as presupposed by the thesis of the omnipresence of domination. For if
it could be shown that ideological and politico-military power
can – as historical materialism requires – be explained in terms
of the prevailing forces and relations of production, then it
would cease to be legitimate to rule out the possibility of the
eradication of these forms of domination, should the appropriate
mode of production turn out, after all, to be feasible. Weberian
theorists of course deny that such a reduction (as they see it)
can be effected. For Mann, as we saw (section 3.1 above), the
various power sources come and go – rather like the women in
Prufrock who 'come and go / Talking of Michelangelo', moving
according to the eddies of history, with none able to pretend to
a permanent, structurally determined primacy over the others.
How do proponents of this conception of historical causation
go about finding support for it?

Mann and Runciman represent two alternative strategies that
are aptly characterized by Chris Wickham: 'Mann ... wants to
conceptualize a narrative historical sociology that will explain
specific historical developments; Runciman wants to develop
sociological categories which will explain historical development
as a concept.'[43] Thus Mann largely eschews comparative explanation on the grounds that human history offers too few
'autonomous, analogical cases' in terms of which comparisons
could be framed, and prefers instead 'careful historical narrative,
attempting to establish "what happened next" to see if it has
the "feel" of a pattern, a process, or a series of accidents and
contingencies'.[44] Runciman, by contrast, constructs a typology
of modes of distribution of (primarily political) power involving
comparisons across wide stretches of historical time (thus the
Roman Empire, Sung China, Norman Sicily and England, Ottoman
Turkey and Tokugawa Japan are all instances of absolutism), and
conceptualizes social change as the outcome of the competitive
selection of practices which confer an advantage on their carriers
in the unending struggle for power.[45]

Different though these approaches undoubtedly are, both can be
seen as accentuations of two sides of Weber's work, both evident
in *Economy and Society*: on the one hand, its historical richness
and depth; on the other, the almost obsessive care with which
conceptual typologies are formulated. Plainly, nothing I say here
can do justice to texts of the quality of Mann's and Runciman's,
particularly given the range of historical knowledge both can
command.[46] All the same, it is possible to say something, however

inadequate, about their success in accounting for the nature and development of human societies on the basis of the claim that forms of domination are irreducibly plural, and therefore (I suggested above), a permanent feature of human existence. I concentrate here on three issues: (1) ideological power; (2) military competition; (3) scarcity and conflict.

(1) *Ideological power* Mann's narrative of power is organized around an account of the rise of 'the most powerful human society, modern Western civilization'. Two concepts play a central explanatory role in this account. First, Europe by AD 1000 was, like the federations of Sumerian, Phoenician and Greek city-states before it, a 'decentralized multi-power-actor civilization'. No imperial state existed with the coercive power necessary to extract the resources required in turn to sustain the empire in the first place – a pattern which Mann calls 'the dialectics of compulsory co-operation'. Mediaeval European society was composed of an immense variety of different power-centres; even when these were progressively absorbed into centralized bureaucratic states, no one Great Power could secure stable domination of the others. Modern Europe thus constituted itself as a plurality of competing states. Secondly, this potentially anarchic condition was contained and regulated through the 'normative pacification' provided by Christianity:

> Christendom combined in a contradictory, indeed in a dialectical way, the two main organizational characteristics of ideological power. It was *transcendent*, yet it reinforced the *immanent* morale of an existing social group, a ruling class of lords. This combination helped ensure a basic level of normative pacification, confirming property and market relations within and between the cells. Second, each local power network was relatively outward-looking, feeling itself to be part of a much larger whole and thus potentially expansionist. Previous civilizations had provided infrastructure of extensive power only at great cost ... Now enough of this was provided by ideological means, by Christianity without a state, that expansion and innovation could burst from the local intensive cell. The early feudal economically centred dynamic was primarily intensive because extensive power was already provided for by Christendom. The economic infrastructure, the village-manor economy, which produced such crucial innovations as the heavy plough and the three-

field system, and the urban-centred trading economy themselves depended on the 'infrastructure' of Christianity.[47]

Mann thus radically extends Weber's claim that Calvinist
ethics and the spirit of capitalism had an elective affinity for
one another; now it is Christianity *tout court* which provided the
indispensable normative framework for the economic dynamic
that led to modern capitalism. The argument is not without its
precedents. Contemporary historical sociology more generally can
be seen, in its preoccupation with inter-state competition, to be
seeking to generalize from one of the main themes of modern
historiography since its inception in the eighteenth century. It
was, after all, the Göttingen historian Heeren who sought in
1809 to characterize Europe (which Voltaire had already called
'une espèce de grande république') as a 'states-system', that is,
'the union of several contiguous states resembling each other in
their manners, religion and degree of social improvement, and
cemented together by a reciprocity of interests'. Heeren's successors, from Ranke to contemporary historians of international
relations, have sought to identify the various mechanisms, both
formal (international law) and informal (the pursuit of the balance
of power), which imposed various restraints on the conduct of
states towards one another, prevented any power from establishing what Mann calls an empire of domination, and thereby made
Europe not an anarchy, but an international *society* of states
rooted in a common set of values and beliefs.[48]

Original or not, Mann's conception of Europe as a norma-
tively integrated but 'multiple acephalous federation' must confront two difficulties if his claim that it explains the rise of
the West is to hold up.[49] First, there are surely other cases
of normative pacification. Anderson points out that '[w]hatever
else it may have lacked, Byzantium certainly did not want for
normative regulation by religion. But the same is true, of course,
of the Islamic world, let alone of early imperial China.' Mann
is able to ignore these apparent counter-examples, Anderson
suggests, because of his methodological disdain for historical
comparisons: thereby 'he has denied himself indispensable empirical controls over too many of his hypotheses.'[50] Secondly,
many vital political and economic relationships cut across the
boundaries of zones of normative pacification. Steven Runciman's
great *History of the Crusades* offers a valuable case-study precisely because it is concerned with one of the main meeting
points of Christendom and Islam. Runciman explores in detail

the complex relationship of co-operation as well as conflict which developed between the crusading states of Outremer and their Muslim neighbours: 'the wiser statesmen amongst the Franks saw that their kingdom could only last if the Moslem world were kept disunited,' a policy which led to a kaleidoscope of changing alliances among the endlessly squabbling Christian and Muslim principalities of the near east. The plight, moreover, of the crusader states was hopelessly – and, from their point of view, disastrously – compromised by the interest of Venice, Genoa and Pisa in their rapidly developing commerce with the Islamic world. Thus when Prince Edward of England arrived at Acre in 1271, intending to unite the Christian states and ally them to the Mongols against the most powerful Islamic ruler, Sultan Baibars of Egypt, he was discomfited 'to find that the Venetians maintained a flourishing trade with the Sultan, supplying him with all the timber and metal that he needed for his armaments, while the Genoese were doing their best to force their way into this profitable business and already controlled the slave-trade of Egypt'.[51]

Frontier regions are frequently zones of ambiguity, where starkly counterposed identities merge and blur, as they seem to have in Outremer.[52] But Ranke points to a more spectacular case of Christian–Muslim co-operation when he notes how central it was to the grand strategy of the French monarchy in its long struggle with Habsburg Spain and Austria during the sixteenth and seventeenth centuries that it could find a ready ally in the shape of the Ottoman Empire, at the very time that the Turkish threat to Latin Christendom was at its greatest: thus Ottoman dominance of Hungary throughout this period gave France a means of turning Austria's flank, even though this meant siding with the infidel against fellow Christians.[53]

Alliances of this kind can be dismissed as mere cases of instrumental calculation. One final example is less easy to treat in this way. Janet Abu-Lughod argues that between AD 1250 and 1350 a 'world system' took shape that bound together the Old World from north-western Europe to China through exchanges primarily of manufactured goods. The trade between the Italian city-states and Egypt which so embarrassed the Lord Edward was one of the chief mechanisms binding the 'European subsystem' to the 'Mideast heartland' of this world economy. One of the most striking features of this very extensive network through which commodities circulated was that it did not involve the existence of a zone, common to all the actors, of normative pacification. On the contrary, Abu-Lughod observes, what is noteworthy in the world system of the thirteenth century is that a wide variety of cultural systems coexisted and cooperated, and that societies organized very differently from those in the west dominated the system. Christianity, Buddhism, Confucianism, Islam, Zoroastrianism, and numerous other small sects often dismissed as 'pagan' all seem to have permitted and indeed facilitated lively commerce, production, exchange, risk taking, and the like. And among these, Christianity played a relatively insignificant role.[54]

The theoretical issue highlighted by these examples is perhaps best brought out by this remark of Mann's:

> Christianity as a *normative* system has been neglected as a causal factor in the emergence of capitalism. It was not only the psychological impact of its doctrines (as in Weberian approaches to the problem) that boosted capitalism, but also that it provided normative pacification, in a Durkheimian sense.[55]

So Mann goes beyond Weber not just in stressing the contribution of Christianity as a whole, rather than merely the more radical forms of Protestantism, to the development of capitalism, but in conceptualizing the role of Christianity as lying in the form of normative integration it provided. But one of the main criticisms of Durkheimian sociology – most obviously in its Parsonian form, though Althusserian Marxism often bears a strong family resemblance to this variant of bourgeois social theory – has long been that it tends to conceive society as constituted by the values and beliefs that prevail within it, and therefore to underestimate the degree of dissent, especially among the popular classes, and of social antagonism. One way of making the point is to ask whether society is best seen as a nexus of antagonistic interests, which the acceptance of particular beliefs may help to articulate, or as a system of shared values, whose breakdown gives rise to conflict. Mann's treatment of Christianity as normative pacification takes him close to the latter view – surprisingly so, since he has himself made an important contribution to casting in doubt the existence of a value consensus in modern liberal democracies.[56]

(2) *Military competition*   Not all Weberian theorists are as strongly committed to conceiving society as constituted by value

consensus as Mann's account of Christianity as a form of ideological power seems to require him to be. Giddens, indeed, is
strongly critical of variants of social theory which make appeal
to the concept of normative integration.[57] In precapitalist class-
divided societies, he argues, it was the military violence of the
state which was chiefly responsible for system integration, required to ensure the reproduction of the social structure; societal
integration, involving the sharing of beliefs and values, operated
through the medium of tradition and kinship to bind together
rural communities rather than to subordinate them to the dominant
class. Perhaps more than any other Weberian theorist, Giddens
highlights the autonomous role of organized coercion, not merely
to secure the acquiescence of the mass of the population in
the status quo, but as the most important form in which the
plurality of rival powers making up the state-system interact with
each other. Thus he argues that this system, 'far from being
ephemeral, is integral to the world capitalist economy – which
is at one and the same time a world military order', and complains that 'Marxism has no tradition of theorizing violence either
as an integral and chronic feature of repression or as the "world
violence" of the contemporary system of power blocs and nation-
states.'[58]

Giddens is in any case here highlighting a point made by
other Weberian theorists. Mann, for example, takes Marxism to
task for failing to give proper weight to the role of military and
political organization in classical antiquity.[59] It is a point which
some Marxists have been quite ready to concede. Thus Wickham,
in perhaps the most effective critique of Mann's work so far to
have appeared, declares: 'Economic processes and political/military
power must be recognized, more explicitly than Marxists often
recognize them, as being in a permanent dialectical relationship
in history, although ... ideological power does not seem quite
as autonomous as the other two.'[60] How, then, is this relationship
to be conceptualized? Christopher Bertram has sought to take
'explicit account of the facts of inter-societal conflict *within* a
revised historical materialism'. He argues that societies are subject
to a process of Darwinian natural selection which compels them
to adopt, in the interests of competitive survival, social structures
that will promote the development of the productive forces:

Countries and cultures have engaged in both economic competition of various kinds and in military conflict. In all these
forms of conflict and competition, possession of a higher

level of technological development increases the *chance* that a given culture or state will survive ... Cultures may adopt social structures (and indeed legal and political super-structures) for all sorts of reasons. The proximate cause may be religious or political, for example. But those countries or cultures that fail to select structures conducive to the development of the productive forces will either be eliminated (or assimilated) by their rivals, or will undergo a crisis that will force them to select anew their basic structures. In either case, the unsuccessful, if they survive, will tend to adopt structures resembling those of their successful rivals. A pattern will emerge in history, as structures conducive to the development of the productive forces at a particular point of their development are diffused.[61]

Bertram's attempt to integrate inter-societal competition into historical materialism seems to have been prompted both by what Mikhail Gorbachev liked to call 'life itself' – the fate of the Stalinist regimes is after all a dramatic illustration of what happens to societies which do not develop the productive forces as fast as their rivals – and by recent debates over the the conceptual structure of the Marxist theory of history. Critics of Cohen's version of the Primacy Thesis – the claim that the nature of the prevailing production relations is functionally explained by their tendency to promote the development of the productive forces – have argued that functional explanations are invalid unless they specify a feedback mechanism, that is, unless they provide a further, causal explanation of how, in this case, the existence of a given set of production relations arises from its being conducive to the development of the productive forces. Marx's theory of the capitalist mode of production comes with a feedback mechanism ready-made, since he argues that competition between capitals compels them to introduce cost-cutting technological innovations and thereby to increase the productivity of labour. But Marxist conceptualizations of precapitalist modes of production have not come up with any comparable processes giving rise to a tendency for the productive forces to develop: indeed, Robert Brenner has argued that prior to capitalism neither exploited nor exploiting classes had any systematic interest in productivity-enhancing innovations. Bertram seeks to offer a way out of this impasse by offering

a possible feedback mechanism. Social structures exist in an environment partly constituted by other social structures.

Those social structures that fail to provide a favourable climate for the development of the productive forces gradually disappear, to be replaced within the population of social structures by those that do tend to have this beneficial consequence.[62]

There are precedents for Bertram's strategy within Marxism.[63] It is not, however, with these that it invites comparison, but rather with W. G. Runciman's attempt to conceptualize social evolution as the outcome of 'the competitive selection of practices', so that 'the most elaborate forms of culture and the most complex patterns of structure are the product of an intense, unremitting, and all too often violent competition for power between rival armies, classes and creeds.' It is true that Runciman does not require that the acquisition of competitive advantage consist in the adoption of a social structure more conducive to the development of the productive forces; but, like Bertram, he thinks of social evolution as proceeding along Darwinian lines, with there being, in particular, no necessary connection between what Bertram calls the 'proximate causes' of social change and its outcome:

As in genetic evolution, *mutation* and *recombination* of practices can come about in all sorts of different and unpredictable ways. But the social theorist can and must treat the emergence of variants as random – that is, ... not as uncaused and therefore inexplicable, but as independently caused and therefore explicable only at a different level. The roles and institutions which are the outcome of the emergence of these practices then survive, or fail to survive, to the extent that they do demonstrably confer on the roles and thereby systacts carrying them competitive advantage in the context of the pre-existing distribution of power.[64]

The similarities between Runciman's and Bertram's theories of social evolution highlight the difficulty which the latter must confront in as much as he is trying to revise rather than reject historical materialism. Runciman, consistent with his Weberian theoretical commitments, treats as, in general, indeterminate the relative contribution made by the three dimensions of power – economic, politico-military and ideological – to the process of competitive selection; his clumsy neologism 'systact' serves to identify any group of persons having a common interest by virtue of the role they share in the social structure – orders, estates, classes, status-groups, castes, factions and age-sets are all promiscuously gathered beneath it.[65] Bertram, however, cannot adopt so relaxed an attitude. More specifically, by treating the existence of inter-societal conflict – both economic and military competition – as a premiss of his theory not itself requiring further explanation he risks collapsing historical materialism into a Weberian theory of history as governed by Runciman's 'unremitting ... competition for power between rival armies, classes, and creeds'.

Bertram does at one point take sight of this problem, when he touches on the part played by military competition in his theory:

> If we are to assign a significant role to military power in the diffusion of technological progress, it is not clear that we are remaining within the bounds of historical materialism, ... At the very least we need some theory that systematically reduces the military dimension to that of economic development.[66]

Now, Marxists certainly have often treated the pressure of military competition as a source not merely of 'technological progress' but (consistent with Bertram's general model of social evolution) also of social change. Thus Trotsky put down the peculiarities of Russian historical development to the 'constant pressures from the more developed social and state relations of Western Europe', in which 'a decisive role was played by military relations between states. First and foremost, the social influence of Europe found expression in the form of military technology.'[67] The question posed not merely by Bertram's attempt to use inter-societal competition to explain the development of the productive forces but also by Weberian historical sociology is whether this kind of account can in fact be accommodated within historical materialism.

Bertram may be imposing too strong a requirement when he suggests that giving a positive answer to this question must involve having a 'theory that systematically reduces the military dimension to that of economic development', if the burden of 'systematically' here is to demand a trans-historical explanation of military conflict. It is hard to see how such an explanation could avoid lapsing into an anthropology of war which abstracted from the immense variety of forms of military conflict revealed in the historical record. Recall that while historical materialism specifies the existence of universal mechanisms of change, namely the development of systemic contradictions between the forces and relations of production, and the intensification of class struggle produced by such a structural crisis, the forms taken by these mechanisms vary according to the nature of the mode of production in question (see section 3.1 above). The Marxist theory of history thus involves a tension between theoretical generality and historical specificity; we might then conclude that what is required to see off the Weberian challenge posed to Marxism by the existence of inter-societal conflict is not a *general* theory of military competition but rather an explanation which takes account of the structural differences between modes of production.

It is easy enough to show, in the first place, that the Marxist theory of the capitalist mode of production does in fact give proper weight to inter-societal conflict, or, more precisely, to military competition between states. Contrary to the impression given, for example, by the 'capital-logic' theories fashionable in Germany during the 1960s and 1970s, Marx does not think of the dynamics of capitalism as the consequence exclusively of the class struggle between workers and bourgeois. On the contrary, his analysis in *Capital* identifies two levels of determination: first, 'capital in general', constituted by the extraction of surplus value from workers in the immediate process of production, and second, the sphere of 'many capitals', where individual capitals compete with each other in order to maximize their share of total surplus value. Competition is not an inessential or phenomenal aspect of capitalism. Without it the social equalization of labour of which Marx seeks to give an account in his theory of value could not take place. As we saw above, it is the competitive struggle among capitals which compels them to seek cost-cutting innovations and thereby to increase the productive forces. Finally, Marx believes that this process of technical change is itself responsible (via the effect it has on the organic composition of capital) for the tendency for the rate of profit to fall that underlies capitalism's inherent propensity to economic crises.[68]

The significance of all this for the issue of inter-state competition is twofold. First, Marx is concerned not simply with the strains endogenous to individual capitalist societies, but with a process of global accumulation and competition whose effects may be experienced in these societies as exogenous pressures and constraints. This has implications beyond Marxist economic theory narrowly defined. Thus, for example, strictly speaking the capitalist state cannot be conceptualized in terms which seek to

define it exclusively with respect to domestic class relations, but
must be understood as one of a plurality of states competing on
a world scale.[69] Secondly, the most important single extension of
the analysis of *Capital* since Marx's time is the body of writing
by, among others, Hilferding, Luxemburg, Bukharin and Lenin
that goes under the name of the theory of imperialism. This is
concerned less with providing a critique of the relationship between the dominant Western powers and the rest of the world
(though it does include that) than with analysing a series of
structural changes within the advanced economies towards the
end of the nineteenth century, which led both to the concentration
of economic power and to a tendency for private capital and
the nation-state to fuse into a single block of interests, and with
the associated changes in the nature of inter-capitalist competition, which ceases to be simply the rivalries of private firms for
market share, and increasingly assumes instead the form of the
military struggle of state capitals for global dominance. The
theory of imperialism thus provides a Marxist explanation of the
relapse of the European *grande république* into anarchy during
the two world wars.[70]

Of course, there is much more to be said about the Marxist
theory of inter-state competition under capitalism: I return to some
of the issues involved in section 3.3 below. Nevertheless, it is
clear enough that considerably more than the rudiments of such
a theory exists. What about precapitalist modes of production?[71]
Here I believe Brenner has made a fundamental contribution. He
argues that the nature of property relations (the expression he
prefers to use when referring to what are normally called in
Marxist theory the relations of production) in precapitalist class
societies systematically impeded them from pursuing 'modern
economic growth', based on investments aimed at increasing the
productivity of labour, and produced a 'long-term developmental
trend towards stagnation'. These property relations had, according
to Brenner, 'two defining traits':

> *First*: the direct producers held direct (i.e. non-market) access
> to their full means of subsistence, that is the tools and land
> needed to maintain themselves.
> *Second*: in consequence of the direct producers' posses-
> sion, the members of the class of exploiters (if one existed)
> were obliged to reproduce themselves through appropriating
> a part of the product of the direct producers *by means of
> extra-economic coercion.*[72]

Under these conditions neither exploiting nor exploited required access to the market in order to reproduce themselves. In the case of the feudal mode of production, for example, the peasants supplied their needs by working on their plots of land, while the lords maintained themselves by using their judicial and military power to extract rent, in labour services, kind or cash, from their tenants. Neither class depended for its survival on the purchase and sale of commodities. Neither, therefore, was under the kind of pressure which market competition imposes on economic actors to cut costs and thereby to reduce relative prices. It is this pressure which, under capitalist property relations, induces investment in productivity-enhancing innovations. It is the absence of this mechanism that gives rise in precapitalist societies to a tendency towards economic stagnation.

It does not follow, according to Brenner, that these societies exhibit no pattern of development. That pattern, however, is not an economic trend, but rather a tendency towards 'political accumulation', that is, towards the construction of powerful states as a result of military competition within the lordly class itself:

> In view of the difficulty, in the presence of pre-capitalist property relations, of raising returns from investment in the means of production (via increases in productive efficiency), the lords found that if they wished to increase their income, they had little choice but to do so by *redistributing* wealth and income away from their peasants or from other members of the exploiting class. This meant they had to deploy their resources toward building up their *means of coercion* – by investment in military men and equipment. Speaking broadly, they were obliged to invest in their politico-military apparatuses. To the extent that they had to do this effectively enough to compete with other lords who were doing the same thing, they would have had to maximize both their military investments and the efficiency of these investments. They would have had, in fact, to attempt, continually and systematically, to improve their methods of war. Indeed, we can say that the drive to *political accumulation*, to *state-building*, is the *pre-capitalist* analogue to the capitalist drive to *accumulate capital*.[73]

The analogy Brenner here draws between capital accumulation and 'political accumulation' should not be taken too far. As Anderson points out, the structure of

inter-capitalist competition ... is typically additive: rival
parties may both expand and prosper – although unequally
– throughout a single confrontation, because the production
of manufactured commodities is inherently unlimited. The
typical medium of inter-feudal rivalry, by contrast, was
military and its structure was always potentially the zero-
sum conflict of the battlefield, by which fixed quantities of
ground were won or lost. For land is a natural monopoly: it
cannot be indefinitely extended, only redivided.[74]

Brenner's own account, indeed, provides a fuller explanation
of the disanalogy between feudal and capitalist competition: it is
less the peculiar economic properties of land than the inherent
limits imposed by precapitalist property relations on any attempt
to increase the productivity of the peasant communities working
the land that makes conflict within the lordly class a zero-sum
game. Since total output stagnates or grows only very slowly, it
is rational for lords seeking to enhance their income to attempt
to seize others' share of this output (or rather, of the land on which
peasants produce it). This, however, points to the major difficulty
with Brenner's argument: did precapitalist societies actually display 'a long-term developmental trend towards stagnation'? The
historical record contains major counter-examples to Brenner's
claim – among the most important are the substantial growth of
output and technical innovation which took place in Sung China
and early mediaeval Europe at roughly the same time, between
the tenth and thirteenth centuries AD.[75] It is true that the centuries of expansion were followed in China by the loss of technological dynamism, and in Europe by profound social and economic
crisis.[76] But this in turn highlights a further problem. Brenner
offers a general structural account of the limits imposed on the
development of the productive forces by precapitalist property
relations that abstracts from the differences between modes of
production prior to capitalism. Yet these differences are potentially of great significance for historical interpretations: thus Guy
Bois bases his claim that the year 1000 saw a 'feudal revolution'
in part on the divergent socio-economic patterns implied by slave
and feudal relations of production.[77] Any attempt properly to
conceptualize these patterns would have to include an account of
the mechanisms specific to each precapitalist mode which made
possible some development of the productive forces, however
limited this might seem relative to the unprecedented dynamism
of capitalist economic growth.[78]

Nevertheless, even when these and other difficulties with Brenner's attempt to rethink the Marxist theory of modes of production are taken into account (see also section 3.3 below), his account of political accumulation contains an essential core of truth. It predicts how members of a precapitalist exploiting class will react to stagnant output – namely by expanding militarily at each other's expense. This prediction is especially valuable when set into the historical context which Brenner's generalizations about precapitalist societies are largely an attempt to explain: the emergence of capitalism in late mediaeval and early modern Europe.[79] The military struggle between rival lords from which the absolute monarchies of early modern Europe took shape represented a rational response to the crisis of feudal production relations. The competition thus unleashed gave rise to the struggle between the Great Powers which constituted the object of modern historiography as it was formed at the end of the eighteenth century. This struggle, however, was not an autonomous process of military competition but rather, if Brenner's argument is correct, a consequence of the nature of feudal relations of production. From this perspective, the Marxist theory of imperialism identified the point at which the military–territorial conflicts of the Great Powers became integrated into the dynamics of capital accumulation: on the one hand, by the late nineteenth century military power came to depend on the advanced productive forces which only capitalist production relations could provide – hence, for example, the alliance of Junker and industrialist on which Bismarckian Germany was built; on the other hand, as capital itself became increasingly nationally organized, the military power of the state became an indispensable means of advancing its interests against its rivals on the world stage.

(3) *Scarcity and conflict*   A Weberian might react in one of two ways to this argument, which seeks to explain military competition by the patterns of development specific to particular modes of production. She might, in the first place, question the historical interpretations on which it depends. How well Marxism and Weberian historical sociology respectively deal with the historical evidence must, ultimately, be the decisive test between them if they are, as I argue, scientific research programmes rather than philosophies of history. I have already indicated that deciding this question falls outside the scope of this book. I have simply sought to show above how historical materialism might handle an aspect of the record apparently resistant to its central

claims. The second response a Weberian might make, however, highlights the different philosophical underpinnings of the two programmes.

This response would consist in a refusal to credit the possibility that historical materialism could come up with a reduction of military competition – that is, could explain it in terms of the forces and relations of production, with the implication, in principle at least, that a mode of production could exist which did not provide the material basis for military conflict. But how would such a denial in principle of the possibility of a reduction of military competition be justified? It is here that the figure of Nietzsche, standing behind Weber, assumes its proper stature. For Nietzsche, conflict and the struggle for domination are an inherent feature not merely of the human condition, but of nature *tout court*. The will to power runs through the physical and social worlds alike. Here, then, are strong reasons for resisting any reduction of military competition – too strong, in fact, for most Weberian theorists. Accepting the doctrine of the will to power is a high price to pay for upholding the claim that relations of domination are irreducibly multiple and universal. Giddens is perhaps the Weberian theorist who comes closest to relying on a general theory of domination.[80] Runciman typifies an apparently more cautious approach:

> It might be argued that to analyse societies and define their constituents in this way [i.e. in terms of 'the institutional distribution of power'] is to presuppose that conflict of interest is 'fundamental' to human relations. But it only does so to the degree that resources being limited and their distribution unequal, all persons are thereby in actual or potential competition with one another – a truism from which it is surely difficult for any rival observer from whatever theoretical school to dissent.[81]

What would make this 'truism' genuinely indisputable is the truth of its premiss – that resources are scarce and unequally distributed. In turn, it is surely the scarcity of resources that gives the thought its force: in conditions of real abundance inequality might lose much of its edge, so long as everyone enjoyed at least a generously defined minimum. But is scarcity really so secure a basis on which to posit the omnipresence of power and conflict? In the first place it seems doubtful that scarcity is genuinely a universal feature of human existence. Thus consider

Marshall Sahlins's famous description of hunter–gatherer society as 'the Original Affluent Society': the !Kung Bushmen of the Kalahari, for example, 'lived in a kind of material plenty', satisfying their wants out of an average of fifteen hours a week's labour per adult worker. Of course, this state of affairs was made possible, as Sahlins makes clear, by the simplicity of the hunter–gatherers' wants: 'Want not, lack not.'[82] Nevertheless, to treat the adjustment of wants and resources represented by hunter–gatherer societies as a special case is to appeal to something resembling one of the basic assumptions of neo-classical economics, that wants are insatiable, so that any given level of development of the productive forces is inherently unstable, since existing wants will expand and new wants emerge; the resulting scarcities, particularly if accompanied by inequalities in the distribution of resources, will generate social conflict and pressure for further economic growth. But this conception of human desires as insatiable is in its own way as metaphysical as the Nietzschean doctrine of the will to power. If – as research on hunter–gatherer societies suggests – stable wants coexisted with a low level of development of the productive forces during the longest single period of the human species' existence, why could not a much wider and more complex set of wants achieve a condition of relatively stable equilibrium with a far higher level of development of the productive forces, as Marx's conception of advanced communism requires?

There is, of course, a great deal more to be said about the nature of scarcity and the feasibility of communism.[83] My purpose here has simply been to establish the one-sided character of Weberian theorists' preoccupation with domination and conflict. Historical materialism, of course, does not ignore the existence of scarcity: on the contrary, the relatively low level of the development of the productive forces is critical to its explanations of the existence of exploitation and of the impulses to technological progress.[84] But, the foregoing argument suggests, the role played by scarcity is a historically variable one: correlatively, wants do not expand to infinity, but tend rather to adjust to the prevailing level of development of the productive forces, which set the boundaries of the socially possible. Rather than explicitly acknowledge the enabling – and constraining – role thus played by the productive forces, Weberian theorists tend at best tacitly to presuppose it.[85] They do so in part because, focusing single-mindedly on power, they lose sight of what Marx calls the labour process – the co-operative activity through which human beings

work together to control nature, and which lies at the basis
of the development of the productive forces. We reach here
the central analytical weakness of Weberian sociology, despite all
the historical and conceptual insights it has to offer – relative
to the fundamental Marxist couplet of the forces and relations of production, which conceptualizes human social life as
simultaneously the co-operative transformation of nature and
(in class societies) the antagonistic struggle between exploiter and
exploited.[86]

3.3   CAPITALISM AND ABSTRACTION

Any theory of history involves a set of relatively abstract concepts
and general propositions intended to articulate what it claims to
be the structure of societies and to analyse the mechanisms it
postulates as the causes of social transformation. These theoretical concepts and generalizations naturally invite the suspicions
of empirically minded philosophers and historians, who tend to
dismiss them as metaphysical abstractions incapable of capturing
the concreteness and the diversity of human social life. There is,
for example, a very well-known debate among analytical philosophers of history provoked by Carl Hempel's famous attempt to
show that historians' explanations, if properly laid out, include
among their premises universal laws.[87] I shall not discuss this
issue here, since there is a well-established concept of scientific
law – where it is conceived as a tendency the initial conditions
of whose operation are often not fulfilled – which is not vulnerable to the standard objections to lawlike generalizations in
historical inquiry, namely that they involve strict determinism and
ignore the distinctive, because intentional, character of human
action.[88]

The problem remains of how theoretical concepts and generalizations relate to the accounts, narrative or otherwise, given by
historians of particular events or episodes. Max Weber's theory
of ideal-types offers one solution to this problem, though one
deeply flawed by his relativist epistemology.[89] I wish, however,
to consider here how well the Marxist theory of history fares
as a theory committed to quite a strong version of what is
sometimes called scientific realism, since it holds that concepts
such as those of the capitalist and feudal modes of production
are not simply mental constructs which may be of heuristic value
in helping us to understand concrete historical situations (as

Weber seems to have believed of his ideal-types, at least some of the time), but have referents, actual social formations, which exist independently of our thinking and talking about them.[90]

Consider, then, these remarks of Roberto Unger's, which come from a critique of Marxism:

> Every attempt to make the definition of capitalism more concrete comes up against the same hurdles. Every addition to the list of defining traits produces another category that seems to include both too much and too little and to have an arbitrary relationship to the more abstract conceptions of capitalism. If you go far enough, you no longer have a concept at all but the summary description of particular developments that took place in particular countries, with the particular outcomes that resulted from time to time.[91]

This passage is intended to describe the defects of Marxism as a form of 'deep-structure social theory' which claims to have discovered the underlying global structures which set limits to the range of possible social change.[92] Yet it is striking how closely Unger's condemnatory characterization of how Marxist analyses of capitalism proceed shadows Marx's own account of his method in the Introduction to the *Grundrisse*. Here he argues that 'the method of rising from the abstract to the concrete' is 'the scientifically correct method'. The alternative, to proceed inductively, from the concrete – from concepts which empirically summarize the way in which the world presents itself – will lead merely to 'a chaotic conception of the whole', whose structure will only begin to emerge through the formulation of more abstract concepts capable of functioning as tools of analysis and therefore permitting its reconstruction as 'a rich totality of many determinations and relations':

> The concrete is concrete because it is the concentration of many determinations, hence unity of the diverse. It appears in the process of thinking, therefore, as a process of concentration, as a result, not as a point of departure, even though it is the point of departure in reality and hence also the point of departure for observation and conception. Along the first path [i.e. proceeding inductively from concrete to abstract] the full conception was evaporated to yield an abstract determination; along the second, the abstract

determinations lead towards a reproduction of the concrete
by way of thought.[93]

To some degree, these remarks are part of Marx's prolonged
(indeed, never completed) settling of accounts with his Hegelian
philosophical past.[94] They involve, however, three points of
substance. First, social formations are not collections of discrete
practices, but totalities which are at once internally complex
and structurally integrated: the concrete, Marx says, reveals itself
once the appropriate method of inquiry is applied to it as 'a
rich *totality* of many determinations and relations', '*unity* of the
diverse'. It is this more than anything else that attracts the ire
of Unger, who wants to treat society as a congeries of diverse
activities that can be dismantled and reassembled in an indefinite
variety of ways. Secondly, the nature of social formations is not
directly accessible to observation: Marx uses numerous metaphors in order to convey his belief that the capitalist mode of
production has a concealed, inner structure, for reasons that
have much to do with the dominant class's interest in preventing
workers from recognizing their exploitation. Thirdly, this systematic divergence between how things are and how they appear
to be requires that resort be made to the 'power of abstraction'
in order to isolate the hidden structure of the capitalist mode.[95]
Marx's preferred 'method of rising from the abstract to the
concrete' indicates how the social totality is to be reconstructed,
starting from the abstract concepts which delineate its essential
features. In his attempt actually to deploy this method in *Capital*
and its manuscripts Marx makes its character more specific. Thus,
for example, he takes Ricardo to task for merely juxtaposing
abstract determinations isolated by his theory and concrete features of economic life without seeking to establish their connection
'through a number of intermediary stages'.[96]

Marx's conception of his method is not without its conceptual
difficulties.[97] It does, however, represent a coherent attempt to
address the question posed at the beginning of this section of
how the abstract concepts and propositions of historical theory
relate to the accounts given by historians. Whether it does so
successfully – whether Unger's diagnosis is correct and 'rising
from the abstract to the concrete' degenerates into the endless
complication of theoretical concepts till they coincide with a
description of their *explanandum* – is ultimately an empirical
matter to be settled by the relative success of Marxism and its
rivals in accounting for the evidence confronting them. I wish

here, however, simply to illustrate the relevance of the issue, and to show that there are right and wrong ways of 'rising from the abstract to the concrete', by considering the case of a historian whose work we have already touched on, in section 3.2 above, Robert Brenner.

It is, I think, fair to say that a conception of capitalism occupies centre stage in Brenner's writing. His most influential and widely debated essays are concerned with the singular role played by English agrarian capitalism in early modern European economic history (and, by implication, in the transition from feudalism to capitalism). Brenner has devoted an enormous monograph to tracing the role played by a particular group of capitalists, the 'new merchants' involved in opening up colonial enterprises in the New World, in the English Revolution. And, engaging with the present, he has analysed the dynamics of capitalist crisis in the West, and, by contrast, of Stalinist collapse in the East.[98] Considered as a whole this body of work is one of the most impressive contemporary demonstrations of the continued vitality of historical materialism. Yet it is not without its difficulties, many of which can be traced back to the way Brenner uses his account of the capitalist mode of production.

This account lays particular stress on the nature of capitalist property relations (as Brenner prefers to call the relations of production) and their role in stimulating the peculiarly dynamic development of the productive forces characteristic of modernity:

Under what conditions, then, will economic actors adopt patterns of economic action conducive, in the aggregate, to modern economic growth? In my view, they can be *expected* to do so, only where all the direct producers are separated from the means of subsistence, *above all the land*, and where no exploiters are able to maintain themselves through surplus extraction by extra-economic coercion. It is only where the organizers of production and the direct producers (sometimes the same) have been separated from direct access to the means of subsistence, that they *must* buy on the market the tools and means of subsistence they need to reproduce themselves. It is only where the producers must buy on the market their means of reproduction, that they must be able to sell *competitively* on the market, i.e. at the socially necessary rate. It is only in the presence of the necessity of competitive production – and the correlative absence of the possibility of cutting costs, or otherwise

raising income, by forcefully squeezing the direct producers
– that we can expect the systematic and continual pressure
to increase the efficiency of production that is the *sine qua
non* of modern economic growth.[99]

These conditions are typically met, Brenner argues, when the
direct producers are separated not merely from the means of
subsistence, but also from the means of production, that is, when
they are 'free' wage labourers in the double sense Marx often
gave the word 'freedom', of being free to sell their labour power
but free also of the property in other productive assets which
would allow them to live any other way.[100] The critical contrast
here is with precapitalist modes of production, where direct
producers and exploiters alike have non-market access to the
means of subsistence – the peasant through his possession of a
plot of land, the lord thanks to the juridico-military power that
allows him to extract surplus product from the peasant. As we
saw in section 3.2 above, it is these features of precapitalist
property relations which, Brenner claims, account for the tendency towards economic stagnation found where they prevail.
We also saw that he ignores the cases of substantial economic
growth which took place in precapitalist societies. This is, I
think, at least partly a consequence of the way in which capitalist
property relations are counterposed to those characteristic of
precapitalist societies, which in turn are not differentiated into
distinct modes of production (though in fact Brenner's account
is plainly based on the case of feudalism). The resulting picture
depicts so stark a contrast that the real productive achievements
of precapitalist societies dwindle when set alongside the unprecedented economic performance of capitalism.
    Brenner's procedure here is not in itself indefensible: the styl-
ized economic history he offers may serve to make an important
analytical point. But it is an instance of a more general tendency
on his part to use his account of capitalism as a normative
model rather than as the starting point of analysis and interpretation. The difficulty is not so much with the account of
capitalism itself; for what it's worth, Brenner is impeccably orthodox in the way he highlights the connection between capitalist
production relations – notably the institution of free wage labour
– and the dynamics of competitive accumulation.[101] The problem
is more how he uses this account. Brenner tends to isolate forms
of economic behaviour which directly correspond to his model
of capitalism; these forms then tend to assume a privileged role

in the explanations he gives. The effect is often to undermine these explanations.

Take, for example, Brenner's interpretation of the origins of modern capitalism. Famously, this allocates the decisive role to English agrarian capitalism.[102] Only in England did the late mediaeval crisis of feudalism lead to the emergence in agriculture of the distinctively capitalist trinity – commercial landlord, capitalist tenant farmer and wage labourer. In France the peasant communities were strong enough to wrest control of the land, forcing the lords to rely on the absolutist state and the centralized form of extra-economic coercion it represented; east of the Elbe the lords were strong enough to reduce the peasants to the status of serfs. The exceptional English pattern of development involved precisely the consequences Brenner assigns to capitalist property relations: the rapid expansion of agricultural productivity made possible the transfer of a growing proportion of the population to urban, industrial pursuits and helped stimulate the rapid expansion of the home market. 'Agricultural revolution thus continued to help pave the way not only for ongoing industrial growth, but for continuing commercial revolution.'[103] In this way were the foundations of the first industrial capitalism laid.

This account has come under strong criticism from other Marxists, notably Chris Harman, for ignoring the essential – even, Harman argues, decisive – contribution made to the development of modern capitalism by the urban merchant class. In focusing so exclusively on the genesis of agrarian capitalism, Harman charges, Brenner is guilty of 'a sort of rustic economism'.[104] To put the point in more general terms relevant to the point under discussion, Brenner, by seeming to treat as the sole genuine case of full-blown capitalism English commercial agriculture, involving as it did the exploitation of free wage labour, occludes the role played by transitional forms, such as the putting-out system characteristic of what economic historians tend now to call proto-industrialization, where merchants would supply raw materials and sometimes money to artisans responsible for production of finished commodities in their own households, and the production of cash crops in the slave plantations of the New World, which represented the partial subsumption of labour under capital.[105] Brenner does occasionally admit the existence of some such forms which allow 'a *more or less* direct transition to formally capitalist class relations and co-operative labour under the pressure of competition on the market'.[106] But these 'social-productive forms'

have yet to be integrated into his overall account of the development of capitalism.

The effect is to introduce a dissonance between this account
and Brenner's study of the London merchants in the English
Revolution. For this latter work involves drawing a sharp distinction between the dominant force in the City oligarchy before
the Civil War, the company merchants whose dependence on
'politically constituted forms of property' – royal charters grant-
ing them the monopoly of particular lines of trade – bound
them to the monarchy, and the new merchants, drawn from a
more plebeian background and oriented towards the unregulated
commerce with the American and West Indian colonies. One of
the most significant features setting the latter apart was that they
tended to form partnerships with colonial planters and thereby
to exercise a degree of supervision over production on the plantations in which they invested; the grandees who dominated the
trade with the Levant and the East Indies were, by contrast, 'mere
merchants', specializing exclusively as intermediaries in the international circulation of commodities. These structural differences
between the two groups of merchants corresponded broadly to
their political allegiances: while the company merchants sided with
the Crown, the new merchants took up the cause of Parliament,
playing a crucial role in mobilizing the London crowd against the
king in 1641–2, backing the New Model Army when it assumed
control at the end of the Civil War and helping to shape the
foreign and commercial policies of the Commonwealth.[107] Brenner
thus delineates, in the new merchants, a cohesive and politically
active group of capitalists with interests at odds with those of
Stuart absolutism rooted in their participation in what looks like
a transitional form, the exploitation of unfree slave and indentured
labour in the plantations of the New World. The result is what
even as sympathetic a critic as Perry Anderson calls 'a deep
paradox': 'The detractor of merchant capital in principle has been
the first to establish, in spellbinding detail, its role as demiurge
in practice.'[108]

One conclusion suggested by these reflections is that it is necessary to distinguish between the abstract model of the capitalist
mode of production outlined by Marx in *Capital* – of which
Brenner's account of capitalist property relations is a development
– and more concrete models of different *kinds* of capitalism.
The first is intended to isolate the essential features of capitalism,
common to all its variants; the second seek, within the limits
set by these features, to identify the diverse historical forms they

have assumed. This distinction is well established in Marxist theoretical writing. Lenin's theory of imperialism, for example, aims to identify a particular phase of capitalist development (indeed, he argues, the 'highest stage') possessing a combination of characteristics which set it apart from earlier phases.[109] While it is insufficient to seek to account for particular variants of capitalism simply by situating them historically, so that they correspond to a specific phase of capitalist development, since different forms may coexist, Lenin's approach seems basically sound. Models of the variant forms of capitalism represent an 'intermediary stage' between the most abstract level of analysis represented by *Capital* and empirical accounts of the behaviour of definite capitalist societies.

Brenner's failing as an historian of early modern Europe might then be that, by equating capitalism with the economic form corresponding most closely to the abstract model of *Capital* – English commercial agriculture – he evades the necessity of constructing a model of capitalism as it took shape in the sixteenth and seventeenth centuries. Such a model would have to account for the way in which certain forms of merchant capital (in particular those involved in proto-industrialization and plantation slavery) constituted the framework within which a transition was effected to capitalism proper, itself prefigured by the social relations crystallizing in the English countryside.[110] The importance of fully understanding this kind of transitional capitalism is supported by the research of other Marxist historians: Edward Thompson's brilliant essays on eighteenth-century England are concerned precisely with the forms taken by the class struggle in a society that was no longer feudal but in which the transformation of labour power into a commodity – the prevalence of wage labour – had not yet been fully achieved.[111]

Recognizing the existence of different variants of capitalism is essential to understanding the present as well as the past. Thus when we turn from Brenner's historical writings to his interpretation of Stalinism, we encounter once again the stark contrast between the abstract models of capitalist and precapitalist property relations central to the former. For Brenner's analysis amounts to answering in the affirmative the question posed by Eero Loone when he suggests that the evidence of the Soviet Union's failure to develop the productive forces at a comparable rate to that achieved by the Western capitalist economies 'provides sufficient grounds for asking whether Soviet society might belong to a kind of pre-capitalist rather than post-capitalist formation'.[112] Thus

Brenner argues that the most important feature of the 'bureaucratic social-property system' that prevailed in the Soviet Union is that 'the bureaucracy constitutes and reproduces itself as a ruling class by virtue of its ability to take a surplus *directly by force* from the collectivity of the direct producers, the working class.' The extraction of surplus labour by extra-economic coercion is, of course, the most general defining characteristic of precapitalist modes of production. And, as one would expect, given Brenner's theory of the structural limits imposed on the development of the productive forces by precapitalist property relations, he argues that, 'since its inception, the bureaucratic economic system has developed for the most part, *by extension* – increasing its surplus basically by bringing in new workers (generally from the countryside where they were less productive) and furnishing them with machines – rather than *intensively* – transforming the means of production available to each worker.' Thus Stalinism, true to its destiny as a precapitalist social formation, shows the same tendency towards stagnation to which feudal societies were prone.[113]

This interpretation of Stalinism must confront three kinds of difficulties – conceptual, empirical and comparative. The first is simply the problem already familiar from Brenner's analysis of precapitalist property relations, namely its lack of specificity. The crisis of the feudal mode of production spanned five centuries: what was it about 'the bureaucratic economic system' that doomed its entire existence, embracing both growth and decline, to, at most, a mere seventy years? The generality of Brenner's explanation of precapitalist societies' tendency to stagnation once again seems to obviate any account of the specific mechanisms – what Marx would call the 'laws of motion' – at work within particular kinds of 'social-property forms'.

Secondly, how well does Brenner's interpretation accord with the actual workings of the Stalinist societies? I shall merely mention here what seem to me two of its most serious defects. First, Brenner claims that 'in the bureaucratic system, *labour-power is not a commodity*'; indeed, 'the system of bureaucratic surplus-extraction depends on the suppression of a labour market.'[114] This seems to me greatly to exaggerate the role played by coercion in the Stalinist economy. Even during the era of the first two Five-Year Plans (1928–37), when violence was at its most pervasive in Soviet society, workers in the Soviet Union were not serfs or slaves. Levels of labour turnover were exceptionally high throughout the 1930s. In the period of relative 'normality' attained by the Soviet Union after the Second World War a labour market functioned to allocate workers to competing sectors, regions and enterprises through a variety of mechanisms including variations in wage rates and the illegal incentives often offered by managers to attract or retain skilled personnel. Secondly, Brenner is also in my view guilty of overstating the relative inefficiency of the Stalinist economies. Thus the East European economies experienced much higher growth rates in the immediate postwar era, when they had been incorporated into the Stalinist system, than they had achieved in the interwar era. The Soviet economy proved itself capable of producing complex technological products representing what Brenner calls the intensive development of the productive forces, especially in the military sphere; the respect in which the Soviet Union was most obviously economically inferior to the West – the production of consumer goods – was itself in large part a consequence of the overriding priority in the allocation of resources given to the military-industrial complex. Brenner, in failing to acknowledge the existence of certain forms of intensive growth in the Soviet Union, falls victim to the general tendency of analysts of various political and intellectual persuasions to read back the final economic collapse into the entire sixty-year history of Stalinism.[115]

Finally, Brenner's interpretation of Stalinism potentially disables his analysis of the other term of his governing contrast between precapitalist and capitalist property relations. It is, he argues, the pressure of market competition that compels direct producers and exploiters alike under capitalism to co-operate in intensively expanding the productive forces. Plainly, this mechanism was largely absent from the Soviet Union: resources were allocated to enterprises by bureaucratic direction rather than through the medium of fluctuating market prices, and foreign trade played at best a secondary role. Another form of competition was, however, formative of the Stalinist system: the priority which, as I have mentioned, was given to production for military purposes reflected the protracted struggle which the Soviet Union waged as a Great Power with the major Western states – Britain in the 1920s, Germany between 1939 and 1945, the United States and its allies after the Second World War. Now, as we saw in section 1.1, state direction of the economy for the purposes of military competition was a pervasive feature of Western capitalism in the first half of the twentieth century. Nor can the forms of state regulation and control involved be seen simply (as is claimed by some vulgar Marxist interpretations based on an instrumentalist theory of the state) as expressions of the interests of private capital. To take the most important example, the *Reichswerke*, set up by Göring in June 1937 as part of a more general shift in Nazi policy from political regulation of the economy to state control of productive capital, was by the outbreak of war the largest industrial enterprise in Europe. As Richard Overy puts it, 'Göring poured into the *Reichswerke* any industrial assets that came his way: Jewish firms compulsorily aryanized, coal mines taken through the bullying and harassment of the Ruhr coal-owners, the bulk of the heavy industry captured in Austria and Czechoslovakia and state-owned armament works in the Reich.' These productive assets were accumulated in competition with private capital. Thus after the German reannexation of Silesia and Lorraine in 1939–40 the Ruhr industrialists expected the 'repatriation' of the coal and steel industries which they had controlled before 1918. Göring tried to grab them for the *Reichswerke* – successfully in Silesia, less so in Lorraine. The growth of the state sector existed in symbiotic relation with German military expansion: the concentration of productive resources in the hands of the National Socialist regime was justified by appeals to the needs of military, whose victories in turn contributed to the amassing of yet more state assets.[116]

Now, the ordering of industrial economies according to the priorities of inter-state competition poses a dilemma for Brenner. On the one hand, the role he accords to market competition in his abstract model of capitalist property relations might lead him to treat this phenomenon as amounting to an intrusion of a non-capitalist logic. He might, for example, interpret twentieth-century military competition as a continuation of the process of political accumulation which he claims is the main developmental pattern of precapitalist societies (see section 3.2 above). This then poses the question of the relationship between the capitalist mode of production and – what would one call it? 'bureaucratic statism', perhaps? – in modern industrial societies. How would the articulation of these different 'social-property forms' be conceptualized? More to the point, how would the claim that they were genuinely different social forms embodying distinct developmental patterns be justified? On the basis of Brenner's interpretation of Stalinism one suspects that the answer to this question would rest on the idea that the statist mode of production would be capable only of extensively developing the productive forces. Loren Goldner offers a hint of what this line of thought might look like when he argues that 'bureaucratic statism' in twentieth-century France represented 'the absence of full-blown capitalism' and amounted to 'a positive hindrance to further economic development'.[117] But even if it could be demonstrated empirically that economic forms involving state control are necessarily incapable of making productivity-enhancing investments – which seems highly unlikely – this kind of argument is uncomfortably close to that axiom of neo-classical economics that claims private enterpreneurial capitalism as the unique engine of productive progress. Even if this collapse into the uncritical celebration of the market could somehow be avoided, why not, having sought to establish that military competition even in industrial societies operates according to a different logic from that of capitalism, go the whole hog and join Michael Mann and the other Weberian historical sociologists in treating the dynamics of politico-military power as autonomous of and irreducible to those of economic class relations?

The other horn of the dilemma facing Brenner is to give up his insistence on treating as capitalist only those forms of economic behaviour which directly correspond to his abstract model of capitalism as market competition plus wage labour. The Marxist theory of imperialism, after all, provides a more concrete model of a particular variant of capitalism in which the military rivalries between states are conceptualized as a form of competition between capitals (see section 3.2 above). Making this move would not be without a price: it would be hard to resist the extension of this model to the case of Stalinism. Cliff's theory of state capitalism, which I outlined in section 1.1, amounts essentially to such an extension: on this interpretation, it was the pressure of military competition with the West which forced on the *nomenklatura* the dynamic of capital accumulation, in the specific form of the priority given to armaments production and related heavy industries in the allocation of resources.[118] So Brenner must choose between hanging on to an abstract and normative theory of capitalism, in which case much of the history of the West in the twentieth century falls outside its ambit, and dropping this theory and the interpretation of Stalinism it entails, and instead conceptualizing the Soviet Union as a particular variant of capitalism. Taking the latter horn of the dilemma seems – to me at any rate – not to be too tough an option; differentiating between an abstract account of the essential structure of the capitalist mode of production and the concrete models of its historically specific variants offers historical materialism a considerable gain in explanatory power.

The Stalinist societies have almost all now joined the inventory of defunct social forms. This does not mean, however, that the relationship between capital accumulation and military competition has ceased to be a pressing theoretical and political issue. East Asia – the zone of the world economy that has experienced the most dynamic growth since the late 1980s – is also the site of a major arms race: countries such as China, Taiwan and South Korea, hailed as the vanguard that will lead market capitalism into the twenty-first century, are building themselves up as regional military powers by modernizing their armed forces, importing advanced weapon systems, developing their own arms industries, and expanding their ability to manufacture and deliver chemical and nuclear weapons.[119] Developing a proper understanding of the interactions of economic and military power – one of the main themes of this chapter – continues to be an urgent task of any serious theory of history. This reflection provides a natural cue for turning, finally, to consider the relation between such a theory and the future.

4

HISTORY AS PROGRESS

It is closing time in the gardens of the West.

Cyril Connolly

4.1   MEANING IN HISTORY

Theories of history discern a pattern in the process whose dynamics they analyse – the development of the productive forces in the case of Marxism, the growth of social power in the case of Weberian historical sociology. But does this feature not amount to what has generally been seen as one of the principal faults of speculative philosophy of history, namely the attempt, unsupported by evidence, to impose a meaning on history? Let us consider this criticism more closely, taking as our guide perhaps the most careful discussion of the difference between ordinary historical inquiry and speculative philosophy of history, by Arthur Danto.

Danto argues that historians often use narrative sentences. Such sentences refer to at least two events separated in time, though they describe only the earliest of these events. Take, for example, this statement: 'The Thirty Years War began in 1618.' This fulfils the conditions of a narrative sentence: though the sentence is about the outbreak of the Thirty Years War, it implicitly refers to the end of that conflict in 1648. But notice that this sentence, indeed any containing the expression 'Thirty Years War', could not have been used before the Treaty of Westphalia was signed on 24 October 1648. It follows, Danto suggests, that 'there is a sense in which we may speak of the Past as changing; the sense in which an event at $t - 1$ acquires new properties ... because the event at $t - 1$ comes to stand in different relationships to events that occur later.' This is a consequence of the (perhaps obvious) fact that the historical significance of an event depends on those which followed it. (So there is something to be said for the famous remark, attributed variously to Mao Zedong and Zhou Enlai, that it is too early to tell what the significance of the French Revolution was.) Understanding past events depends on knowing their future. Now, some of *their* future is known, since it forms part of *our* past: we can, for example, trace not simply what happened during the Thirty Years War, but also its impact on later Great Power rivalries, the effect it had in Germany, and so on. But, of course, we do not know what our future contains, and it may include developments which cast a different light on the past. It follows, Danto argues, that 'any account of the past is *essentially* incomplete', since 'a complete account of the past would presuppose a complete account of the future.' The philosopher of history seeks to provide a theory of 'the whole of history, past, present, and future,' when in fact he 'does not have before him the whole of history' but 'at best a fragment – the whole past'. It is the philosopher's attempt to give a complete account of history when a necessary condition of such an account – knowledge of the future – is missing that leads Danto to agree with Karl Löwith that 'this way of viewing history is essentially theological.'[1]

There is an important kernel of truth in the consequences Danto draws from his analysis of narrative sentences. Plainly, the weight we attach to past phenomena is partly a matter of what follows them, and, since time flows on relentlessly, what follows changes, and so, therefore, may our weighings up of the past. Some recent remarks by the journalist James Morgan provide a good example of this process. Arguing that the collapse of Stalinism has ushered in a 'New Imperialism', a new epoch of Western ascendancy over the rest of the world, he declares:

> It is daunting to think that the cataclysmic events since 1913 are insignificant historically, but it is obvious that the Russian Revolution will not play the role in history that is assigned to the French. The period 1914–1990 has already been called the 'short twentieth century' and appears even now as an aberration.[2]

The assertion that the Russian Revolution is 'insignificant historically' would have been dismissed as nonsense by most people, whatever their political views, for much of that 'short century'. It may be that it will fall victim to the same process of retrospective revision which makes it now, not nonsense, but an expression of sound common sense, and that in a few years' time Morgan's remarks will be cited as an instance of the short-lived complacency that engulfed the Western establishment in the aftermath of the East European revolutions.

It is perhaps necessary, given how judgements of historical significance may change, to lay stress on two of their features. First, Danto's analysis of narrative sentences does not license an anti-realist view of the past according to which (in its most relativist versions) the past exists only in the accounts we give of it. Danto seeks to clarify the idea of a changing past: 'The Past does not change, perhaps, but our manner of organizing it does.'[3] It is not that the Thirty Years War or the Russian Revolution cease to exist because our interpretations of them change. Rather, one reason why our interpretations change is because these events come to stand in relationship with events which had not occurred when the interpretations were first framed: to put it banally, the Russian Revolution looked different from the perspective of 1945 from how it looks from the perspective of 1990. Secondly, these judgements of historical significance are not essentially evaluative: as is implied by Danto's analysis, they are concerned with the *causal* relationships in which events occurring at different times stand towards each other. Morgan no doubt thought the Russian Revolution was a Bad Thing before 1990; it is only the collapse of the regimes issuing from it, however, that allows him now – i.e. after 1990 – to treat it as insignificant. Of course, getting the causal relations among historical phenomena right is itself a complex and difficult matter: notoriously there are many rival accounts of the connections between the October Revolution and Stalinism. Nevertheless, an event's historical significance is a matter of its causal role.[4]

Reference to the fact that historical interpretations involve causal judgements serves to highlight what is distinctive about speculative philosophy of history. Danto complains that it seeks to include the future in its account of history. Earlier I argued that it is their reliance on teleological explanations which sets philosophies of history apart from theories of history (sections 1.4 and 3.1 above). Now, teleological explanations necessarily make reference to the future. In general, this future need only be that of the *explanandum*: event E_1 occurring at time t_1 is explained teleologically by event E_2 occurring at time t_2. (Frequently, however, explanations which appear to be teleological are in fact causal: a person's doing E_1 may be explained by the goal she has selected, E_2, but it is her mental state at t_1, and in particular the beliefs and desires which pick out E_2 as her goal, and E_1 as her preferred means of achieving it, that actually cause her – on some theories of causation, at least – to act.[5]) But a teleological explanation of the historical process – one, that is, which accounts for the whole course of history in terms of the final state of affairs in which it culminates – necessarily makes reference to the future of the person offering the *explanans* (unless, of course, Kojève and Fukuyama are right, and the End of History is now upon us).[6]

Theories of history, I also argued, use causal rather than teleological explanations (sections 1.4 and 3.1). Yet they range over the whole of history. The time has come to clarify this latter assertion. Theories of history cover the entire course of history in two respects: first, they involve explanatory concepts applicable to the entire range of human societies (theories of structure and transformation); secondly, they discern an overall pattern in the succession of these societies (theories of directionality). The generality of these explanatory concepts implies no restriction of them to past and present, while the patterns discovered with their aid are usually projected into the future. But it does not follow that theories of history foreclose the future in the way in which a teleological explanation of the entire historical process must. For one thing, the interactions of the mechanisms held responsible for historical change may occur in such complex ways that no theory can be given of the future consequences of these interactions. Such certainly is the import of Weberian historical sociologies, which stress the contingency of the connections formed between different power relations; I return in section 4.2 below to the question touched on in section 3.1 above of whether historical materialism also leaves the future open. For another, the patterns theories of history claim to have detected are typically extensions of the kind of explanations they give: the development of the productive forces and the devising of new forms of domination account for historical change as well as, according to Marxists and Weberians, being its outcome. In theories of history explanation shapes outcome; in teleological philosophies of history the reverse occurs.

We have thus come across two senses in which the question of meaning arises in history. The first is that of what I called historical significance – the causal relationships in which an event stands to other events occurring at different times. The second sense arises from the resort to teleological explanations in philosophies of history: the meaning of an event here derives from the position it occupies with respect to the goal of the historical process. Assigning an end to history is closely related to a third respect in which it can be given a meaning, namely the ethical judgements we pass on historical events. Thus Hegel calls his philosophy of history 'a theodicy' which 'should enable us to comprehend all the ills of the world, including the existence of evil'. World history, 'this spectacle of passions', will be redeemed through the philosophical demonstration that the self-seeking and destructive actions which occupy centre-stage contribute to the development of the consciousness of freedom and thereby to the attainment – beyond history – of Absolute Knowledge.[7] There is, of course, no reason why evaluations of historical occurrences should take the form of this kind of teleology. Acton was perhaps the major figure who insisted most strongly on the autonomy of the moral judgements the historian not merely could but should pass on the processes she reconstructed. His chief difference with the German historical school, to which Acton was so greatly indebted intellectually, lay in what he believed to be its tendency to accept 'a theory which justifies Providence by the event, and holds nothing so deserving as success, to which there can be no victory in a bad cause; prescription and duration legitimate; and whatever exists is right and reasonable' – a vulgar Hegelianism which after 1871 could easily degenerate into a celebration of the power of Bismarckian Germany.[8] Acton's famous letter to Mandell Creighton, where he declares that '[p]ower tends to corrupt, and absolute power corrupts absolutely. Great men are almost always bad men,' was a defence of the idea that 'History' should be 'the upholder of that moral standard which the powers of earth and religion itself tend constantly to depress'.[9]

Acton's position is thus an extreme expression of the fact that the historian is under no obligation, logical, methodological, or ethical, to endorse the outcome of the processes of which she gives an account. I sought, in section 3.1 above, to make a similar point about theories of history, arguing that to claim to have detected a form of historical progress – the development of the productive forces, say, or the growth of social power – does not amount to holding that this process contributes to the good (whatever ethical theory of the good one may happen to accept). Theories of history are an extension of ordinary historical inquiry, covering as they do a far greater expanse of space and time, and involving the explicit articulation of a set of explanatory concepts, but they are not a different kind of discourse. It does not follow, however, that developing a theory of history – or, indeed, a straightforward historical account of some episode or phenomenon – involves the suspension of moral judgement. To suppose otherwise is to accept a positivist conception of discourse as separated into distinct 'descriptive' and 'evaluative' domains which seems to me, particularly where the study of human beings is concerned, simply to be untenable. This is not a view for which I intend to provide arguments here, though it is supported by some of the most important recent contributions to moral philosophy.[10] Rather, I wish to make clear that what I have just said does not amount to the withdrawal of the arguments I made earlier. To reject a philosophy of language which treats fact and value as radically distinct forms of discourse is not to say that fact is value, that 'whatever exists is right and reasonable'. It is rather to say that attempts to reconstruct historical processes – or *the* historical process, though governed by canons of theoretical consistency and empirical progress common to all the sciences, will always involve ethical judgements, even if they cannot be reduced to them. There is, however, no reason why these judgements need be positive ones, as is shown by the examples offered by Acton and by Gibbon, who famously defined history as 'little more than the register of the crimes, follies, and misfortunes of mankind'.[11]

Theories of history, like ordinary historical accounts, may therefore attach two kinds of meaning to the events and processes with which they are concerned. They will seek, as an essential part of the giving of explanations constitutive of all historical inquiry, to locate these events and processes within a broader set of causal relationships, and they are likely, tacitly or overtly, to pass ethical judgements on what they recount. The sense in which it is illegitimate for theories of history to discern a meaning comes when they take the form of objective teleology, for this involves precisely collapsing the distinction between fact and value, and simultaneously explaining and redeeming events by their position with respect to the immanent goal of the historical process.

What, then, is there to be said about the two main theories of directionality, those which conceive history as taking a progressive or a cyclical form? (As we saw in section 3.1 above, it is more usual to see regress as a phase within a historical cycle than it is to think of the entire course of history as a process of regression.) At issue here is what one might call the strong theory of historical progress. The weak theory merely claims that the course of history involves the growth of some quality;

the strong theory goes further, asserting that this growth makes a positive contribution to the good. The crucial ethico-political difference between a strong theory of progress and many cyclical theories lies in the stance they tend to adopt towards modernity. As J. B. Bury notes, the first clear formulations of the concept of historical progress came during the *querelle des anciens et des modernes* at the end of the seventeenth century, when Perrault, Fontenelle and others sought to vindicate the claim that the scientific discoveries and technical developments made since the Renaissance represented a decisive advance over, not merely the Middle Ages, but also classical antiquity.[12] The idea that modernity constitutes the most significant instance of progress began to take shape.

Löwith, however, denies that the concept of progress has any original and distinctive character. He argues that it is nothing but a secularized version of Christian eschatology. Where Augustine distinguished between two narratives, a profane history of man's sinful striving for wealth and power, and a sacred history of divine creation and human disobedience, of incarnation and redemption, modern philosophers of history run the two together: 'There would be no American, no French, and no Russian revolutions and constitutions without the idea of progress and no idea of secular progress without the original faith in a Kingdom of God.'[13]

Löwith offers remarkably little argument or evidence to support this claim in an essay that often reads like a piece of Christian apologetics but whose 'secularization thesis' has nonetheless come to form part of the common sense of contemporary social theory.[14] It has been the object of a critique of great conceptual acuity and enormous erudition by Hans Blumenberg. He offers an historical interpretation which stresses the significance of late mediaeval nominalism. By treating the world as bereft of meaning, the arbitrary expression of the will of a God who hides himself from man (*Deus absconditus*), nominalism set the stage for the decisive moves beyond classical metaphysics involved in the seventeenth-century scientific revolution – curiosity ceases to be a sin and acquires legitimacy, theory is no longer the blissful contemplation of God and involves instead active interference in its object, mathematics stops being a mere aid to understanding a world that is qualitatively differentiated and becomes instead the key to reading the book of nature, which is (as Galileo put it) written in the language of numbers, and the universe itself comes be thought of as infinite. The effect is to instal a conception of knowledge which is no longer, as it was for mediaeval scholasticism, the repetition of inherited truths, but rather a process of self-improvement extending indefinitely into the future – a conception which the Enlightenment applied to history in general. This historical reading, which stresses the ways in which the formation of the modern conception of knowledge involved a radical break with the assumptions of Christian theology, supports the conceptual considerations also advanced by Blumenberg, notably the 'manifest difference that an eschatology speaks of an event breaking into history, an event that transcends and is heterogeneous to it, while the idea of progress extrapolates from a structure present in every moment to a future that is immanent in history'. At most, modern philosophy of history seeks to address questions inherited from the Middle Ages, about 'the totality of history', but it seeks to do so using 'the means available to a post-mediaeval age'.[15]

It is clear that there is a close connection between the concepts of modernity and progress. Blumenberg calls the idea of progress that of 'the continuous self-justification of the present, by means of the future that it gives itself, before the past, with which it compares itself'.[16] As Reinhart Koselleck has shown, the concept of modernity took shape at the end of the eighteenth century: it could only be formulated through the rejection of the classical conception of history, inherited by the Middle Ages and Renaissance, in which nothing qualitatively new can occur ('while empires age,' said Bodin, 'history remains eternally young'), and the recognition that 'no longer can expectation be satisfactorily deduced from previous experience'. While modernity could only be conceived as a 'new time' (*Neuzeit* is the German for 'modernity') once expectations had thus broken loose from the past, Koselleck argues that ' "[p]rogress" is the first genuinely historical concept which reduces the temporal difference between experience and expectation to a single concept.'[17] It is easy then to see how theories of history which make explicit the differentiation of distinct social forms implicit in modern historical discourse should also tend to conceive the movement from one form to another as a progressive one (see section 2.2 above).

Those thinkers who, by contrast, have sought to rehabilitate the classical conception of history as a series of cycles have characteristically done so as part of a critique, if not an outright condemnation, of modernity. Nietzsche's doctrine of the eternal recurrence of the same is the most obvious example of this style of thinking. Richard Schacht observes: 'One reason why he seizes upon this idea is that it enables him at a stroke to express his complete rejection of all views according to which the world develops in a linear, teleological manner, proceeding towards some pre-established final goal or end-state.'[18] It is true that, as Löwith points out, Nietzsche's thought is in no sense an authentic return to the ancients. The stress he lays on the will strikes a note distinctive to both Christian and modern philosophy; it was precisely Nietzsche's subjectivism which ultimately turned Heidegger against him.[19] (One should, however, point out that Nietzsche does not conceive the will as anything like a mental faculty; he calls the will to power 'a *pathos*', a disposition inherent in the nature of things, physical as well as human.[20]) The fact remains that the idea of eternal recurrence forms an organic part of Nietzsche's critique of modernity (a principal theme of which is in turn his relentless polemic against the idea of progress). Spengler's biological philosophy of history, which conceives civilizations as organisms following a cycle of youth, growth, maturity, and decay, serves in a much more direct and crude fashion as the vehicle of German conservative-revolutionary politics for which Western bourgeois modernity represents a decline into decadence.[21] Toynbee is a more complex case, since he sees history following a course that is a composite of progressive and cyclical movements; however, especially in the later volumes of the *Study*, condemnation of what he tends to call the West's 'Post-Modern Age' (which began in 1875) for its spiritual bankruptcy becomes increasingly the dominant note.[22]

Contemporary social theorists have made a more modest and limited resort to cyclical conceptions. Jacques Bidet, for example, offers a theory of modernity intended as an alternative to the 'monoteleological Marxist philosophy of history ... which places socialism after capitalism as a quite different type of society'. Bidet distinguishes between the 'metastructure' of modernity, common to both capitalism and socialism, and the structures specific to different variants of modern society. The metastructure includes contractuality, the voluntary 'inter-individual' relationship constitutive of the market, and domination, the hierarchy of power inherent in the state. Modern societies vary according to the precise articulation of contractuality and domination they involve. The 'dialectic of modernity' takes the form of a circle, 'that which "makes the rounds" [*fait le tour*] of the limit-conditions of modernity'. The unregulated market necessitates the existence of a state which establishes the framework in which contracts may be struck; soon the stronger market actors come to dominate

the state, and it becomes capitalist. This stark class polarization
gives rise, in response, to the working-class movement which
presses, with increasing success, for the regulation of the market;
at the limit, this process leads to the establishment of 'historical
Communism', which abolishes the market; but, since this state
of affairs works to the benefit of the *nomenklatura* alone, a
reaction sets in, and it's back to the market and the start of
the cycle again.[23] This pattern should ring a bell, since it is a
stylized summary of the past two hundred years of Western
history. Bidet calls a simplified version a 'fable which helps us
to break out of the progressivist [*progressiste*] philosophy of
history ... And which reactivates a form of cyclical thought
which we have too often neglected. Not that history repeats
itself. But it spins. And we are caught in this whirlwind.'[24]

Bidet's theory of modernity seems to me untenable for reasons
which are not directly relevant to the subject under discussion.[25]
What is of interest here is the conception of historical cycles as
a fatality. History is a whirlwind in which we are caught up,
like Dorothy spinning in her house way above Kansas. A similar
conception of cycle as fate is to be found in the work of Roberto
Unger. Thus he argues that both Western and Eastern economies are subject to 'cycles of reform and retrenchment' which
are 'reasonless' in the sense both of being unexplained (until he
came along) and of there being 'no good reason to acquiesce
in them'.[26] Similarly, Unger claims that 'cycles of reversion to
natural economy were central to the history of the agrarian-
bureaucratic societies' that were the main form of developed
civilization prior to the Industrial Revolution; only late mediaeval Europe and Tokugawa Japan were able to break out of this
cycle.[27]

Unger brings out more clearly than Bidet does a weakness
that is in fact common to both their theories. Both, when giving
explanations which appeal to the structures constitutive of a
given society (what Unger calls its 'formative context'), tend to
offer some sort of cyclical account. This is not always true:
Unger's explanation of how Europe and Japan escaped the 'reversion cycle' does not take this form; it stresses rather the distinctive role played by smallholding peasants (Unger consistently
champions the cause of what Marxists tend to call the petty
bourgeoisie – he is the Proudhon of contemporary social theory).
Nevertheless, there is a strong bias towards cyclical theories. But
cycles are fate, a barrier to human intervention. 'The reform
cycles', Unger tells us, 'challenge the primacy of the will.' Unger

does not want us simply to accept this fatality; he believes in 'the primacy of the will'. We should seek to increase our 'individual and collective mastery ... over the shared terms of [our] ... activity'. Unger calls this mastery 'negative capability'.[28] But this very formulation highlights the difficulty of conceptualizing social transformation on Unger's theory. His voluntarism makes it seem sometimes that we can simply shake off a burdensome 'formative context'. Now, one such context has in fact been overthrown, bringing to an end the reform cycle of the Eastern bloc, since Unger first advanced his theory. How is this transformation to be understood – as an assertion of 'the primacy of the will', or a consequence of strains that had developed within the structures of the Stalinist societies?

Opting for the second response to this question implies a recognition that social structures enable as well as constrain, that they are not simply 'frozen politics', imprisoning a will that struggles to escape from their confines.[29] On this conception of social structure – first clearly formulated by Anthony Giddens – human beings are able to find even in subordinate and exploited positions resources allowing them to struggle and sometimes even to transform social systems.[30] Once we abandon a negative conception of structure as simply setting limits to action, we need no longer restrict historical agency to the mere 'making the rounds' of variant combinations of contractuality and domination, as Bidet does, or conceive it as an inexplicable leap beyond the existing 'formative context', as Unger does. In any case, it does not seem as if even their relatively cautious cyclical theories offer an attractive alternative to 'monoteleological' Marxism.

4.2   THE DIALECTICS OF PROGRESS

The most popular theory of history (if it is proper to describe it thus) sees in the tale of human doings neither progress, nor repetition, nor regression: it consists in the denial that any such pattern exists. The Liberal politician and historian H. A. L. Fisher gave this view classic expression when he wrote:

> I can see only one emergency following upon another as wave follows upon wave; only one great fact with respect to which, since it is unique, there can be no generalizations; only one safe rule for the historian: that he should recognize

in the development of human destinies the play of the contingent and the unforeseen.[31]

The test of any strong theory of historical progress – strong
in the sense not merely of discerning in the course of history
the growth of some property but also of regarding this progress as something, ultimately, to be welcomed – is that it
should be able to encompass an understanding of the horror
of history and of its contingencies. Any theory of progress which
were to seek simply to reproduce the view of history expressed
by some of the *philosophes* – Condorcet, for example – as
a straight line moving forward and upward indefinitely into
the future ('Up and Up and Up and On and On and On', as
Ramsay MacDonald liked to say) would be literally incredible
now, at the end of a century which has made Gibbon's 'crimes,
follies, and misfortunes' seem too mild a description.[32] Walter
Benjamin's vision of history as 'one single catastrophe which
keeps piling up wreckage after wreckage' seems much more to
the point. Benjamin's 'Theses on the Philosophy of History' –
written at midnight in the century, after the Hitler–Stalin pact
and the outbreak of the Second World War – represent the
most serious attempt, within the Marxist tradition, to undertake
a 'critique of the concept of progress itself'.[33] But even he did
not advocate simply the abandonment of this concept. As Susan
Buck-Morss notes, Benjamin attacked both 'the assumption that
rapid change is historical progress', and 'the conclusion that
the modern is no progress', a view expressed, for example, in
the version of the doctrine of eternal recurrence developed by
Blanqui.[34]

How, then, to think simultaneously of history as progress and
as catastrophe? It is precisely the claim of classical Marxism
that it can do so. It inherits from Hegel a dialectical conception of history as a spiral movement, in which each advance
contains within itself an element of regress.[35] Nowhere is this
conception of history more forcefully expressed than in those
famous pages in the *Communist Manifesto* where Marx both
condemns the capitalist mode of production as yet another form
of class exploitation and praises the bourgeoisie for the 'most
revolutionary part it plays', 'constantly revolutionizing the instruments of production, and thereby the relations of production,
and with them the whole relations of society'.[36]

Fredric Jameson brilliantly captures the intent of this passage:

Marx powerfully urges us to do the impossible, to think this development positively *and* negatively all at once; to achieve, in other words, a type of thinking that would be capable of grasping the demonstrably baleful features of capitalism along with its extraordinary and liberating dynamism simultaneously within a single thought, and without attenuating any of the force of either judgement. We are somehow to lift our minds to a point at which it is possible to understand that capitalism is at one and the same time the best thing that has ever happened to the human race and the worst.[37]

Many argue, of course, that what Marx advocates is indeed impossible, and that his attempt to develop a dialectical conception of historical progress all too easily collapses into the naïve celebration of Western capitalism's domination of the rest of the world. Marx's 1853 article, 'The British Rule in India', is frequently seen as the *locus classicus* of this collapse. Here he argues that the British conquest of India, for all its vileness – 'the misery inflicted by the British on Hindostan is of an essentially different and infinitely more intensive kind than all Hindostan had to suffer before' – is, by sweeping aside the stagnant world of 'Oriental despotism', the means of future progress:

England, it is true, in causing a social revolution in Hindostan, was actuated only by the vilest interests, and was stupid in her manner of enforcing them. But that is not the question. The question is, can mankind fulfil its destiny without a fundamental revolution in the social state of Asia? If not, whatever may have been the crimes of England, she was the unconscious tool of history in bringing about that revolution.[38]

For Edward Said, this passage represents the triumph of Orientalism in even the most critical European thought: 'as human material the Orient is less important than as an element in a Romantic redemptive project.'[39] Others have claimed that Eurocentrism is built into the conceptual structures Marx inherited from Hegel. Thus Robert Young argues that 'the construction of knowledges that all operate through forms of expropriation and incorporation of the other mimics at a conceptual level the geographic and economic absorption of the non-European world by the West.'[40] I consider this larger charge in section 4.4 below.

My concern here and in the following section, however, is with the more concrete issue of whether Marx is able to formulate a dialectical conception of progress irreducible to an ethnocentric apologia for Western capitalism.

There are several respects in which 'The British Rule in India' is highly unsatisfactory. First, formulations such as 'can mankind fulfil its destiny' and 'the unconscious tool of history' have a strongly teleological ring about them. [41] Secondly, the concept of 'the Asiatic mode of production' employed by Marx in this and other texts is untenable on both theoretical and historical grounds. Perry Anderson has definitively established its 'inherent weakness of functioning essentially as a generic residual category for non-European development, and so blending features found in distinct social formations into a single, blurred archetype'. [42] Finally, it is true that some theorists have used Marx's writings on India to support a one-sided rendering of capitalism's impact on non-European societies which tends almost without qualification to underwrite its role as an instrument of progress. A striking example is provided by Bill Warren, who, in his eagerness to correct the undoubted error committed by dependency theorists who deny that any economic development has occurred in the Third World in the era of Western domination, ends at the opposite extreme of concealing the real ills wrought by colonialism. Thus he writes of 'the virtual elimination of famines [in India] after the beginning of the twentieth century', ignoring the Great Bengal Famine of 1943 in which three million people died. [43]

Whether Marx's own views on the question are similarly one-sided is, however, another matter. Another 1853 article, 'The Future Results of British Rule in India', in which Marx 'concludes' his earlier 'observations', repays careful inspection. It shares with the preceding piece the conception of the Asiatic mode of production as static and unchanging: 'Indian society has no history at all, at least no known history. What we call its history, is but the history of the successive intruders who have founded their empires on the passive basis of that unresisting and unchanging society.' And, in trying to sum up the impact of British capitalism on India, Marx resorts again at times to quasi-teleological language. Thus, 'England has to fulfil a double mission in India: one destructive, the other regenerating – the annihilation of old Asiatic society, and the laying of the material foundations of Western society in Asia.' But, despite these defects, there is no attempt to gloss over or justify the destruction wrought by British

Imperialism: 'The profound hypocrisy and inherent barbarism of bourgeois civilization lies unveiled before our eyes, turning from its home, where it assumes respectable forms, to the colonies, where it goes naked.' The concluding paragraph of the article, where Marx seeks to grasp the historical meaning of the British conquest of India is worth quoting in full, since it captures something of the complexity of his views:

> The devastating effects of English industry, when contemplated with regard to India, a country as vast as Europe, and containing 150 millions of acres, are palpable and confounding. But we must not forget that they are only the organic results of the whole system of production as it is now constituted. That production rests on the supreme rule of capital. The centralization of capital is essential to the existence of capital as an independent power. The destructive influence of that centralization upon the markets of the world does but reveal, in the most gigantic dimensions, the inherent organic laws of political economy now at work in every civilized town. The bourgeois period of history has to create the material basis of the new world – on the one hand universal intercourse founded upon the mutual dependency of mankind and the means of that intercourse; on the other hand the development of the productive powers of man and the transformation of material production into a scientific domination of natural agencies. Bourgeois industry and commerce create the material conditions of a new world in the same way as geological revolutions have created the surface of the earth. When a great social revolution shall have mastered the results of the bourgeois epoch, the market of the world and the modern powers of production, and subjected them to the common control of the most advanced peoples, then only will human progress cease to resemble that hideous pagan idol, who would not drink the nectar but from the skulls of the slain.[44]

This passage is of great importance, for three reasons. First, whether or not we think Marx's views on colonialism, capitalism, or indeed history *tout court* are correct, it is clear that they do not involve ignoring or explaining away what he after all calls the 'crimes' of the British bourgeois on the grounds that they acted as 'the unconscious tools of history' in India. The final sentence in particular, with its arresting image of progress as a monstrous god battening on human suffering, is an example of the kind of thinking described by Jameson, which at once captures both the dynamism and the horror of capitalism. Passages such as this one belong, as Aijaz Ahmad puts it in his outstanding discussion of Marx's writings on India, to

> an enraged language of *tragedy* – a sense of colossal disruption and irretrievable loss, a moral dilemma wherein neither the old nor the new can be wholly affirmed, the recognition that the sufferer was at once decent and flawed, the recognition also that the history of victories and losses is really a history of material production, and the glimmer of a hope, finally, that something good might yet come of this merciless history.[45]

Secondly, Marx gives in this passage a brief indication of why progress, in the sense of the development of the productive forces, is to be welcomed as potentially increasing human well-being; it is because it represents an expansion of human capacities. The English phrase used by Marx, 'the productive powers of man', captures this dimension of progress better than the expression 'the productive forces', which connotes an autonomous and objective process (*Productivkräfte*, usually translated as 'productive forces', is in any case Marx's rendering into German of the concept of 'productive powers' developed by the British classical economists).[46] The following passage from the *Grundrisse* is, once again, worth quoting at length, for it brings out the sense in which Marx believes that capitalism constitutes progress over its predecessors because of the expansion of human potential it represents:

> the old view [i.e. that of classical antiquity], in which the human being appears as the aim of production, regardless of his limited national, religious, political character, seems to be very lofty when contrasted to the modern world, where production appears as the aim of mankind and wealth as the aim of production. In fact, however, when the limited bourgeois form is stripped away, what is wealth other than the universality of individual needs, capacities, pleasures, productive forces etc., created through universal exchange? The full development of human mastery over the forces of nature, those of so-called nature as well as of humanity's own nature? The absolute working-out of his

creative potentialities, with no presupposition other than the previous historical development, which makes this totality of development, i.e. the development of all human powers as such the end itself, not as measured on a *predetermined* yardstick? Where he does not reproduce himself in one specificity, but produces his totality? Strives not to remain something he has become, but is in the absolute movement of becoming? In bourgeois economics – and in the epoch of production to which it corresponds – this complete working-out of the human content appears as a complete emptying-out, this universal objectification as total alienation, and the tearing-down of all limited, one-sided aims as sacrifice of the human end-in-itself to an entirely external end. This is why the childish world of antiquity appears on the one side as loftier. On the other side, it is really loftier in all matters where closed shapes, forms and given limits are sought for. It is satisfaction from a limited standpoint; while the modern gives no satisfaction; or, when it appears satisfied with itself, it is *vulgar*.[47]

This remarkable passage, like the *Manifesto*, does convey something of the sense of exhilaration at what Joseph Schumpeter called 'the process of creative destruction' unleashed by capitalism that Marshall Berman claims is inherent in the experience of modernity.[48] Plainly it implies an ethical theory which defines well-being as the full exercise by human beings of their creative powers, of which specifically productive powers are a sub-set. There are, of course, some important objections to this theory. One, particularly influential since the rise of the contemporary ecological movement, homes in on the idea of 'human mastery over the forces of nature', which is condemned for licensing the wholesale destruction of the earth. The issues raised by this objection are too complex and far-reaching for me to do more here than offer the merest gesture in place of a proper reply. Every human society of which we have any record, from bands of gatherer–hunters to modern industrial capitalism, has intervened in its physical environment in order to secure the reproduction of that society and of its individual members. One can indeed argue that any organism will act on its environment in order to make that environment more amenable to its needs. The peculiarities of the human species – its great intellectual powers, capacity to engage in an indefinitely large range of activities rather than a limited, genetically programmed repertoire, and manipulative abilities – mean, however, that the extent and intrusiveness of human intervention in nature are qualitatively different from anything to be found in any other organisms. Long before the advent of modern industrial capitalism, human interference in the physical world had produced local ecological collapses: two examples are given in section 4.3 below. The effort to impose some control over nature, or at least over that segment of the physical world directly accessible to the society in question, is a constant in the history of the human species. The only choice concerns the appropriate form of intervention in nature, and even that is constrained by the nature of the society in which the choice is made, and its material presuppositions.

It is a strength of Marxism that it starts from these unavoidable facts about human beings and their relationship to nature, facts which the urgent search for a solution to the developing ecological crisis must take into account. Talk of 'mastery over nature' sits ill with current tastes, but the following remarks of Reiner Grundmann may help to relieve some of the anxiety it arouses:

> As far as the phrase 'domination of nature' is concerned, there seems to be nothing wrong with it if it denotes 'conscious control'. In this sense we speak of 'taming' a river or of taming wild animals. To take another example: imagine a musician who plays her instrument with virtuosity. We call her play 'masterly'; in German one would say *'sie behersscht ihr Instrument'*. It is in this sense that we have to understand the domination of nature. It does not mean that one behaves in a reckless fashion towards it, any more than we suggest that a masterly player dominates her instrument (say a violin) when she hits it with a hammer.[49]

A second objection focuses on the idea of human beings realizing themselves through 'the absolute working-out of [their] ... creative potentialities'. Why should we see 'the absolute movement of becoming' through which human capacities are expanded as necessarily desirable? Terry Eagleton points out that 'war is a form of creation, and the building of concentration camps is a realization of human powers.'[50] We might take this kind of criticism as less a refutation of Marx's tacit ethical theory than a demand that it be properly articulated into a fully worked out conception of the good. Marx famously defines communism as 'an association, in which the free development of each is the condition for the free development of all'.[51] This amounts to imposing a significant constraint on the exercise of human powers: collective well-being is defined in terms of individual well-being, and therefore, presumably, proper scope must be provided to allow individuals to pursue their own chosen form of self-realization. Ground that has been well trod by political philosophers at least since Mill's *On Liberty* comes into sight, as well as some of the neighbouring plots: does well-being consist solely in the full exercise of our creative powers or has the good other ineliminable dimensions? Would not a communist society require some principle of justice to regulate the distribution of resources? And so on.[52]

Whatever reservations one might have about defining the good in terms of the full exercise of human capacities, it is clear that Marx sees capitalism as a very limited realization of the good: if antiquity is 'childish', modernity is 'vulgar'. Elsewhere in the *Grundrisse* he rejects both romantic nostalgia and triumphalist liberalism: 'It is as ridiculous to yearn for a return to that original fullness as it is to believe that with this complete emptiness history has come to a standstill.'[53] The development of the productive forces under capitalism represents largely a *potential* increase in well-being. For this potential to be fulfilled – and this is the third respect in which the passage cited above from 'The Future Results of British Rule in India' is significant – 'a great social revolution' is necessary. Such a revolution would place 'the modern powers of production' under 'the common control of the most advanced peoples'. The latter phrase seems to suggest a Eurocentric reliance on the working class of the developed countries to bring freedom to India, but elsewhere in the same article Marx makes it clear that he envisages the Indian people being agents of their own emancipation:

> The Indians will not reap the fruits of the new elements of society scattered among them by the British people, till in Great Britain itself the now ruling classes shall have been supplanted by the industrial proletariat, or till the Hindoos themselves have grown strong enough to throw off the English yoke altogether.[54]

As Ahmad observes, 'no influential nineteenth-century Indian reformer ... was to take so clear-cut a position on the issue of Indian Independence; indeed Gandhi himself was to spend the years of World War I recruiting soldiers for the British Army.'

Consistent with this stance, Marx supported the 1857 Rebellion as a 'national revolt' against British rule.[55] The suffering wrought by British colonialism – and more generally by the development of capitalism – is thus redeemed, not by whatever contribution it may make to some expansion of the productive forces, but by revolutionary action on the part of the oppressed and exploited. This is not so far removed from Benjamin's conception of revolution as a Messianic irruption into 'the homogeneous course of history', where the proletariat is 'the avenger that completes the task of liberation in the name of generations of the downtrodden'. Social democracy, wedded to a conception of history as a linear and irresistible progression, 'thought fit to assign to the working class the role of the redeemer of future generations', and thereby made it 'forget both its hatred and its spirit of sacrifice, for both are nourished by the image of enslaved ancestors rather than that of liberated grandchildren'.[56]

There are important differences between Marx's and Benjamin's conceptions of revolution. Both, however, are concerned to establish a relationship between past (and present) suffering and future revolution, though they do so in different ways. For Benjamin, the thought seems to be that avenging 'enslaved ancestors' provides both psychological motivation and ethical justification for revolutionary violence; Marx's concern, by contrast, is that the only way (in Ahmad's words) in which 'something good' might come out of 'this merciless history' of capitalist development is if its victims develop the strength to take power for themselves, and only thereby to 'reap the fruits of the new elements of society'. Both Marx and Benjamin in any case seem a long way from the view of history satirized by Edward Thompson: 'However many the emperor slew / the scientific historian / (while taking note of contradiction) / affirms that productive forces grew.'[57]

Yet this view of history is securely lodged within the Marxist tradition; it is closely associated with that strand of Second International Marxism – taken over and carried on by Stalinism – which considers social revolution to be inevitable. It would be silly to pretend that this variant – sometimes called orthodox historical materialism – can draw no authority from Marx's own writings. The existence of a significant ambiguity in his thought can be measured in the first chapter of the *Manifesto*. 'The history of all hitherto existing society is the history of class struggles,' its opening sentence declares. Marx goes on to describe this class struggle as 'an uninterrupted, now hidden, now open fight, a fight that each time ended, either in a revolutionary reconstitution of society at large, or in the common ruin of the contending classes'. The bulk of the chapter is devoted to Marx's account of the dynamics of the class struggle under capitalism – this mode of production's revolutionary character, its constitutive instability and injustice, and the emergence from within its bowels of an exploited class, the proletariat, with both the power to and an interest in abolishing class society itself. The chapter concludes thus: 'What the bourgeoisie, therefore, produces, above all, is its own grave-diggers. Its fall and the victory of the proletariat are equally inevitable.'[58]

So, on the one hand, the class struggle in the past was always open to alternative outcomes – '*either* ... a revolutionary reconstitution of society at large, *or* ... the common ruin of the contending classes' – but, on the other hand, socialist revolution is inevitable. While not amounting to a formal inconsistency, these assertions are a source of tension in Marx's thought. It is here that the presence of Hegelian teleology makes itself felt: socialist revolution is inevitable because it leads to a communist society which both explains and vindicates the course of history.

But to note the existence of an ambiguity is not to claim that it governs the entire history of Marxism. An important part of the contribution to the classical Marxist tradition made by Lenin and Trotsky lay in their rejection of the idea that socialist revolution is inevitable: the concept of a vanguard party, for example, is unintelligible if combined with the doctrine of historical inevitability. Nor can this be seen simply as a voluntarist aberration from Marx's own thought. For his theory of history postulates the existence of two mechanisms of change: the development of systemic contradictions between the forces and relations of production, and the intensification, in these conditions, of the class struggle. Now, there is no *a priori* reason why these mechanisms should necessarily operate in a co-ordinated and synchronized fashion. The relative strength of antagonistic classes is only partly determined by their material bases in the relations of production; it also depends on forms in which subjectivity and agency play an irreducible part – organization, ideology, leadership. Depending, then, on the contingencies of how these are worked up on both sides, the outcome of the historical crisis of a mode of production will vary. The fate of capitalism may, in the end, turn out to be the 'common ruin of the contending classes' – or, as Rosa Luxemburg put it, 'socialism or barbarism'.[59]

It was considerations such as these which led Erik Olin Wright, Andrew Levine and Elliott Sober to argue that historical

materialism is 'a theory of historical trajectories', which claims
that history takes a progressive direction, but denies that 'directionality implies a unique path and sequence of development'
(see section 3.1 above).[60] Eero Loone has independently sought to
develop an alternative to the idea that the sequence of modes
of production must form 'an elementary oriented series' – say,
the succession of Asiatic, slave, feudal and capitalist modes of
production which Marx seems to postulate in his 1859 Preface
to *A Contribution to the Critique of Political Economy*. Loone
argues for the rejection of this 'unilinear conception of social
development, which allows only acceleration or braking of processes, but not choice between possibilities that differ in principle
both in relation to the preceding stage and among themselves'.
He constructs a number of 'non-elementary, coherent, alternative
graphs', in which several different sequences of modes of production are possible depending on the choices taken at given
junctures. In this way, '[t]he idea of *regularity* in social development is retained, though the question of the *necessity* of social
development is shunned.'[61]

If history on this view does not quite assume the contorted
shape described by Borges in 'The Garden of the Forking Paths',
where divergent times representing the realization of every possibility coexist, it certainly loses the linear form which the idea that
social revolution is inevitable imposes on it. Once the Marxist
conception of historical progress has been enlarged in this way to
include the possibility of alternative outcomes to the crisis of a
mode of production, then it can encompass apparent dead ends,
cases of what Joshua Cohen calls 'blocked development', for
example, the long stagnation of Chinese technology between AD
1300 and 1800.[62] W. G. Runciman, who, though not a Marxist,
seeks to defend the concept of social evolution, makes some
useful distinctions. There is, to begin with, catastrophe, 'the
destruction of a society' – say, the collapse of Minoan or Mayan
civilization. Here 'social evolution has not so much been arrested
as obliterated.' Then there is regression – 'evolution in reverse'
– which may take one of two forms. First, and more straightforwardly, 'the mode of distribution of power reverts to what
it was before' – for example, the disintegration of the Carolingian
empire into 'a larger number of smaller and weaker patrimonial
societies'; secondly, the dominant 'systact' preserves its position
by adopting practices which 'function to the competitive dis-
advantage of the society as a whole at the level of competition
with others' – thus the institutions designed to make the Spartiates

a closed aristocracy made them eventually vulnerable militarily, as Sparta's defeat at the hands of Epaminondas of Thebes showed. This second form of regression seems to merge, finally, with the case of a dead end, that is, 'the continuance of a set of existing institutions ... when the environment is changing in a way which, if these institutions do not change too, will cause the society to lose so much power relative to others that they cease to be workable.'[63] It is in this sense that China after 1300 became a dead end, since its long technological stagnation made possible its subjugation by and effective partition among the militarily superior European powers in the nineteenth century.

Historical materialism, understood thus as a theory of historical trajectories, does not seem vulnerable to the charge that it is a secularized theodicy, and one which to boot justifies Western domination of the world. The suffering consequent on the development of the productive forces is not denied or explained away; at best it may be redeemed when revolution allows the victims of progress, or their proletarian descendants, to take control of these forces. This revolution is itself not inevitable. Each historical crisis has more than one possible outcome, and the general course of history does not follow a predetermined, linear path. The actual, contingent outcome of progress may be catastrophe, 'the common ruin of the contending classes'. Nowhere is this possibility more clearly expressed than by Benjamin, when he gave this inflection to Marx's metaphor that revolution is 'the locomotive of history': 'Perhaps revolutions are the reaching of humanity travelling in this train for the emergency brake.'[64]

Some critics, however, argue that attempts to rescue historical materialism from a linear and teleological conception of progress deprive it of any content. Brendan O'Leary, for example, in the course of a searching discussion of the difficulties which the concept of the Asiatic mode of production (AMP) poses for Marxism, claims that 'historical materialism is damned with the AMP and damned without it.' The most obvious difficulty the AMP poses for the Marxist theory of history is that, on Marx's account of it at least, it is a form of social stagnation, in which the productive forces do not develop. This leads O'Leary to pose the following dilemma: 'the AMP is either part of a unilineal schema, in which case it contradicts the theory of historical progress; or it is part of a multilineal schema, in which case historical materialism ceases to be a theory of history and becomes instead a redescription of world history.' Let us leave aside the AMP, which I have already rejected; in the next section, I endorse suggestions that the concept of a tributary mode of production is a far more useful analytical tool in understanding precapitalist societies. Why should a multilineal version of historical materialism, of the sort sketched out in the past few pages, be a mere 'redescription of world history'? The closest O'Leary comes to answering this question is the following passage:

> A theory apparently compatible with every description of historical diversity explains nothing. Multilineal schemas may be superficially 'empirical' but they are philosophically banal. So far, they remove necessity from Marx's theory of history, converting it into redescription rather than explanation.[65]

This looks more like a reassertion of the claim demanding justification than an argument for it. The line of thought it traces does not seem at all compelling. For one thing, *any* version of historical materialism, unilineal or multilineal, will be inconsistent with plenty of 'descriptions of historical diversity' – for example, with Michael Mann's claim, discussed in section 3.2 above, that Christian 'normative pacification' played a decisive role in mediaeval Europe's Great Leap Forward. For another thing, if Marxist explanations do not treat outcomes as inevitable, does that make them any less explanations? To tie together the concepts of explanation and necessity in the way O'Leary appears to in the last sentence cited is a move requiring careful argument, which he completely fails to provide. Explanation in the physical sciences is usually a matter of giving an account of the mechanisms responsible for certain phenomena. Using concepts such as those of the forces and relations of production to specify the mechanisms involved in the reproduction and transformation of societies seems like a variant of the same species of explanation. O'Leary seems to be launching a pre-emptive strike, by attempting to demonstrate *a priori* that explanations of this kind cannot work, or at least fail to meet the conditions required of any explanation. The dilemma with which he confronts historical materialism is in fact a variation of a fork on which followers of Althusser seeking to extricate themselves from Marxism used some years ago to impale their more orthodox brethren. *Either*, they said, Marxism is an interesting, but evidently false theory – deterministic, teleological or whatever – *or*, once the exciting falsehoods have been excised, all that is left is a collection of truisms which any Weberian or even a card-carrying empiricist could accept. The sensible Marxist response to these manoeuvres is to refuse to be caught on either horn of the dilemma. Almost all that is interesting and controversial in historical materialism is capable of being stated in a philosophically defensible form that is open to empirical corroboration. Whether or not it is, in addition, true is another matter; but this is too important a question to be settled by the kind of question-begging devices employed by O'Leary.

4.3 THE RISE OF THE WEST

Many believe that *any* defence of historical progress, however nuanced, is inescapably a celebration of the modern West. Eurocentrism has become a central issue in what Pat Buchanan called at the 1992 US Republican Convention the 'cultural war' between right and left in American society. Many left-wing intellectuals (for it is largely as intellectuals located in the academy that the American left survives) have been drawn towards various forms of cultural relativism as a means of historically situating modern Western society and highlighting the forms of oppression it involves of both various groups within its own boundaries and the peoples of the Third World; from this standpoint, the idea that this society might in any respect represent progress over its predecessors is abhorrent. Correlatively, the ideologues of the New Right (with the help of many liberals) have sprung fiercely to the defence of what they call Western culture, with its unique values of freedom, objectivity and tolerance. I consider the political and theoretical issues involved in what is sometimes trivialized as the 'political correctness' debate in section 4.4 below. For the time being, however, I wish to concentrate on Eurocentrism as a historical question.[66]

But to do so requires that we confront the implication of historical discourse itself in Eurocentrism. If by this term we mean the privileging of the pattern of development held to be distinctive of Western Europe and its North American extension as the norm by which all societies and peoples are to be understood and judged, then Eurocentrism is deeply embedded in modern historical thought. Hegel famously (or infamously) declared that in sub-Saharan Africa 'history is in fact out of the question. Life there consists of a succession of contingent happenings and surprises. No aim or state exists whose development could be followed, and there is no subjectivity, but merely a series of subjects who destroy one another.'[67] Note the implicit definition of history which this remark offers, with the internal relationship it establishes between the state and subjectivity – a connection whose truth is only fully articulated when freedom comes to self-consciousness in modern Europe. Hegel's philosophy of history is an explicitly and avowedly Eurocentric discourse.

Empirical historiography has shown itself little better than speculative philosophy of history in this regard. Herbert Butterfield points out that in eighteenth-century Göttingen, where the essential features of modern professional history-writing first took shape, 'the conception of "general history", so far as the modern period was concerned, came to be identified with that history of the modern European state-system which had been establishing itself in German university teaching.'[68] Ranke was the greatest exponent of this conception of history. The expressions 'world history' and 'universal history' recur in his writings, but their referent is the European state-system, each of its component units a living organism possessing a unique individuality but developing thanks to its relationship, at once harmonious and antagonistic, with its fellows. India and China, on the other hand, are 'a matter of natural history'. Their 'eternal repose' makes them 'a hopeless starting point' for the student of universal history. 'The nations can be regarded in no other connection than that of the mutual action and reaction involved by their successive appearance on the stage of history and their combination into one progressive community.' *These* nations, the proper object of world history, are those of modern Europe, locked in an 'unceasing struggle for dominion', for '[i]t is in and through this conflict ... that the great powers of history are formed.'[69]

These passages make clear, not simply how deeply imbued Ranke was with the Orientalist style of thinking denounced by Said, in which Asia is depicted as Europe's inert and sensual other, but also the extent to which, despite Ranke's criticisms of Hegel's absolute idealism, the two shared a remarkably similar conception of history. Georg Iggers and Konrad von Moltke observe: 'Both saw history as a meaningful and essentially benevolent process in which spiritual forces assumed concrete reality in social and political institutions.'[70] Acton claims that Ranke 'discards the teleological argument for history'.[71] Certainly, Ranke says that he does so, but his writings are full of teleological explanations. Consider, for example, his account of the rise of Richelieu. The end of the Wars of Religion had allowed the

French state to re-establish its power, and to adopt 'a bolder line of policy than had been hitherto attempted. This natural tendency inevitably called forth the organs suited to its promotion: men disposed to carry it out to its consequences and capable of doing so.' Hence the emergence of Richelieu, a statesman determined to challenge the Habsburg powers, Austria and Spain, 'for the supremacy in Europe'.[72] This is merely one instance among many of the way in which Ranke tends to think of the balance of power as a kind of self-correcting mechanism which serves not merely to prevent any of the Great Powers achieving hegemony over Europe, but to promote processes which both Hegel and he regard as desirable, notably the triumph of the Reformation and the flourishing of the European nations in all their individuality.

English-speaking historians notoriously shun speculation of any kind. But their writings are deeply imbued with Eurocentrism, not to say sometimes straightforward racism. H. E. Egerton, Professor of Colonial History at Oxford in the early years of the twentieth century, described the European partition of Africa as 'the introduction of order into blank, uninteresting, brutal barbarism'.[73] Two of the most celebrated modern American historians, Samuel Eliot Morison and Henry Steele Commager, could write in 1930 of the antebellum South: 'There was much to be said for slavery as a transitional status between barbarism and civilization.' This assertion reflected what Peter Novick calls the 'nationalist and racist historiographical consensus' established at the end of the nineteenth century and involving a general acceptance of the interpretation of the Civil War and Reconstruction put forward by Southern white historians such as John W. Burgess, and sanctified by Hollywood in films such as *Birth of a Nation* and *Gone with the Wind*. It was left to a black outsider, W. E. B. Du Bois, to challenge this consensus in his masterpiece *Black Reconstruction in America*.[74]

Eurocentric attitudes cannot be reduced to a past embarrassment. Hugh Trevor-Roper, one of the grand masters of postwar British historiography, could write in 1965: 'Perhaps in the future, there will be some African history to teach. But at present there is none, or very little: there is only the history of the Europeans in Africa. The rest is largely darkness, like the history of pre-European, pre-Columbian America.' Hegel's shade hovers over Trevor-Roper's defence of this assertion: 'history ... is essentially a form of movement, and purposive movement at that'; therefore the historian can safely ignore 'the unrewarding

gyrations of barbarous tribes in picturesque but irrelevant corners
of the globe'.[75] Fast-forward to 1991 and we find another doyen
of the historical profession, Arthur M. Schlesinger Jr, entering
the lists against proponents of Afrocentricity in the United States:
'As for tribalism, the word *tribe* hardly occurs in the Afrocentric
lexicon; but who can hope to understand African history without
understanding the practices, loyalties, rituals, blood-feuds of
tribalism?'[76] This assertion is more telling as a revelation of
Schlesinger's prejudices than as a criticism of his opponents.
Contemporary scholars, while they may disagree over the interpretation of tribalism in Africa, accept that it cannot be projected back into the continent's precolonial past. As Leroy Vail
puts it, 'empirical evidence shows clearly that ethnic consciousness is very much a new phenomenon, an ideological construct,
usually of the twentieth century, and not an anachronistic cultural
artifact from the past.'[77] Perceiving African history as the tale
of unremitting 'blood-feuds' among 'barbarous tribes' is as much
a feature of the discourse of Eurocentrism as the Orientalist
ideology explored by Said.

The strength of Eurocentrism's hold is perhaps most evident
in the case of some of those seeking to break from it. Toynbee's
philosophy of history is a case in point. It is not simply a matter
of his stereotyped view of Africa, evident in the remark that
'[t]he Black races alone have not contributed positively to any
civilization – as yet': so much then for the West African empires
of Ghana, Kanem-Bornu, Mali and Songhay, and for the succession of states which controlled the trade routes connecting the
Zimbabwean plateau with the east coast of Africa, whose most
spectacular monument is the stone citadel of Great Zimbabwe.[78]
Toynbee nevertheless does genuinely attempt 'to read the map
of history from a non-Western angle of vision' in order 'to see
in true perspective the whole history of a species of Society of
which the Western civilization was but one representative'. But
the vantage point from which he seeks to gain this 'true perspective' is that constituted by Toynbee's making his interpretation of the decline and fall of the 'Hellenic Society' of classical
antiquity, which he dates from the outbreak of the Peloponnesian
War in 431 BC, the basis of his general account of the breakdown of civilizations – above all that of the modern West which,
Toybnee fears, began with the First World War. Thus, '[t]here
was a sense in which the two dates AD 1914 and 431 BC were
philosophically contemporaneous.' Toynbee's philosophy of history
was thus a generalization from 'a comparison in two terms',

between Western modernity and the civilization to which it traced its origin, classical antiquity.[79]

Really overcoming Eurocentrism depends chiefly on the historian taking two steps, one ethico-political, the other conceptual. First, no historical discourse can hope to attain genuine universality unless it involves the recognition of, and gives proper weight to, the crimes perpetrated during the establishment and maintenance of Western domination over the globe. Of these, three in particular stand out: the European conquest of the Americas and the demographic catastrophe which it precipitated – within fifty years of Cortez's expedition in 1518, the population of central Mexico had been reduced by disease, war, and forced labour from thirty million to three million;[80] the transatlantic slave trade, with the appalling suffering it directly caused and the terrible legacy of racism it left behind it; and the Holocaust, which itself can, to some degree, be seen as an intensification on European soil of the ideologies and techniques used by the Western powers (including those fighting Nazi Germany) in their 'race wars' in other continents.[81]

Such a moral reorientation must be accompanied, secondly, by the conceptual decentring of historical discourse. This involves, above all, the refusal to treat the pattern of development associated with any particular region or country as a model in terms of which happenings elsewhere are to be understood. I advocate *de*centring rather than the discovery of the *real* centre of human history somewhere outside Europe. Afrocentric historiography, which treats Africa as the origin of civilization, not merely in the sense that the human species itself in all likelihood originated there, but as the source from which all the known high cultures, from the near east to Mesoamerica, can be traced, merely mimics the fantasies of Eurocentrism – the attempt, for example, by colonial ideologues to explain away Great Zimbabwe as the work of Phoenicians who for these purposes at least could be regarded as white, rather than acknowledge that it was made by the ancestors of the Shona-speaking Africans who form the majority in modern Zimbabwe. Afrocentrism is entirely understandable as a reaction to the experience of Western racism – and not just in the writing of history; but, in as much as it, quite literally, says black where Eurocentrism says white, it reproduces what is objectionable in the discourse to which it is responding, namely the reduction of world history to the destiny of a particular portion of humankind.[82]

This is not to say that the process of decentering does not
involve pointing to the respects in which the flow of cultural
influence has often been from Africa and Asia to Europe. Martin
Bernal has forcefully reminded us in *Black Athena* of the belief of Herodotus and other ancient historians – occulted by
nineteenth-century classicists concerned to construct a continuous
'Aryan' civilization from Homeric Greece to Wilhelmine Germany
– that the culture and perhaps also the rulers of the Hellenic
poleis had come from Egypt. When the intellectuals of the mediaeval West began to rediscover Greek scientific and philosophical thought, they sought it, not where it was available in the
original among their fellow Christians of Byzantium, but in the
brilliant Islamic centres of learning that had developed in Sicily
and southern Spain. 'The drawback that the Greek works were
here found at one remove from their original language – in
Arabic – was more than balanced by finding them surrounded
by a body of living thought,' Richard Southern observes. The
first Latin translation of Ptolemy's *Almagest* was made from the
Greek *c.*1160 in Palermo, under the Norman kings a meeting
point for Catholic, Orthodox and Islamic cultures, but it fell
into disuse once a translation from the Arabic appeared a few
years later. It was this 'one-way traffic in ideas which,' Southern
claims, 'hesitatingly in the eleventh century, but with rapidly increasing impetus throughout the twelfth century, transformed the
scientific knowledge of the Latin West'.[83]

Discovering what Loren Goldner calls the 'non-European roots
of Europe' does not, however, imply the displacement of the
centre of world history to Africa or Asia,, but rather the refusal
of any form of thought which requires that there be a centre.[84]
From Hegel and Ranke to Toynbee and Trevor-Roper there is a
close association between Eurocentrism and reliance on teleological
explanations: recall, for example, Trevor-Roper's appeal to the
concept of 'purposive development' to justify writing Europe into
and Africa out of history. The connection is easy enough to
understand. Teleological theories explain events according to their
relationship to the state of affairs constituting the culmination of
the process: the full flowering of Western modernity – or, in
Fukuyama's terms, of liberal capitalism – is an obvious candidate
for the role of the end, in the sense at least of the *telos*, of
history. A theory of history that is non-teleological in the respects
in which I argued in chapter 3 that both Marxism and its
Weberian rivals, in principle at least, are, is of its nature in-
hospitable to Eurocentrism.[85]

Surely, however, historical materialism is obviously Eurocentric, since the focus of its concern is with the capitalist mode
of production, which after all first became dominant in Western
Europe? Now there is a sense in which, as Tim Mason puts it,

> [a]ll good history writing begins at the end ... Where the
> end is judged to lie in time, what its character is, how it is
> defined – in taking these decisions about any piece of work,
> historians necessarily make their judgement about the general
> significance of their particular theme or period. And this
> judgement in turn determines where they start. [86]

In this respect Marx, throughout his career, is concerned with
the end of a particular history, namely the process through which
capitalism became the dominant mode of production in Europe.
His reasons for doing so were, however, political not metaphysical:
as a revolutionary socialist striving to overthrow capitalism he
needed to understand its origins and dynamics. Marx was notoriously cautious about the claims he made for his own attempt to
outline the prehistory of English capitalism in part 8 of *Capital*,
volume I. He attacked N. K. Mikhailovsky for trying 'to meta-
morphose my historical sketch of the genesis of capitalism in
Western Europe into a historico-philosophical theory of general
development, imposed by fate on all peoples, whatever the historical circumstances in which they are placed'. [87] More generally,
there seems to be no reason in principle why any attempt to
explain why capitalism first became dominant in Europe – surely
an undeniable fact, at least on Marx's definition of capitalist
dominance – should require setting Europe aside as the privileged
centre of world history. [88]
  Samir Amin has essayed such an explanation on a non-
Eurocentric basis. He argues that the 'family of formations that
is most widespread in the history of pre-capitalist civilizations' is
that in which what he calls 'the tribute-paying mode of production' prevails. Here society is divided into 'two main classes:
the peasantry, organized in communities, and the ruling class,
which monopolizes the function of the given society's political
organization and exacts a tribute (not in commodity form) from
the rural communities'. The great centres of ancient civilization
in the Old World (Egypt, Mesopotamia, India and China) and
the New (for example, the Inca, Maya and Aztec empires) were
all 'tribute-paying formations'. They represented 'the normal path
of evolution' of humankind before the onset of capitalism. The

precapitalist modes of production particularly associated with European development – slavery and feudalism – were marginal variants of the tribute-paying mode. The societies where they predominated – respectively, classical antiquity and mediaeval Christendom – were 'peripheral precapitalist formations', on the edge of the main centres of civilization. It was indeed the peculiarity of these social forms which made possible an 'exceptional line of evolution in the west of the Old World'. European feudalism involved 'an absence of political, administrative, and economic centralization', and consequently, by the standards of the Asian mainstream, 'a surplus of modest size'. But 'this weakness ... was to become its strength':

> This low level of centralizing capacity was to allow freedom to the commercial sectors ... Under their stimulus, agriculture made great progress, and the surplus produced naturally by agriculture grew naturally, so that the dialectics of increasing trade could get under way, leading in turn to the rise of capitalism.[89]

At a very general level a number of attractions are offered by this interpretation. It makes the onset of capitalism not a consequence of uniquely European virtues but rather an instance of what Trotsky calls the 'privilege of historic backwardness', which in the capitalist era itself has allowed peripheral economies to leapfrog over the advanced – Germany and the United States over Britain in the late nineteenth century, Japan over the United States a hundred years later.[90] Moreover, the concept of the tribute-paying or tributary mode of production offers a means of conceptualizing the distinctive characteristics of the ancient empires while avoiding the pitfalls of Marx's sketches of the Asiatic mode of production, in which the Orient appears as stagnant and historyless. Nevertheless, in rightly claiming that the tributary mode was the predominant form of precapitalist class society Amin tends to blur the differences which set it apart from other precapitalist modes of production. The resulting lack of specificity is most clear in his claim that the entire period from 300 BC to the Renaissance constitutes a single 'mediaeval' epoch: Alexander's unification of western Asia and the Mediterranean created 'a unique cultural area' which was destroyed only when the development of capitalism allowed the 'semi-barbarous West' to break away from, and eventually to conquer, 'the more civilized Orient'. Amin's main concern in advancing this interpretation is with the understanding of 'tributary culture': thus he seeks to show how neo-Platonism, the product of Alexandria, intellectual capital of the Hellenistic world created by Alexander's conquests, provided the philosophical matrix from which developed the most sophisticated version of tributary ideology, Islamic metaphysics, and its 'peripheral' variant, Latin Christian scholasticism. As a cultural analysis this is quite plausible, though not without its difficulties: thus in depicting the Renaissance as an empiricist break with scholastic metaphysics Amin fails to confront the profound influence of Platonism on Renaissance thought, and, above all, on Galileo and the seventeenth-century scientific revolution.[91]

Whatever the continuities or discontinuities that may exist at the level of culture, the main issue is whether the modes of production dominant in precapitalist Europe can be treated merely as peripheral variants of the tributary mode. The recent work of a number of historians suggests that they cannot. Ellen Wood, for example, has sought to bring out the specificity of the Greek *poleis* in the classical era by comparison with the ' "redistributive" kingdoms' of Minoan and Mycenean Greece, which, like 'most known advanced civilizations of the ancient world', were based on tributary production relations; the admiration expressed by Plato and Aristotle for societies such as Egypt and Crete where these relations still prevailed reflected the hostility of the Athenian aristocracy to the democratic political forms which, uniquely in the ancient world, had enfranchised the smallholding peasantry. The institutional structures of the *polis*, most democratically developed in Athens, in turn presupposed certain decisive technical and social innovations – above all, the development of an intensive peasant agriculture made possible by iron ploughs and axes, and the emergence of the hoplite citizen infantry, recruited from the better-off farmers, whose military superiority was reflected first in the employment of Greek mercenaries by near east kingdoms, then in the defeats inflicted on the armies of the Great King by the Hellenic city-states, and finally in the conquests of Alexander of Macedon. The Hellenistic civilization which emerged from Alexander's victories was undoubtedly dominated by a variant of the tributary mode of production, but its creation is only comprehensible once one takes into account the characteristics which set apart the Greek *poleis* from the other ancient civilizations.[92]

Of far greater importance, however, is Chris Wickham's attempt to give an account of the nature and dynamics of the tributary

mode of production, one of the most significant contributions
to historical materialism in the past few years. Wickham takes
over Amin's basic definition of the tributary mode as 'a state
bureaucracy taxing a peasantry'. But he seeks sharply to distinguish it from the feudal mode of production, which is based on
'rent-taking ... backed up by coercion'. Both modes of production
involve the extraction of surplus labour from a smallholding
peasantry on the basis of extra-economic coercion. Nevertheless,
'state tax-raising and coercive rent-taking by landlords cannot be
conflated. They represent two different economic systems,' involving 'divergent interventions in the peasant economy'. Thus, in
the tributary mode, 'it is not in the state's purview to control the
production process'. It 'does not need to control the economic
and social lives of its subjects; it just needs the funding that
enables it to pursue its objectives'.[93]
The feudal mode, by contrast, implies a much more intimate
involvement by the dominant class in the process of production:

> Landowners relate to peasants more closely. Their interest is
> not just in the amount of surplus, though this is important
> enough: it is in the recognition of local power, local control
> ... But this control is not just political, i.e. coercive; it
> extends to involvement in production itself. This involve-
> ment is structural, rather than necessarily conscious ...
> everywhere, landlords control access to the land, even if in
> practice how much power this gives them is very variable,
> and largely dependent on the degree of peasant resistance ...
> It is thus in this arena that class struggle tends to happen
> between peasants and landlords; over control of the pro-
> duction process, and, at a more mediated level, over the
> conditions in which one side or the other must be able to
> exert such control: protection of local customs on one hand,
> judicial subjection on the other.[94]

One implication of this analysis is that 'feudalism was a world
system', rather than a peculiar social form confined to the periphery of the great tributary civilizations: '*empirically* there have
been few if any class societies that have not experienced some
form of landowning and coercive rent-taking.' Typically, the
empires of the precapitalist Orient represented an articulation
of the tributary and feudal modes of production, in which the
former's dominance was constantly contested by landowners seeking to expand their local power, and therefore their control over

the peasants' surplus labour. These were societies whose history was that of the working-out of 'the structural antagonism ... between the state ... and the landed aristocracy'.[95] Wickham even argues that the 'ancient mode of production' mentioned by Marx in the 1859 Preface must be seen as 'one subtype' of the tributary mode, involving 'the control of a city-based citizen body over the immediate countryside', with 'tribute or tax taken from proprietors in the subject countryside and, in the case of Rome itself, other subject cities'. The collapse of this mode in the West reflected, not the decline of slavery, which had become economically marginal in late antiquity, but the growing power of the landowning class. The barbarian invasions acted as a catalyst in this process because 'they cracked the power of the state'; though the Germanic successor states sought to maintain 'the financial mechanisms of the empire', the army, 'the major item of expenditure for the late Roman state', was now based on landowning. Rent replaced taxation as the main form of surplus-extraction. 'Private landowning was henceforth no longer the means of obtaining power; it was itself power.'[96]

From this perspective the question of the peculiarity of the Western pattern of development can be reformulated in these terms: 'the mediaeval and post-mediaeval West was one of the few societies where feudalism has *dominated*.'[97] In the more advanced precapitalist civilizations – in the Islamic world, for example, and China – the state bureaucracy was able to hold the landowners in check. In Western Europe, however, the landlords became the dominant class; this transformation unleashed a process of development which in certain important respects created the conditions for the formation of capitalist relations of production. I shall mention two of these conditions. First, the lords' involvement in production to a greater degree than the state bureaucracy of tributary society contributed to the considerable advance in agricultural output and productivity which unfolded between the tenth and thirteenth centuries, making possible the growth of trade and of urban life which was an essential ingredient in the formation of capitalism. Secondly, the local character of lordly power made for a far more fragmented and decentralized society than that characteristic of a developed form of the tributary mode. This may have promoted the circulation of commodities; it certainly allowed the crystallization of nodes of development, particularly in the towns, outside the control of either feudal lords or a tributary bureaucracy. Of course, other conditions were required for capitalism to begin to take shape in a developed form – above all, the separation of labour power from the means of production and its subsumption under capital; we touched on some of the issues raised by this condition in sections 3.2 and 3.3 above. But here too, a tributary state has a structural interest in preserving cohesive peasant communities working the soil as the source of its tax revenues; there are, by contrast, circumstances in which landowners may directly benefit from the differentiation of the peasantry into tenant farmers and wage labourers, as did many English lords in the early modern period, or may be too weak to resist the proletarianization – often in the partial form of proto-industrial artisan households producing for urban merchants – of at least a section of the peasantry. It is plausible, then, to conclude that capitalism could only first develop out of a feudal society: the peculiarity of Western Europe is thus reduced to the fact that mediaeval Christendom is the main instance of such a society.[98]

One advantage of the style of analysis pursued by Wickham and other Marxist historians is that, by using the concept of mode of production in order to understand ancient civilizations and therefore homing in on such issues as the form of surplus-extraction prevailing within them, it provides an antidote to any tendency to idealize them. This tendency is understandable enough as a reaction to the crimes perpetrated by the modern West, but it is an obstacle to arriving at a proper historical judgement of capitalism and its precursors. Paul Buhle illustrates the pitfalls involved in the nostalgic celebration of precapitalist societies. Challenging Loren Goldner's qualified defence of capitalism as a progressive force in world history, Buhle argues that 'conquest or domination' often 'brings a one-way catastrophe disguised as the advance of particular classes within societies that hardly knew of their existence previously, and gain little from their presence compared to the losses endured'. Among such victims of progress are 'many American Indian populations, such as the cliff-dwellers of the west, who had achieved an admirable balance of scarce natural resources utterly unlike the increasingly destructive economies to follow'.[99]

Buhle implies that ecological collapse is a peculiarity of modern industrial societies. This claim is wholly untenable. Take the case of one Native American cliff-dwelling people, the Anasazi of the south-west. One of the most impressive of their settlements is Tyuonyi, in the Frijoles Canyon, New Mexico (now the Bandelier National Monument). Embracing cave-rooms, substantial stone buildings and *kivas* (underground structures used in religious

rituals), Tyuonyi came into existence in the late twelfth century.
By the time the Spanish reached northern New Mexico four
hundred years later, the canyon was deserted. It seems likely
that intense farming, hunting, plant-collecting and tree-cutting
exhausted the available resources; as returns diminished the
population dispersed in search of more fertile land.[100] Nor does
this pattern seem particularly exceptional or aberrant. The magnificent stone ruins at Great Zimbabwe were once the capital of
a state which flourished between AD 1300 and 1450 thanks to
its control of the gold trade with the ports of east Africa. But
this state, according to David Beach, 'seems to have come to a
relatively sudden end by the beginning of the sixteenth century'.
His explanation of this abrupt collapse

> is that Zimbabwe simply grew too big to be supported by
> its environment ... the mere presence of so many people at
> one spot [between 5,000 and 11,000 people lived in Great
> Zimbabwe at its height] would have seriously affected the
> ability of its site territory to supply crops, firewood, game,
> grazing, and all the other necessities of life. A *shangwa*
> [drought or other natural disaster] at a point where the
> population had reached critical level would have destroyed
> the ability of the site territory to support it, and in the
> absence of a technology that could transport sufficient sup-
> plies over long distances the only alternatives would have
> been to disperse the people or move the state structure
> itself.[101]

Precapitalist societies are in general no more likely to achieve
what Buhle calls a 'balance of scarce natural resources' than
capitalist ones: if other examples are required, the appalling
Malthusian crisis of overpopulation which gripped late mediaeval
Europe should suffice.[102]

It is equally misleading to suggest, as Buhle does, that the
ancient civilizations supplanted by the modern West 'hardly knew'
of the existence of classes. To take the case of pre-Columbian
America, the Aztec and Inca empires were both products of
processes of expansion and conquest which had occurred comparatively shortly before the Spanish conquest. Both societies
were instances of the tributary mode of production, with a steady
flow of surplus product fuelling the consumption, rituals and
war-making of the dominant class. The conquistadores were able
to exploit the internal tensions of both states – particularly those

between more and less recently conquered areas – in order to destroy them.[103] There is much to admire in these civilizations: it would be an impoverished historical imagination that could not respond to the great city of the Mexica (as the Aztecs are more properly known), Tenochtitlan, with its 200,000 inhabitants participating in a complex urban life. Inga Clendinnen has recently provided a remarkable reconstruction of how this society was experienced by its members. But she unflinchingly focuses on how this experience was pervaded by ritual human sacrifice, so that Aztec society presented to its destroyers 'an unnerving discrepancy between the high decorum and fastidious social and aesthetic sensibility of the Mexica world, and the massive carnality of the killings and dismemberings: between social grace and monstrous ritual'. She argues, with great subtlety and sympathy for the Mexica, that these rituals served at once to celebrate 'cosmically sanctioned human power' and to dramatize the fragility and dependence of human existence.[104] The reader is left both impressed by the force of this interpretation and, inescapably, overcome by the beauty and horror of the Mexica world – a world in the face of which one is caught between two impossibilities, celebration and condemnation. The ambivalence Marx displayed towards all cases of historical progress acquires a peculiar intensity here.

But in what sense can one talk of progress at all? Let us respond to this question obliquely, by returning to the case of the European transition from antiquity to feudalism. Guy Bois has made a remarkable recent contribution to the understanding of this process. He argues that we must date its turning point, not as Wickham does in the fifth century, but *c.* AD 1000. Carolingian Europe was, in its basic structures, a continuation of antiquity; the fundamental division remained that between the free citizens, entitled whatever their socio-economic status to participate in public life, and the unfree, slaves, enjoying some advantages compared to their classical counterparts (for example, the right to marry and live with their families) but still the property of their masters. Bois traces the gradual process of transformation along several dimensions – the erosion of monarchical power, the radical reordering of town–country relations, the build-up of agrarian growth central to which were 'the enlargement and consolidation of small-scale peasant production on the economic and technical level' – which precipitated around the millennium the revolution from which feudalism proper emerged. The main legatee of this upheaval was the new dominant class of feudal lords to whom the peasants, freed from slavery, were subordinated. But Bois is not content to leave matters there:

> The paradox ... is that the feudal revolution had supported itself on the movement itself of the peasantry: on its rise in the long term and on its direct intervention in the final phase. This class thus contributed to putting in the saddle those who would dominate and exploit within the seigneurial framework for centuries. But must one retain only this aspect of the event? Can one dismiss as negligible the peasant's access to a new socio-economic status which guaranteed him, through tenure, the stability of his rights to the soil, and which made him an economic agent in his own right, endowed with a real autonomy in production and exchange? The feudal revolution inaugurated the true age of the peasantry. Like other revolutions, it certainly had an oppressive aspect; but it was first of all liberating.[105]

The merit of this weighing-up of the costs and benefits of social transformation is the connection it establishes between two concepts: progress and freedom. This is one of the issues I explore in the following, and final, section.

4.4 IDENTITY AND EMANCIPATION

I have proceeded so far on the assumption that it is possible to formulate a theory of history that is not Eurocentric: whether or not a particular theory meets this requirement is a contingent matter of how it constructs its concepts and handles the empirical evidence confronting it. Another way of making the same point is to say that it is possible to arrive at a genuinely universal theory of history – that is, at a theory of history whose general propositions do not simply mask the conceptual procedures involved in Eurocentrism, where a particular pattern of development is transformed into the norm by which all historical phenomena are to be understood. This assumption is a highly controversial one, because it runs against the grain of contemporary intellectual fashion. It has become part of the commonsense beliefs of large sectors of the Western intelligentsia that every universalism is a masked particularism. Lyotard's critique of metanarratives is one version of this thesis.

Historical materialism is, of course, the grand narrative that is the main object of this critique. Perhaps the most careful attempt to make out the charge of particularism against Marxism is that made by Robert Young: 'Marxism, in so far as it inherits the system of the Hegelian dialectic, is also implicated in the structures of knowledge and the forms of oppression of the last two hundred years: a phenomenon that has become known as Eurocentrism.' Consequently. 'Marxism's universalizing narrative of the unfolding of a rational system of world history is simply a negative form of the history of European imperialism,' so that 'the story of "world history" not only involves what Fredric Jameson describes as the wresting of freedom from necessity but always also the creation, subjection and final appropriation of Europe's "others".'[106]

Young's case is made from a distinctive philosophical standpoint, that of poststructuralism. This is the label attached to the group of Nietzschean philosophers who first came to prominence in Paris during the 1960s. Chief among them were Deleuze, Derrida and Foucault; despite their many disagreements, all shared certain fundamental positions which can be traced back to Nietzsche: the denial of any structure to reality, which is reduced to the play of difference; a preoccupation with power and domination as the fundamental driving force of the human world; a critique of knowledge's claim to truth and its exposure as a particular form of the will to power; the dissolution of the subject into the contingent effect of specific relations of domination. Critics (of whom I am one) argued that poststructuralism's wider reception during the 1980s (when it was repackaged by Lyotard, Baudrillard et al. as postmodernism) represented a depoliticization of radical theory, and its aestheticization, so that the critique of bourgeois society was transformed into striking a knowing, ironic attitude towards both the defenders of the status quo and those still benighted enough to wish to overthrow it.[107] Young's position amounts to a defence of poststructuralism against this charge, a rebuttal which seeks to vindicate this current of thought as articulating a more genuinely radical politics than that of classical Marxism. The central issue at stake here is that of Eurocentrism. 'Postmodernism can best be defined', Young declares, 'as European culture's awareness that it is no longer the unquestioned and dominant centre of the world.'[108]

It is something of an irony that the philosophical tradition which Young claims as the basis of his critique of Eurocentrism should trace itself back to Nietzsche and Heidegger. For both were, as Loren Goldner points out, 'pure products of ... the Greek romance of philosophy', that is, of the very powerful

tendency whose development from the late eighteenth century has been reconstructed by Martin Bernal, which set up an idealized image of classical Greece as the pure origin of modern Europe, writing out of this genealogy the influence of Pharaonic and Hellenistic Egypt on Greek culture, and of the Islamic world on mediaeval Christendom.[109] Nevertheless it is true that, under certain conditions, the esoteric conceptual apparatus of post-structuralism has served to articulate a would-be radical politics. This is what has come to be known as identity politics. 'Identity' has become one of the most widely used terms of contemporary political discourse. In some ways a looser version of the concept of social role in orthodox sociological theory, 'identity' refers to various social labels used in inter-subjective relationships, labels which individuals attach to themselves or which are attached to them by others, and which identify them as members of a specific group. The most important identities in contemporary politics are those arising from gender, race, nationality, sexual orientation and religion. In a broad sense, identity politics is simply any political action which is legitimized by appeal to some identity. On this criterion, the Balkan war is an example of identity politics. But a narrower version of identity politics re-presents itself as a strategy of the left based on the militant assertion of their specific identities by various oppressed groups. The radical American political scene in the late 1980s and early 1990s offered a number of examples of this kind of identity politics – the gay and lesbian activists of ACT-UP and Queer Nation, the militant feminists of the Women's Action Committee, and a variety of radical African-American, Latino and Native American groups.[110]

It is easy enough to see the elective affinity of poststructuralism for this narrower form of identity politics. This philosophical current denies that social formations (or indeed anything else) have an intrinsic unity: the very idea of a social totality harbours within itself a will to power. The Nietzschean problematic of power tends to displace class exploitation as the main object of radical critique; instead, a multiplicity of power relations gives rise to irreducibly different forms of oppression. Resistance therefore of necessity takes a plural form. Each oppressed group cannot transcend its particular identity; the closest the oppressed can arrive at any broader unity is a coalition of autonomous move-ments, each separate but equal.[111] This theoretico-political posi-tion can be worked up without much difficulty into a critique of Marxism as a phoney universalism. Thus Ernesto Laclau has purported to reveal a 'logic of incarnation', originating in Christianity but at work in Western modernity, one of whose features is 'the *privileged agent of history*, whose particular body is the expression of a universality transcending it'. Eurocentrism is an instance of this logic: 'European imperial expansion had to be presented in terms of a universal civilizing mission.' In Marxism a particular class, the proletariat, became an incarnation of the universal. 'The same type of logic in Eurocentrism [*sic*] established the ontological privilege of the proletariat.[112]

To a significant degree arguments such as those put forward by Young and Laclau presuppose claims which I have criticized above – for example, Löwith's reduction of modern historical discourse to a secularized version of Christian eschatology (section 4.1), and the widespread dismissal of Marxism as a speculative teleology (sections 3.2 and 4.2). Here I wish to concentrate on their attack on Marxism's universalism, both as a theory of history and as a political tradition. The issue is best considered at three levels: (1) the concept of theory itself: (2) Marxism's contribution to the struggle against imperialism; and (3) the political goal of human emancipation.

(1) *The imperialism of theory* Consider these claims by Young, some of which I cited in section 4.2 above:

> what is at stake is the argument that the dominant force of opposition to capitalism, Marxism, as a body of knowledge remains complicit with, and even extends, the system to which it is opposed. Hegel articulates a philosophical structure of the appropriation of the other as a form of knowledge which uncannily, simulates the project of nineteenth-century imperialism; the construction of knowledges which all operate through forms of expropriation and incorporation of the other mimics at a conceptual level the geographical and economic absorption of the non-European world by the West. Marxism's standing Hegel on his head may have reversed his idealism, but it did not change the mode of operation of a conceptual system which remains collusively Eurocentric.[113]

Hegel in this context is a bit of a red herring, since the vast philosophical debates provoked by Lukács and Althusser in the 1920s and 1960s respectively have established one thing beyond any doubt – namely, that the relationship between Hegel and

Marx is an extremely complex one. It is also, in my view, one which cannot be reduced to either direct continuity (as Lukács claimed) or radical discontinuity (as Althusser argued).[114] This is not to say that Young's critique has no target; behind the metaphors of 'appropriation', 'expropriation' and 'incorporation' lies what one might call the realist conception of theory, according to which knowledge is arrived at through the construction of a set of theoretical concepts designed to identify the essential structures of the real, which are usually inaccessible to direct observation.[115] Now, poststructuralists have good reasons, from their point of view, for rejecting this conception of theory, since they are anti-realists for whom (in Foucault's formula) the will to truth is merely a form of the will to power: Young's argument amounts to an attempt to give this anti-realism a more directly political inflection, by claiming that the realist conception of theory is intrinsically Eurocentric.

It is hard to see what would count as a formal proof – or disproof – of this claim. I shall try to erode whatever plausibility it might seem to have by making some observations about the historical conditions and consequences of the realist conception of theory. For there is no doubt that this conception was not simply accepted by Marx but has played an important part in the modern Western intellectual tradition. It can be traced back to classical Greek philosophy – specifically to the concept of philosophical thought itself developed by Plato and Aristotle, of *theõria*, the disinterested contemplation of objective reality. Gadamer calls *theõria* 'pure presence to what is truly real':

> to be able to act theoretically is defined for us by the fact that in attending to something it is possible to forget our own purposes. But *theõria* is not to be conceived primarily as an attitude of subjectivity, as a self-determination of the subjective consciousness, but in terms of what it is contemplating. *Theõria* is a true sharing, not something active, but something passive (*pathos*), namely being totally involved in and carried away by what one sees.[116]

This conception of thought, in which the theorist detaches himself from the immediate preoccupations and purposes of everyday social practice in order to penetrate to the core of the real, is taken over – with one very significant modification which I discuss below – by the sciences of Western modernity. It is, however, by no means the exclusive property of the West. Samir

Amin argues, as we saw in section 4.3 above, that 'the Neo-
platonic synthesis of Hellenism' perfected by Plotinus in the third
century AD formed 'the core of mediaeval metaphysics'.[117] Through
this medium, the concept of *theõria* served to articulate the
self-understanding of intellectuals in that vast, but relatively
culturally unified, mediaeval civilization which stretched from
northern India to, on its semi-barbarous western periphery, the
British Isles. One consequence has been to make the intellectual
products of that civilization accessible to its successor cultures.
One of the masterpieces of mediaeval thought, Ibn Khaldûn's
The Muqadimmah, is a case in point. Numerous Western commentators have been struck by both the modernity and the intellectual grandeur of this work. For Toynbee it is 'undoubtedly
the greatest work of its kind that has been ever yet created by
any mind in any time or place'.[118] Toynbee's bitter antagonist
Hugh Trevor-Roper is little more restrained in his praise of Ibn
Khaldûn, whom he calls 'the profoundest, most exciting historical writer between Antiquity and the Renaissance.[119] Yves
Lacoste sees him as Marx's precursor, the founder of the science
of history.[120] Yet what makes Ibn Khaldûn's writing a text with
which modern Western theorists and historians can directly engage
is surely in part that he is engaged in essentially the same kind
of intellectual enterprise, characterized in the same way, as that
of the Greek thinkers who represent the origin of both his own
thought and that of his interlocutors. Set *The Muqadimmah* alongside another great historical work, also written in north Africa,
albeit nearly a thousand years earlier, Augustine's *City of God*,
and one is confronted, as Toynbee puts it, with 'two strikingly
similar but entirely independent works', with both of which the
modern reader can enter into dialogue, despite the fact that they
were written to vindicate the world-views of, respectively, Islam
and Latin Christianity.[121]

The modern realist conception of theory can thus trace its
origins back to a concept – *theõria* – that became part of the
common intellectual heritage of mediaeval civilization, Islamic
and Christian alike. Nevertheless, the scientific revolution of the
seventeenth century introduced a radically new dimension of theoretical activity: it now became legitimate to intervene in the
physical world in order both to know and to control it. Thus
theory is for Francis Bacon, as Hans Blumenburg puts it, 'no
longer the reposeful and bliss-conferring contemplation of things
that present themselves – as the ancient world had regarded
it – but rather is understood as work and a test of strength'.

Hence the significance of Galileo's use of the telescope: 'the discovery of unseen realities' showed that 'curiosity is rewarded', but it did so in a form which, 'unlike any experimental intervention in the objects of nature, ... could be adapted to the classical ideal of the contemplation of nature'.[122] But the subsequent evolution of the physical sciences made such intervention a necessary condition of the acquisition of knowledge, since the corroboration of hypotheses in disciplines such as physics and chemistry typically requires the creation of artificial conditions in order to test experimentally whether or not the relationships postulated by the hypotheses actually hold. The result is a dynamic conception of theory, which retains the classical conception of knowledge of the essential structures of the real but combines it with the modern presupposition that it is necessary to interfere in the real in order to uncover this structure.

The idea that knowing nature is inseparable from acting on it is of course one aspect of the broader historical significance of the modern physical sciences which derives from their role in the transformation of the physical world under capitalism. Marx argues that 'general social knowledge has become a *direct force of production*' in bourgeois society.[123] It is precisely because of the close connection between the theoretical development of the physical sciences and their technological applications in greatly enhancing (albeit often in what turn out to be highly costly and destructive ways) human control of nature that it is tempting to offer an entirely instrumentalist interpretation of theory as nothing but as a means of intervention in and domination of the physical world; it is then an easy step to argue that the use of theory to know the social world plays a similarly 'appropriative' role, serving to legitimize the Western conquest of the rest of the world. But this interpretation fails to capture what one might call the classical moment of the modern realist conception of theory – the fact that it is the physical sciences' success in providing knowledge of the structure of reality which makes possible technological control of nature. The gargantuan apparatus of intervention into the physical world that is such a dominant characteristic of modernity would be inconceivable unless, as a matter of fact, theoretically driven scientific research had come up with a series of fairly close approximations to the truth about the physical world.

The same point is made by Charles Taylor, a philosopher who has shown himself to be extremely aware of the costs of modernity but is at the same time unwilling to ignore its genuine achievements. He stresses the differences between – even the incommensurability of – the premodern and modern conceptions of theory: 'One view ties understanding nature to wisdom and attunement, the other dissociates them.' Nevertheless, the 'technological pay-off' of the modern sciences puts the burden of proof on their classical and mediaeval predecessors:

> once a spectacular degree of technological control is achieved, it commands attention and demands explanation. The superiority of modern science is that it has a very simple explanation for this: that it has greatly advanced our understanding of the material world. It's not clear what traditional Platonism could say about this phenomenon, or where it could go for an explanation ... In this way, one set of practices can pose a challenge for an incommensurable interlocutor, not indeed in the language of this interlocutor, but in terms which the interlocutor cannot ignore. And out of this can arise valid transcultural judgements of superiority.[124]

Notice that this argument makes no claims that the consequences of technological control are all welcome from an ethical or political point of view. It merely suggests that the best explanation for the instrumental success of the modern physical sciences is that they offer an understanding of nature superior to that provided by their premodern ancestors. This argument bears at least a family resemblance to that put forward by Michael Devitt for Scientific Realism, the doctrine which holds that most of the unobservable entities posited by scientific theories exist independently of the mental. 'If Scientific Realism, and the theories it draws on, were not correct,' Devitt contends, 'there would be no explanation of why the observed world is as if they were correct: that fact would be brute, if not miraculous.'[125] This line of thought poses a challenge to all those who put forward an instrumentalist interpretation of the sciences – not merely poststructuralists like Young but also pragmatists like Richard Rorty and neo-Kantians like Jürgen Habermas (Habermas's apparent inability to comprehend the physical sciences is one of the weakest points in his entire theoretical position). If it is correct, then Young's mobilization of metaphors of appropriation and the like is beside the point. They do not cut to the heart of the modern realist conception of theory, which turns out, quite simply, to be, as it asserts, that the objective of theoretical activity is to establish the essential structure of the real.

(2) *Anti-imperialism in theory and practice* Historical materialism is, of course, the most important attempt to extend this conception of theory to the understanding of the social world, which is itself conceived historically, as a process of development and transformation. Young claims that Marxism has from start to finish been complicit in the subjugation of the peoples of the world to Western imperialism. Anyone who seriously consults the historical record rather than, as Young does, reading it through the distorting lens offered by the literary and philosophical divagations of the Parisian intelligentsia, will soon establish that this assertion is – not to put too fine a point on it – demonstrably false. Far from defending Western domination of the world, Marxism has played a central part in the twentieth-century history of the movements which have challenged that domination.

Much is made in discussions of this issue of the Stuttgart Congress of the Second International in 1907, when the increasingly assertive right wing of the socialist movement, led by Eduard Bernstein, defended colonialism because of 'the need of civilized peoples to act somewhat like guardians of the uncivilized'. What is less often noticed was that this position was rejected by the congress after being fiercely attacked by, among others, the Polish revolutionary Julian Marchlewski, who said: 'We Socialists understand that there are other civilizations besides simply that of capitalist Europe. We have absolutely no grounds to be conceited about our so-called civilization nor to impose it on the Asiatic peoples with their ancient civilization.'[126] More significantly in the longer term, this very period before the First World War saw the formulation of the Marxist theory of imperialism, which sought to establish a connection between the partition of the world among the Great Powers of the West and the transformation of the advanced economies themselves. The significance in this context of Lenin's version of the theory lay in the further link it forged between a primarily economic analysis of imperialism as a particular stage of capitalist development and a political strategy for overthrowing it. The distinctive feature of this strategy – which could only begin to be properly pursued after the collapse of the Second International and the formation of its revolutionary rival, the Third or Communist International – was the alliance it sought to forge between incipient socialist revolution by the working class of the imperialist countries and the developing nationalist revolts in the colonies.[127] A remark by Trotsky admirably captures the novelty of this strategy: 'What characterizes Bolshevism on the national question is that in its attitude towards oppressed nations, even the most backward, it considers them not only the object but also the subject of politics.'[128] Whereas previously even the strongest Marxist critics of imperialism had tended to see the peoples of the colonies primarily as victims, now they were regarded as the agents of their own liberation, participants in a global revolutionary process which would mark the end of capitalism itself.

The subsequent history of the Communist movement in what we now call the Third World is a long, complex and ultimately tragic tale inseparable from the larger story of the development of Stalinism in the Soviet Union itself.[129] Yet one thread running through it is the essential role played by the Communist Parties in the development of movements for national liberation in Asia, Latin America, Africa and the Arab world. Two examples must suffice. In India the relationship between the Marxism of the orthodox Communist movement and the nationalist struggle for independence was so intimate as to be problematic, and thus was one factor in the emergence (partly under poststructuralist influence) of the intellectual current around the journal *Subaltern Studies*, which in reaction has, in Dipesh Chakrabarty's words, 'developed a critique of nationalism as an ideology and of the (nation) state as a social formation'.[130] The Iraqi party was the most important Communist Party in the Arab world. In one of the great historical works of recent years, which combines an almost obsessively detailed analysis of socio-economic structures with vivid political narrative, Hanna Batatu has traced the history of Iraqi Communism, its development into the leadership of a mass movement against the Hashemite monarchy and the latter's British backers, and the role it played in the tragedy of the 1958–9 Revolution, whose ultimate outcome was the Ba'ath dictatorship.[131]

But perhaps the most extraordinary examples of the ability of the Communist movement to act as an instrument of struggle against forms of oppression distinct from class exploitation come from the United States. Two remarkable studies have reconstructed the considerable degree of success the Communist Party of the USA achieved in winning the support of black people during the 1930s. Mark Naison shows how the predominantly white party was able to build up a substantial base in Harlem during the early 1930s, despite the fierce competition from the black nationalists of Marcus Garvey's Back to Africa movement.[132] But far more striking is the story told by Robin Kelley of how, in Alabama, the heart of the deep South, the CP was able to

win the loyalty of hundreds of black people, some of them mill
and mine workers in Birmingham, but many others sharecroppers
in rural Alabama.[133] The Comintern's decision in 1928 to extend its general support for national liberation to backing black
self-determination in the southern United States (the so-called
'Black Republic' policy) was undoubtedly an important factor
in making these achievements possible. But it is noteworthy that
the American CP's greatest successes among black people came
in the early 1930s, when, as part of the Comintern's sectarian
'Third Period' line, they stressed very strongly the common
interests of black and white workers; the apparently more ac-
commodating Popular Front strategy of building broad alliances
against fascism, adopted by the Comintern in 1935, actually cost
the CP much of its black support, since in the American context
it implied wooing the Democrats, who ran the South as what
amounted to a collection of one-party regimes in the Jim Crow
era.

Detailed acquaintance with any of these histories would soon
establish the extent to which the Communist Parties were hopelessly compromised by their slavish loyalty to the Soviet Union,
which undermined all their achievements and (in the case of the
Iraqi and other Arab CPs) eventually destroyed them. And Marxism, usually in this distorted Stalinist form, was only one of the
discursive means by which those engaged in the struggle against
imperialism sought to articulate their self-understanding. Nevertheless, any proper balance sheet of Communism in the Third
World would have to enter in the credit column the sincere commitment of Communist activists to the goal of national liberation
and the heroism and self-sacrifice with which they pursued this
objective. (The French Communist Party's miserable record of
complicity in Paris's efforts to hold on to Algeria during the
1954–62 war of independence, though undoubtedly important
in convincing some French intellectuals that Marxism was inherently Eurocentric, stands out as an exception to this general
pattern.[134]) The contribution made by even so distorted and
vulgarized a version of Marxism as that produced by Stalinism to
the movements against imperialism and racism hardly suggests that
historical materialism is a theoretical discourse which can only
act as a tool of Western domination. To continue, in the face
of this history, to insist that Marxism is irredeemably Eurocentric
is not only an insult to the memory of those who have given
their lives to the cause of socialism *and* national liberation – for
example, half a million supporters of the Indonesian Communist

Party who were massacred when the military seized power in
October 1965; it is also to evade the real task of anyone seriously interested in opposing imperialism, namely that of arriving
at a proper historical appreciation of the role played by Marxism
in all its diversity – including, in some cases, Trotskyism as well
as Stalinism – in the various movements for national liberation,
in order to help draw conclusions for future political strategy.[135]

(3) *Human emancipation* I suggested at the end of section 4.3
above that the respect in which a historical transformation can
be regarded as progressive in a strong sense – that is, in ethico-
political terms rather than merely from the standpoint of the
development of the productive forces – lies in the increase in
freedom it involves: thus, if Guy Bois is right, the feudal revolution of *c.* AD 1000 marked a step forward in human progress
because it depended on the real autonomy which hitherto enslaved peasants were able to wrest from their masters. Loren
Goldner makes the same claim for early modern capitalism:

> the European capitalist society which appeared in the post-
> 1450 Renaissance and Reformation eras, prior to and during
> the early phases of Western world ascendancy, was a revolu-
> tionary society without precedent which posed as a (still
> unfulfilled) *potential* the realization of a kind of human free-
> dom, indissolubly social and individual, superior to and more
> truly humane than anything realized in previous or then-
> contemporary Old World state societies (Islam, India or
> China) or in New World state formations (Mayan, Aztec,
> Inca).[136]

The thought seems to be, in the first instance, that it was in
early modern capitalism that the concept of this 'unique *potential
of individual realization*' emerges; Goldner attaches particular
importance to the idea, formulated by two key heterodox Renaissance thinkers, Nicholas of Cusa and Giordano Bruno, that
the universe is infinite, which, as Blumberg puts it, '[s]ince the
subject is now understood as the power of representing the
universe', made it possible to think of each individual person
as unique in the way in which she or he refracts the variety of
creation.[137] This concept of individual freedom begins to acquire
a political dimension, and to be linked to projects of collective
transformation, as a result of the English Revolution of the 1640s,
though it is perhaps only in Kant's writings, themselves heavily

influenced by Rousseau and part of the same epoch as the French Revolution, that it acquires a rigorous, and largely secular, formulation.[138]

It is tempting to relate the emergence of this concept of freedom founded upon the notion of the unique individuality of every human being to one of the principal features of the capitalist mode of production: the fact that, according to Marx, 'the worker ... [is] free in the double sense that as a free individual he can dispose of his labour-power as his own commodity, and that, on the other hand ... he is free of all the other commodities needed for the realization of his labour-power.'[139] The replacement of feudal exploitation, in which the extraction of surplus-labour is secured by extra-economic coercion and therefore presupposes the political subjection of the peasantry, by capitalist exploitation, in which primarily economic pressures lead formally free workers who have no direct access to the means of production to consent to employment on terms which involve their producing surplus value for capital, creates the conditions in which the concept of individual freedom as a political ideal can be articulated. But putting it like this is simply to state the classic Marxist objection to capitalist freedom, namely that it represents only a formal emancipation, since the worker's liberty and equality (for one way of stating this conception of freedom is to say that everyone has an equal right to it) is consistent with her lacking the means to support herself and therefore being compelled to sell her labour power; indeed, the continued existence of capitalism depends, if Marx is right, on her being in this position. This critique of freedom under capitalism does not imply that this mode of production represents no progress over feudalism; on the contrary, the fact that the direct producer is no longer directly subordinated to a lord armed with judicial and military power indicates the respect in which it undoubtedly does mark an advance. The point rather is that the worker's double freedom, and all it implies – above all, the contrast between the formal equality of citizens and their real, socio-economic inequality – indicate it is only an imperfect and limited fulfilment of the idea of freedom.[140]

Marx had argued along these lines long before he developed the theory of surplus value of which the concept of double freedom is part. In 'On the Jewish Question' (1843) he distinguishes between 'political emancipation' and 'human emancipation'. Political emancipation, the outcome of the French Revolution, is the most that can be achieved in capitalist society. It involves a condition of alienation, in which 'man ... leads a twofold life, a heavenly and an earthly life: life in the *political community*, in which he considers himself a *communal being*, and life in *civil society*, in which he acts as a *private individual*, regards other men as means, degrades himself into a means, and becomes a plaything of alien powers.' Civil society, man's '*most immediate* reality,' is a realm of economic competition and class antagonism; in the liberal state, however, whose constitutive principles are liberty and equality, man is 'the imaginary member of an illusory sovereignty, is deprived of his real individual life, and endowed with an unreal universality'. Thus, '[p]olitical emancipation is the reduction of man, on the one hand, to a member of civil society, to an *egoistic, independent* individual, and, on the other hand, to a *citizen*, a juridical person.' Human emancipation, by contrast, seeks to abolish this double life, to do away with the distinction between *bourgeois* and *citoyen*:

> Only when the real, individual man re-absorbs in himself the abstract citizen, and as an individual human being has become a *species-being* in his everyday life, in his particular work, and in his particular situation, only when man has recognized his '*forces propres*' as *social* forces, and consequently no longer separates social power from himself in the shape of *political* power, only then will human emancipation have been accomplished.[141]

There is, no doubt, much that is open to argument in the distinction Marx draws here between political and human emancipation (certainly the idea that the state and civil society must be kept separate has become, in contemporary intellectual fashion, an unquestionable dogma). The virtue of the distinction is that it provides a way of stating the sense in which modernity is, in Habermas's words, 'an incomplete project'.[142] It was Kant who first properly established the connection between emancipation and enlightenment when he defined enlightenment as the transcendence of immaturity ('the inability to use one's own understanding without the guidance of another'), and argued that 'enlightenment of this kind' presupposes freedom (though he tried to make this claim acceptable to the Prussian absolute monarchy of Frederick the Great by limiting the scope of this freedom to intellectual freedom).[143] Marx's concept of human emancipation is plainly a development of this view of enlightenment and liberation, but one which provides the means of criticizing the latter's inadequacies. The degree of freedom attained by capitalist society represents only a limited and incomplete realization of the objective of human emancipation, since, by leaving in place systematic socio-economic inequalities, it represents only a formal – in Marx's terms, political – emancipation which abstracts from the class antagonisms and constitutes itself as the basis of a juridico-political realm of rights and liberties alienated from the realities of everyday life.

The notion of human emancipation can thus be thought of as a reference point from which to assess the extent to which a given society has overcome the different forms of social oppression. Developing this idea plainly requires some attempt to specify the content of the concept of human emancipation. Etienne Balibar has recently offered what amounts to such a specification. Like Marx in 'On the Jewish Question', he gives a reading of the Declaration of the Rights of Man and of the Citizen, the fundamental political document to emerge from the French Revolution. But, whereas Marx sees in this text the opposition between *bourgeois* and *citoyen*, between the private individual of a conflict-ridden civil society and the participant in an abstract political community, Balibar discovers there an equation of man and citizen which he believes to have the most radical consequences. He seeks to sum these up in what he calls '*the proposition of égaliberté*'. *Egaliberté*, or 'equaliberty', is a portmanteau word formed by the fusion of 'liberty' and 'equality'. Balibar is not claiming here to be stating a conceptual truth, the 'identity of the *ideas* of Equality and of Liberty', but rather is announcing what he believes to be 'the historical discovery, which one could perfectly well call empirical [*expérimentale*], that their *extensions* are necessarily identical'. In other words, 'the (*de facto*) historical *conditions* of liberty are exactly the same as the (*de facto*) historical conditions of equality.' Thus:

> *There are no examples* of restrictions or suppressions of liberties without social inequalities, nor of inequalities without restriction or suppression of liberties, even if there are degrees, secondary tensions, phases of unstable equilibrium, compromise situations in which exploitation and domination do not distribute themselves in a homogeneous fashion among all individuals.[144]

Of the implications of *égaliberté* Balibar stresses two in particular. First,

the meaning of the equation Man = Citizen isn't so much
the affirmation of a political right as the affirmation *of a
universal right to politics*. Formally at least – but this is
the very type of a form which can become a material force
– the Declaration opens an indefinite sphere of the 'poli-
ticization' of demands for rights which reiterate, each in its
own fashion, the requirement of a citizenship or of an institutional, public, inscription, of liberty and equality: in
this indefinite opening there inscribe themselves as well –
and as early as the period of the [French] Revolution one
sees the attempt – the demand for the right of wage-earners
or dependants such as women and slaves, later that of the
colonized. This right finds itself formulated later in the
following form: *the emancipation of the oppressed can only
be their own work*, which immediately underlines its ethical
meaning.[145]

Secondly:

An intrinsic part of the truth of our statement [the proposition of *égaliberté*] is its absolute *indeterminacy* ... the
consequences of the statement are themselves indeterminate:
they depend entirely on 'relations of forces' and on their
evolution in the conjuncture, where it is necessary prac-
tically to construct the individual and collective referents of
égaliberté, with more or less 'prudence' and 'precision', but
also with 'audacity' and 'insolence' against the established
powers. *There will be a permanent tension* between the
conditions which historically determine the construction of
institutions which conform to the proposition of *égaliberté*,
and the hyperbolical universality of the statement.[146]

The proposition of *égaliberté* is thus a formula for permanent
revolution, for the continuous radicalization of the Enlightenment. Forms of inequality and oppression which were ignored
when it was initially formulated at the beginning of the French
Revolution – capitalist exploitation, the oppression of women,
of slaves, of the colonized, of black people, of lesbians and
gays – can be made to fall under its scope by virtue of its
capacity for indefinite extension. What Balibar calls the principle's
indeterminacy – perhaps better described as the tension between
its generality and its dependence on specific historical conditions
for its application – provides the basis for criticizing specific

institutional realizations of *égaliberté* as limited and incomplete. Balibar himself seeks to restrict the scope of *égaliberté*. He argues that it cannot satisfactorily be applied to cases of 'anthropological difference' – for example, the oppression of women. This is an instance of 'a relation of collective inequality ... which is reproduced, exercised and verified as a personal relationship'. Women's liberation therefore cannot triumph 'as the restoration of an original identity or as the neutralization of differences in the equality of rights, but as the production of an equality without precedents or models which would be difference itself, the complementarity and reciprocity of singularities'. The struggle for women's liberation thus marks the end of the '*modern* epoch' of politics, the era of *égaliberté*, and the opening of 'a *postmodern* epoch, in which the question is posed of the transcendence of the abstract or generic concept of man at the basis of generalized citizenship'.[147]

This line of argument is quite unpersuasive. For it is surely true of every form of inequality that it involves particular historical conditions, institutional patterns and intersubjective relationships; overcoming inequality will therefore in each case require a specific reordering of social and political relations which can only to a limited extent model itself on other liberations. Undoubtedly there is a disjunction between simply making certain forms of oppression illegal (as most liberal democracies have legislated against discrimination against women, black people and homosexuals, for example) and genuinely eradicating them, which usually requires a much more thorough social transformation. But this tension has been present from the very first formulation of the principle of *égaliberté* – its existence is after all the theme of Marx's critique of the formal freedom and equality of capitalism – and therefore cannot be treated as a problem peculiar to 'postmodern' politics. In any case, the *impulse* behind the demand that some specific form of oppression be removed is always the same, namely that it represents some respect in which the promise of emancipation embodied in the principle of *égaliberté* has not been fulfilled. The ethical grounds for seeking to overcome oppression are not altered by the fact that in some cases it may require, as Balibar (correctly, I think) argues in the case of the subjection of women, some as yet unimagined form of equality.

In broader historical terms Balibar's general account of *égaliberté* (minus the restrictions he attempts to put on its scope) provides support for Habermas's claim that 'there is no cure for the wounds of Enlightenment other than the radicalized Enlightenment itself.'[148] The false universality of political emancipation, whose formal enactment of freedom and equality conceals a congeries of real inequalities, embracing both capitalist exploitation and sexual, racial and national oppression, can only be overcome by seeking to achieve a genuine universality, which more fully realizes in institutional terms the principle of *égaliberté*. Sàbina Lovibond persuasively argues against postmodernist critics of Enlightenment such as Rorty and Lyotard that feminism is 'a typically *modern* movement. The emergence of sexual equality as a practical political goal can be seen as one element in the complex course of events by which tradition has given way, over a matter of centuries, to a way of life that is deeply *untraditional* – in fact, to "modernity".' She takes Marx to be saying in the *Manifesto* that 'the horror of modernity also contains a promise: *sooner or later arbitrary authority will cease to exist.*' From this perspective, the movement for women's liberation, seeking as it does to challenge one particularly entrenched and pervasive form of arbitrary authority, 'should persist in seeing itself as a component or offshoot of Enlightenment modernism, rather than as one more "exciting" feature (or cluster of features) in a postmodern social landscape'.[149]

One reason why this perspective is an attractive one is that it is very hard to see how a critique of oppression can proceed except on a nonrelativist basis. Rorty inadvertently provides corroboration for this thought when he argues that the basis of moral and political action is not some universalistic notion of moral autonomy or human rights but the narrower solidarities which emerge in specific, historically contingent circumstances:

> Consider ... the attitude of contemporary American liberals to the unending hopelessness and misery of the lives of the young blacks in American cities. Do we say these people must be helped because they are our fellow human beings? We may, but it is much more persuasive, morally as well as politically, to describe them as our fellow *Americans* – to insist that it is outrageous that an *American* should live without hope ... our sense of solidarity is strongest when those with whom solidarity is expressed are thought of as 'one of us', where 'us' means something smaller and more local than the human race. That is why 'because she is a human being' is a weak, unconvincing explanation of generous action.[150]

The last sentence quoted is plainly muddled. No doubt in explaining why a person performs some generous action we appeal to facts about her particular character and history. But her own *reasons* for so behaving may well include the thought that the object of her generosity is a human being. The more general difficulty with Rorty's argument is equally obvious. Who are the *we* shared membership of which is to be the basis of moral and political action? Solidarities 'smaller and more local than the human race' necessarily exclude as well as include. The politically effective 'we' in the antebellum American South excluded slaves. Abolitionists challenging the 'peculiar institution' appealed, among other things, to the very fact that black slaves were as much human beings as free whites. Looking back, we condemn various historically constituted solidarities as too narrow in an ethically relevant sense – classical Athens, for example, for excluding women, slaves and metics from the 'we' of free citizens. But how is that condemnation to be grounded? Rorty says he welcomes modern 'moral progress . . . in the direction of greater human solidarity', of 'the ability to think of people wildly different from ourselves as included in the range of "us"'.[151] But how did this extension in the scope of what Adam Smith called the sentiment of sympathy take place? Rorty is unable to give any answer because the widening 'in the range of "us"' involves precisely the *transcendence* of particularism, the recognition of the inadequacy of the narrower solidarities of nation or race or religion.

This is not to say that Rorty's critique of universalism does not articulate with particular clarity the *doxa* of identity politics. One important element in this common sense is what one might call the hypostatization of culture. 'Culture' in this context refers to the distinctive complex of traditions that constitutes a specific identity. These days it tends to be conceived as a closed totality, sufficient unto itself and requiring no communication with other cultures; correlatively, appeal to the speaker's particular culture has come to count as providing good reasons for a wide range of actions. Instances of this latter feature of contemporary usage of the term 'culture' run from the silly to the sinister. Susan Sontag, for example, justified her idiosyncratic form of aid to the besieged people of Sarajevo in 1993 – staging a production of *Waiting for Godot* – with these words: 'I know that suffering is the same all over the world but these people are European. They belong to my culture.'[152] Doubtless the people of Angola, who were at the time suffering even more greatly than the Bosnians but who had the bad luck not to share Sontag's culture,

could cope with being denied her help, but the remark sums up
the ethnocentric blindness with which Western media and poli-
ticians agonized ineffectually over the war in Bosnia but ignored
the even bloodier one in Angola. 'Culture' has come to conceal
a multitude of sins. Chief Gatsha Buthelezi, leader of the Zulu
tribalist Inkatha Freedom Party, would frequently defend his supporters' use of assegais and pangas in their ferocious attacks
on the people of South Africa's black townships by saying that
these were 'cultural weapons', sanctified by time-hallowed Zulu
tradition.

This kind of hypostatization of national cultures is merely
one aspect of a more general efflorescence of particularism.
But however much it may have come to be intellectually respectable, not simply in its postmodernist forms but also in at least
some versions of the communitarian critique of liberalism developed by some contemporary English-speaking philosophers,[153]
identity politics, even in its 'radical variants', is vulnerable to
the most serious historical, philosophical and political criticisms.
Historical: some of the most exciting recent scholarship has un-
covered the fragile, contingent, constructed character of national
identity in particular – its dependence, for example, on 'invented
traditions' as a means of imagining a past capable of legitimizing
its present coherence and demands for the future.[154] Philosophical:
as even some of its more sophisticated proponents acknowledge,
particularism is barely coherent; a specific identity is typically
constituted in contrast and sometimes opposition to other identities, and its demands, generally couched in terms capable of
winning support from the bearers of other identities, are tacitly
universal.[155] Political: to the extent that oppressed groups do
take their stand on the particularity of their oppression, the
effect is likely to be a process of further fragmentation; a good
example is provided by the phenomenon of what one might call
'oppression-trumping' which set in among the declining social
movements from the late 1970s onwards, a process of differentiation *ad infinitum* as various groups formed claiming the special,
and often specially acute, character of *their* oppression – black
women versus white women versus Jewish women, lesbians
versus gays versus bisexuals, Afro-Caribbeans versus Asians versus
Africans ...

The problem here isn't simply that this kind of hyper-
particularism makes any form of unity among the oppressed inconceivable; in the absence of any criterion by means of which
to distinguish genuine cases of oppression from assertions of

identity which may amount to the demand to oppress others, even the most 'rigorous' theorists may end up in strangely uncritical stances. Thus Laclau not long ago took Habermas to task for being 'uncomfortable' in the face of 'the brute fact of German nationalism' renascent after the reunification of October 1990: 'I think that the assertion of a German identity can take place in a variety of ways, not all of them producing reactionary effects.'[156] These remarks were made in November 1991, at a time when the climate of chauvinist hostility to foreigners stirred up by the government of Helmut Kohl would soon lead to the Nazi outrages at Rostock, Mölln and Solingen. But it was not just that Laclau had utterly misread this mood (which Habermas, to his great honour, courageously resisted), but that he offered no way of determining whether a particular assertion of identity is 'reactionary' or not.[157] It is hardly surprising that, faced with all the confusions and inadequacies of identity politics, Edward Said, whose work has until recently been marked by a systematic ambivalence towards universalistic theories, should express his impatience, declaring that '[t]he question of identity – focusing on yourself, are we this, that or the other? – is really in the end one of the less interesting questions in the world', compared to the issue of 'enlightenment and emancipation'.[158]

This judgement seems essentially right. Resistance to oppression can only be coherently justified by a theory that is universalistic in two senses: first, it involves a nonrelativist ethics on the basis of which the transformation or abolition of certain social relationships can be justified – perhaps because they violate the principle of *égaliberté*; secondly, it seeks to establish the relationship between the different forms of oppression in order to identify the common interests which different oppressed groups may turn out to have. One advantage of such a theory would be that it could provide a vantage point from which to set the question of identity in a proper historical perspective. For it is doubtful whether the definition and assertion of identity were often issues in precapitalist class societies, where most of the population lived in isolated peasant communities interacting rarely with those from more than a few miles away. But capitalism, as Marx argues so eloquently in the *Manifesto*, breaks down the divisions separating communities and countries, incorporates every society in a single world system, and drags peoples across the globe – in the slave trade, in the settlement of the white colonies and, most recently, in the great movements of immigrant workers from the Third World to the advanced economies. It is in these conditions that identity becomes an issue, both because, against the universal context created by capital, new forms of differentiation – particularly those of nationality and of race – emerge, and because the anxieties created by bourgeois modernization promote the invention of identity-constituting traditions as a way of ordering chaos. But alongside the crystallization of identities come their assimilation and fusion, a process from which there emerge the heteroclite, eclectic cultures of the great cities of twentieth-century capitalism, so that, for example, the forms of music developed by the descendants of America's African slaves come to dominate popular culture.[159]

It is, of course, a characteristic theme of poststructuralism that identities are fluid and 'impure'. The hybridity of cultures has been explored with great subtlety by 'postcolonial' theorists such as Edward Said and Homi Bhabha. But in Bhabha's thought at any rate (the eclecticism of Said's thought, of which his critics often complain, saves him from any such tendency) cultural difference is theorized in terms of what Bhabha calls the 'language metaphor'. The properties ascribed to language by theorists influenced by Saussure, notably Lacan and Derrida – for example, the 'structure of symbolization' itself and the 'splitting' of the subject it allegedly produces – thus explain the ambiguity and heterogeneity of all identities. Historical struggles are thereby transformed into effects of the process of signification. Not only is this a misleading way of thinking about language – compare, for example, Bakhtin's account of the multiaccentuality of discourse, which treats social conflict as inherent in every utterance – but it tends to depoliticize the struggles of the oppressed. The Freudian category of ambivalence is Bhabha's master-concept: it serves to break down the Manichean opposition of oppressor and oppressed, and to uncover the mutual imbrication of their discourses, but at the price of apparently writing off the possibility of any qualitative transformation. At best, it seems, the oppressed can 'renegotiate' the terms of their oppression: self-emancipation through the revolutionary overthrow of the old order appears too unequivocal an outcome to find any place in Bhabha's 'postcolonialism'.[160]

Other contemporary theorists, more sceptical of poststructuralism, have begun to acknowledge the existence, and explore the dynamics, of the process of identity formation and fusion characteristic of capitalist modernity. Paul Gilroy, for example, resisting 'the continuing lure of ethnic absolutisms in cultural criticism produced both by blacks and by whites', has developed the idea of the 'black Atlantic', of the interchanges between blacks in the United States, Britain and the Caribbean which, he argues, in the work of writers such as Richard Wright and W. E. B. Du Bois produced a veritable 'counter-culture of modernity'.[161] Gilroy's exploration of this theme is suggestive and stimulating. It does not, however, go far enough. Focusing on the transactions among black intellectuals, he imposes artificial boundaries on a process which often embraces influences on and by whites. Where, for example, would that great citizen of the black Atlantic, C. L. R. James, fit in, the brilliant Trinidadian Marxist intellectual who drew on the Western literary and philosophical tradition – Hegel and Aeschylus, Melville and Dostoevsky – in order to develop a critique of contemporary capitalism, and to reconstruct the history of black struggles where these were always seen as part of a process of class emancipation embracing white workers as well?[162]

James's work illustrates the point developed above, namely that the radicalization of the Enlightenment provides the tools by which to remedy its ills. It also raises the question, finally, of the social agency of liberation. Marx believed that universal emancipation required a universal class, the proletariat.[163] Few of his views are more unacceptable to current intellectual opinion. The trouble is that class continues to raise its ugly head in contemporary political debates. One 'post-Marxist' theorist, Stanley Aronowitz, in the course of grappling with the philosophical and political perplexities of identity politics, where '[t]he idea of *difference* becomes, in effect, the new universal that cannot be overcome but must, instead, be celebrated', confronts the fact that class cannot, after all, be wished off the political agenda:

> Rethinking class is plainly a necessary step in any social movement and in any political discourse that takes among its leading premises both equality and autonomy. And we must come to terms with the plain fact that the renunciation of solidarity is a formula for the eternal recurrence of fragmentation among us, and an invitation for the inheritors of the old universalisms to maintain their hold. We were right to throw out the reductionist 'class analysis' that was the theoretical basis of both the old left and, with variations, much of the new left. This version of social and political theory virtually excluded all other considerations or regarded them as displacements of the class struggle. In the course of this rightful rejection, however, class was occluded from the

lexicon of radical terms on the basis of its pernicious history. Yet, in the light of the current debate between and among the two major parties [i.e. the Republicans and the Democrats in the United States] concerning what is euphemistically called the 'working middle class' (more precisely the middle working class), how can questions of class remain outside the discourse of opposition?[164]

How indeed? It is one of the symptoms of the irrelevance of the American left, its confinement to a large degree to the universities where its preoccupation with issues of subjectivity, language and consciousness assumed sometimes the exaggerated forms seized on by the opponents of political correctness, that it should reduce class exploitation to 'classism', just another oppressive 'ism' to be denounced along with all the others. One way out of this mess (only a more extreme form of the general plight of the Western left at this particular *fin de siècle*) is indeed, as Aronowitz suggests, to 'rethink' class. In the absence, however, of any such rethinking, it might be worth taking another look at what Marx had to say, for three reasons.

First, most of the criticisms of Marx's theoretical analysis of the working class are grossly inaccurate. The strategic position of the working class in classical Marxism does not, as Laclau claims, represent its status as a secularized version of Christ's Incarnation. Rather, it derives from an analysis of how capitalist exploitation compels wage labour to organize and resist collectively; this struggle has, Marx claims, a tendency to develop into a generalized confrontation with capital. It is open to argument whether or not this theory is false, but it is in any case an empirical theory rather than a piece of metaphysical speculation, and should be assessed as such. Secondly, the idea that the proletariat is the universal class derives from the claim that its emancipation is inseparable from the elimination of various forms of oppression to be found alongside class exploitation in capitalist society. This claim does not, as Aronowitz alleges, involve ignoring these oppressions or reducing them to epiphenomena of class antagonisms; it is, rather, concerned with the structural connections between capitalist exploitation and racial, sexual and national inequalities. Far from dismissing these inequalities, Marxists have often argued that overcoming them is an essential part of socialist revolution, since a working class that is, for example, racially divided would be incapable of liberating itself. Finally, one reason why Marx believed the working class could unite humankind was that capitalist development would transform a growing proportion of the population into wage labourers. Even now only a minority of the world's population live by wage labour; yet the economic transformations of the past generation have brought us closer to the point where workers are the majority more than ever before. Two developments have been especially important: the rapid incorporation of the majority of women in the advanced economies into the formal wage-earning labour force, and the large-scale industrialization of parts of the Third World (above all, India, southern China and elsewhere in east Asia), which has made the idea of the world working class, invoked by Marx in the *Manifesto* and by Lenin and Trotsky after the October Revolution (but still in those times primarily a theoretical concept), into a social reality. Of course, there is an enormous gap between the objective existence of a world working class and its becoming an active political force. All the same, just now would be an odd moment to say farewell to the idea of universal emancipation, and the class that could still be its bearer.[165]

CONCLUSION

Women, children and revolutionaries have no taste for irony.

Joseph Conrad

Irony is the reigning trope. It can be seen to function at various levels of cultural discourse. Richard Rorty, repackaging post-modernism in a reassuring liberal pragmatist idiom, uses irony to define a new model of the intellectual life. Ironists are those whose

> realization that anything can be made to look good or bad by being redescribed, and ... renunciation of the attempt to formulate criteria of choice between final vocabularies, puts them in the position which Sartre called 'meta-stable': never quite able to take themselves seriously because always aware that the terms in which they describe themselves are subject to change, always aware of the contingency and fragility of their final vocabularies, and thus of their selves.[1]

In parallel with Rorty's 'liberal ironism' is Hayden White's ironic metahistory, which functions to reveal the relativity of every piece of purported historical knowledge, the partiality of every perspective. But there are plenty of more downmarket uses of the trope. Indeed, the adverb 'ironically' has become one of the clichés of contemporary journalistic writing, used to introduce the slightest qualification to, or the vaguest contrast with, the main story-line. This usage is consistent enough with the general picture of the world presented in the mass media, an incoherent chaos of fragments; irony here serves to highlight the fact that the world doesn't fit together, that there seems to be no pattern into which the different pieces can be put. These impressions are closely related to what one might call the commodification of irony – its use by a prosperous, well-educated middle class to consume the products of both high and mass culture that they cannot any longer take at face value, and so must place, as it were, in quotation marks. Umberto Eco imagines a man saying to 'a very cultivated woman': 'As Barbara Cartland would put it, I love you madly.' This allows them, 'in an age of lost innocence', 'consciously and with pleasure' to 'play the game of irony ... But both will have succeeded, once again, in speaking of love.'[2] This little game of love and irony is emblematic of a widespread cultural practice – the knowing and detached appropriation of experiences by an elite that regards itself as too sophisticated for simple pleasures and unqualified commitments.

One is naturally led to inquire about the political implications of this kind of use of irony. Often the cultivation of 'private irony and liberal hope' recommended by Rorty has gone along-side some unremarkably naïve and uncritical political beliefs. Rorty's own bedrock stance seems to be a familiar kind of Cold War liberalism, which had him declare, only a couple of years before the Berlin Wall broke open: 'Not only is Soviet imperialism a threat, but time seems to be on the Soviet side.'[3] We have seen (in section 2.3 above) that White's ironism does not prevent him from adopting a remarkably ambivalent attitude towards nationalism in some of its most regressive forms. In some ways more interesting than these examples (which may after all only tell against the political judgement of the individuals concerned) is the advocacy of irony as the prime intellectual and political virtue. Take, for example, these remarks by C. Vann Woodward. After approvingly quoting Conrad's *bon mot*, cited as the epigraph to this conclusion, that 'women, children and revolutionaries have no taste for irony', the great historian of the American South continues: 'These are certainly not the most propitious times for the cultivation of that taste. Not only is it an abomination to revolutionaries, but also equally abhorrent are mixed motives, ambivalence, paradox, and complexity in any department.'[4] Woodward wrote these words at the end of the 1960s. They reflect the political storms which shook the United States during that decade, and the consequent demands within the academy for a radical historiography which would reflect the experience, and be written from the standpoint, of the oppressed and the exploited, the victims of progress, the marginal and the excluded.[5] Woodward interpreted these demands as an assault comparable to McCarthyism, and has responded to the more recent pressures now labelled as political correctness in the same vein.[6] It is plain enough what the ironic awareness of 'mixed motives, ambivalence, paradox, and complexity' serves to convey in his hands: the recognition of the different sides to every question, of the qualifications to every generalization, and therefore of the futile and self-defeating nature of all efforts radically to transform an oppressive social structure.

In fact, the political and aesthetic uses of irony interweave. In a brilliant essay Franco Moretti argues that the sources of modernism are to be found in Romantic irony:

> And Romantic irony – observed one of its sharpest critics, Carl Schmitt, in *Politische Romantik* – is a frame of mind which sees in any event no more than an 'occasion' for free intellectual and emotional play, for a mental and subjective deconstruction of the world as it is. Devoted to the category of 'possibility', Romantic irony is incapable of decision, and even hostile to whatever resembles one. But decision ... is inseparable from praxis and history ... From this point of view Modernism appears once more as a crucial component of that great symbolic transformation that has taken place in contemporary Western societies: the meaning of life is no longer to be sought in the realm of public life, politics and work; it has migrated into the world of consumption and private life. This second sphere has become incredibly more promising, exciting, and free, and it is within its boundaries that we can indulge our unending daydreams. But they are symmetrical – indeed, they owe their very existence to the bored and blind indifference of our public life. Daydreams – even the most subversive ones – have no interest in changing the world, because their essence lies in running parallel to it, and since the world is merely an 'occasion' for their deployment, it may just as well remain as it is.[7]

Far from having attained a postmodern condition, we live in a culture permeated by the modernist withdrawal from a public sphere conceived as incapable of transformation, into a private life characterized by the adoption of an ironic stance towards the forms of art that have become prime items of consumption. Does this mean that Conrad and Woodward are right, and that the proper stance for those unwilling to give up the idea of revolution to adopt towards irony is at best one of suspicion? Such a position can claim authority from Hegel, for whom irony is the 'supreme form' in which *subjectivity declares itself absolute*.

He selects for special attack Friedrich von Schlegel's doctrine of Romantic irony, in which 'particular selfhood' is

> elevated to divine status in relation to the good and the beautiful. This implies that objective goodness is merely something constructed by my conviction, sustained by me alone, and that I, as lord and master, can make it come and go [as I please]. As soon as I relate to something objective, it ceases to exist for me, and so I am poised above an immense void, conjuring up shapes and destroying them. This supremely subjective point of view can arise only in a highly cultivated age in which faith has lost its seriousness, which now exists only in the vanity of things.[8]

The main obstacle to accepting Hegel's reduction of irony to extreme subjectivism is the systematic use he himself makes of the trope. For what is more ironic than the revelation, at every step of the dialectical process, of the limits inherent in that stage, and of the falsehood it embodies? Similarly, Marx's writings are full of irony, as they explore the illusions under which human actors engage in practice and the unexpected consequences of their efforts. These remarks of White's on 'Hegel's conception of historical knowledge' could be applied equally to Marx:

> the whole of it is a sustained effort to hold the essential Irony of the human condition in consciousness without surrendering to the skepticism and moral relativism into which Enlightenment rationalism had been led on the one hand, or the solipsism into which Romantic intuitionism had had to be led on the other. This aim is to be achieved by the transformation of Irony itself into a method of analysis, a basis for the representation of the historical process, and a means of asserting the essential ambiguity of all knowledge.[9]

That final phrase, 'the essential ambiguity of all knowledge', more accurately reflects White's views than Hegel's or Marx's. That aside, the passage highlights a tension between two concepts of irony, as the 'supreme form' of subjectivism and as 'a method of analysis'. Kenneth Burke's remarkable discussion of irony offers one way of resolving this tension. Burke argues that irony is the properly dialectical trope:

> Irony arises when one tries, by the interaction of terms upon one another, to produce a *development* which uses all the

terms. Hence, from the standpoint of this total form (this 'perspective of perspectives') none of the participating 'sub-perspectives' can be treated as either precisely right or precisely wrong. They are all voices, or personalities, or positions, integrally affecting one another. When the dialectic is properly formed, they are the number of characters needed to produce the total development.[10]

Burke warns against any confusion of this kind of dialectical irony with 'the relativistic':

It is certainly relativistic, for instance, to state that any term ... can be seen from the point of view of any other term. But in so far as terms are thus encouraged to participate in an orderly parliamentary development, the dialectic of this participation produces (in the observer who considers the whole from the standpoint of the participation of all the terms rather than from the standpoint of any other participant) a 'resultant certainty' of a different quality, necessarily ironic, since it requires that all the sub-certainties be considered as neither true nor false but *contributory*.[11]

Irony based on a comprehension of the part played by each in a total process is to be distinguished from 'a brand of irony, called "romantic irony", that might fit in with such a pattern', that might, in other words, be considered relativistic, '–the kind of irony that did, as a matter of fact, arise as an aesthetic opposition to cultural philistinism, and in which the artist considered himself *outside of* and *superior to* the role he was rejecting'.[12] This diagnosis does ring true. What is more characteristic of Rorty's writings, for example, than the superior tone of voice he adopts, the way in which he patronizes all those still benighted enough to think it matters whether our sentences correspond to reality or whether we act rationally? The liberal ironist can afford to luxuriate in his refusal to decide, secure in the knowledge setting him apart, that all attempts to interpret, let alone to change the world must fail. Conrad's tone in the epigraph is the same. Women are put in their place, minding the children, and tacitly reduced to a childlike condition. Revolutionaries, by being set alongside these, the marginal and excluded, are the objects of the same disdain for lacking the mature insight into the complexity of things that would allow them to see through their vain dreams. It is a company in which the revolutionary is happy to be counted, since revolution is the process through which the despised and the silent gain a voice and become the subject of history.

Burke's treatment of irony as dialectic firmly links it to the concept of social totality: the irony derives from each term's failure to see its part in the 'total development'. This concept is, of course, one of the prime targets of Lyotard and other post-modernists, for whom the very desire to comprehend society as a whole is a confession of totalitarian ambitions. Even as genuinely radical and committed a critic of the present, Western-dominated world order as Edward Said declares himself 'temperamentally and philosophically opposed to vast system-building or totalistic theories of human history'.[13] It is certainly true that the concept of totality is liable to be abused. The totalizing dialectic of Fredric Jameson, the ablest contemporary practitioner of Hegelian Marxism, all too often becomes a kind of syncretism into which all oppositions are dissolved, so that apparently contradictory theories are reduced to partial 'moments' of the larger whole.[14]

Jameson nevertheless has a response to his critics which, despite his relentlessly Hegelian mediating of contradictions, seems un-answerable. This is, quite simply, that totality isn't primarily a theoretical concept but a social reality. Capitalism, as it happens, is a world system into which all the human activities on the planet, in all their richness and variety, are integrated; indeed, they are all subordinated to the logic of competitive accumu-lation governing this system. Interestingly, Said adds, after the remark expressing his distaste for totalization which I cited in the previous paragraph, the following proviso: 'But I must say that having studied and indeed lived within the modern empires, I am struck by how constantly expanding, how inexorably inte-grative they were.'[15] And still *are*, he would no doubt agree, as new forms of gunboat diplomacy seek to assert Western hege-mony in the Gulf and Somalia. It is totalizing theory as a critical response to the realities of global capitalism which Jameson champions in this magnificent passage:

> even a fully postmodernized First World society will not lack young people whose temperament and values are genuinely left ones and embrace visions of radical social change re-pressed by a business society. The dynamics of such com-mitment are derived not from the reading of the 'Marxist classics', but rather from the objective experience of social reality and the way in which one isolated cause or issue,

one specific form of injustice, cannot be fulfilled or corrected without eventually drawing the entire web of interrelated social levels together into a totality, which then demands the invention of a politics of social transformation ... Whether the word Marxism disappears or not, in the erasure of the tapes in some new Dark Ages, the thing itself will inevitably reappear.[16]

But surely the Marxist theory of history is vulnerable to one of Lyotard's main objections to the grand narratives, namely that they deny legitimacy to 'the little narrative' [*petit récit*], 'the quintessential form of imaginative invention'?[17] As I have tried to show, there is no necessary opposition between theory and narrative, provided one rejects two false conceptions. The first treats a theory of history as a closed and self-sufficient system, from which all events may be deduced. But provided historical materialism rids itself of teleological explanations, and the associated doctrine of historical inevitability, it cannot be regarded as an instance of this kind of theory. A theory of history which does not postulate some necessary course of development is not merely compatible with, but actually requires, resort to narrative, provided that one rejects the second false conception. This is the account of narrative given by Hayden White. Here narrative serves to impose a form of closure on the disorder of events, and thereby to provide the reader with a reassuring sense of her identity and integration in the social order. This is no doubt *one* possible function of narrative, but it is not the only one. Narratives do not serve only to give a sense of certainty. More importantly, as James McPherson suggests, they allow us to recover the contingencies of the historical process, the junctures at which particular choices and chances tipped the balance between significantly different possible outcomes. A theory of history which rejects the idea of inevitability therefore needs narrative historiography to gain insight into the situations in which events decisively took one course rather than another. It is therefore hardly surprising that two of the greatest historical narratives of this past century – Trotsky's *History of the Russian Revolution* and C. L. R. James's *The Black Jacobins* – seek to reconstruct both the inner logic and the aleatory movements, the advances and retreats, of two momentous struggles for self-liberation. Here narrative is part of the discourse of enlightenment and emancipation we still cannot do without.

Strangely enough, it is Hayden White who gives the best statement of the Marxist view of history:

Both Hegel and Marx knew that things are never for the best in the best of all possible worlds, that mankind sustains genuine losses and mutilations in its efforts to realize itself against a cosmos that is as intractable as it is, at different times and and places, unknowable. But that cosmos can, in their estimation, *be known*; the laws that govern it can be progressively discerned. But the laws governing the cosmos can be known only through practice, through action, through heroic – not to say Promethean – assertions of will. Such assertions are as dangerous to individuals and groups as they are problematical. They carry with them the possibility of genuinely tragic failure and defeat. But if they are truly heroic in their aspiration, men can contribute through their failures and defeats to the human knowledge of the laws that govern both nature and history. And their knowledge of such laws provides the basis for the human transcendence of the limitations they lay upon humanity.[18]

This still seems like a good perspective on the world now, at the end, not of history, but of a century that has seen plenty of 'tragic failures and defeats' suffered by the left, at a time when humankind is confronted by a globally entrenched but peculiarly regressive kind of *laissez-faire* capitalism, whose demands are likely to cause yet more misery and destruction. What Lukács called the present as history is still the terrain on which human beings must strive to make sense of, and transform, their situation.

NOTES

Abbreviations

CW   Marx and Engels, *Collected Works* (50 vols, published/
          in preparation, London, 1975–)
IS   *International Socialism*
NLR   *New Left Review*

Introduction

1 J.-F. Lyotard, *The Postmodern Condition* (Manchester, 1984),
   pp. xxiii–iv.
2 'The *Poverty* and *The Open Society* were my war effort,' K. R.
   Popper, *Unended Quest* (London, 1976), p. 115.
3 See, for example, the discussions of the status of their own discourse in W. G. Walsh, *An Introduction to the Philosophy of
   History* (3rd edn, London, 1967), ch. 1, W. B. Gallie, *Philosophy
   and the Historical Understanding* (London, 1964), pp. 11–12,
   and A. C. Danto. *Analytical Philosophy of History* (Cambridge,
   1965), pp. 1ff. For a stimulating, if partisan, recent overview of
   English-speaking philosophy of history, see F. R. Ankersmit, 'The
   Dilemma of Contemporary Anglo-Saxon Philosophy of History',
   History and Theory, 25, Beiheft 25 (1986).
4 Danto, *Analytical Philosophy of History*, pp. 1–2.
5 H. White, *Metahistory* (Baltimore, 1975), p. xii.
6 Ankersmit, 'Dilemma', p. 26.
7 J. Derrida, *De la grammatologie* (Paris, 1967), p. 227. For a critical
   survey of poststructuralism's influence on recent social history, see
   B. D. Palmer, *Descent into Discourse* (Philadelphia, 1990).
8 P. Joyce, 'History and Post-Modernism', *Past and Present*, 133
   (1991), p. 208. Joyce's article is one in a series of exchanges all
   bearing the title 'History and Post-Modernism' – by Lawrence
   Stone, ibid., 133 (1991), Catriona Kelly, ibid., 133 (1991), Stone
   again, and Gabrielle M. Spiegel, both ibid., 135 (1992). See also

Spiegel's important critique of postmodernist historiography: 'History, Historicism, and the Social Logic of the Text in the Middle Ages', *Speculum*, 65 (1990).

9 S. Schama, *Dead Certainties* (London, 1991), pp. 322, 320.

10 Walsh, *Introduction*, p. 16.

11 R. Koselleck, '*Historia Magistra Vitae*', in *Futures Past* (Cambridge, MA, 1985).

12 F. Fukuyama, 'The End of History?', *The National Interest*, Summer 1989, and *The End of History and the Last Man* (New York, 1992).

13 G. Marsden. Preface to *After the End of History* (London, 1992), p. 6.

14 W. H. McNeill, *Arnold J. Toynbee* (Oxford, 1989), p. 206.

15 H. R. Trevor-Roper, 'Arnold Toynbee's Millennium', *Encounter*, 8: 6, June 1957, p. 26.

16 McNeill, *Toynbee*, pp. 216–17: see, generally, ibid., ch. 9. Toynbee later became disillusioned with the United States, describing it in 1965 as 'the leader of world-wide counter-revolutionary movement in defence of vested interests', quoted in ibid., p. 245.

17 P. Kennedy, *Preparing for the Twenty-First Century* (New York, 1993).

18 S. P. Huntington, 'The Clash of Civilizations?', *Foreign Affairs*, 72: 3, Summer 1993, p. 22.

19 See P. Abrams, *Historical Sociology* (West Compton House, 1982).

20 P. Anderson, *English Questions* (London, 1992), p. 207. See E. Gellner, *Plough, Sword and Book* (Oxford, 1988), A. Giddens, *A Contemporary Critique of Historical Materialism* (London, 1981), M. Mann, *The Sources of Social Power*, vol. 1 (Cambridge, 1986), and W. G. Runciman, *A Treatise on Social Theory*, vol. 2 (Cambridge, 1989).

21 L. Althusser and E. Balibar, *Reading Capital* (London, 1970); G. A. Cohen, *Karl Marx's Theory of History* (Oxford, 1978).

22 White, *Metahistory*, pp. 1–2.

23 F. Nietzsche, *Untimely Meditations* (Cambridge, 1983), pp. 104–5.

24 Ibid., p. 121. For the genealogy of postmodernism, see J. Habermas, *The Philosophical Discourse of Modernity* (Cambridge, MA, 1987).

25 F. Furedi, *Mythical Past, Elusive Future* (London, 1992).

26 D. Cannadine, *The Pleasures of the Past* (London, 1990) and *G. M. Trevelyan* (London, 1993). The ferocity of Cannadine's attacks on Trevelyan's critics, such as G. R. Elton and John Kenyon, becomes easier to understand when one realizes that they form part of one of those Cambridge vendettas that seem to go on for ever.

27 See, for example, J. Clive, *Not By Fact Alone* (London, 1990), the title of one whose sections, 'Why Read the Great Historians?', provides the book with its theme.

28 See Koselleck, '*Historia Magistra Vitae*'.

29 R. Augstein et al., *Historikerstreit* (Munich, 1987), now available
    in a (rather poor) English translation under the title *Forever In
    the Shadow of Hitler?* (Atlantic Highlands, 1993). There is a good
    discussion of the issues involved in C. S. Maier, *The Unmasterable
    Past* (Cambridge, MA, 1988).
30 M. Nolan, 'The *Historikerstreit* and Social History', *New German
    Critique*, 44 (1988), p. 63.
31 Nietzsche, *Untimely Meditations*, p. 106.
32 W. Benjamin, *Illuminations* (London, 1970), p. 259.
33 Koselleck, *Futures Past*, p. 17.
34 J. Joyce, *Ulysses* (Oxford, 1993), p. 34.
35 G. W. F. Hegel, *Elements of the Philosophy of Right* (Cambridge,
    1991), p. 22.

Chapter 1   Sympathy For the Devil?

1   F. Fukuyama, *The End of History and the Last Man* (New York,
    1992), p. 56.
2   Boswell, *Life of Johnson* (Oxford, 1970), p. 333.
3   See, for example, my contribution in F. Fukuyama and A. Cal-
    linicos, 'The End of History?', *Socialist Review*, 152, April 1992.
4   Fukuyama, *End*, p. xii.
5   F. Braudel, *The Mediterranean and the Mediterranean World in
    the Age of Philip II* (2 vols, London, 1975), vol. 1, p. 8.
6   T. W. Adorno, *Negative Dialectics* (London, 1973), p. 8.
7   J.-F. Lyotard, *The Differend* (Manchester, 1988), p. 179.
8   P. Anderson, 'The Ends of History', in *A Zone of Engagement*
    (London, 1992), G. Elliott, 'The Cards of Confusion', *Radical
    Philosophy*, 64 (1993), F. Halliday, 'An Encounter with Fukuyama',
    NLR, 193 (1992), and J. McCarney, 'Endgame', *Radical Philo-
    sophy*, 62 (1992), and 'Shaping Ends', *NLR*, 202 (1993).
9   Anderson, 'Ends', p. 345.
10 See, for example, the late Peter Jenkins's column in *The Inde-
    pendent*, 4 March 1992.
11 Elliott, 'Cards', p. 4.
12 Halliday, 'Encounter', p. 95.
13 Ibid., p. 91. See esp. F. Halliday, *The Making of the Second Cold
    War* (London, 1983).
14 Anderson, 'Ends', p. 336.
15 Elliott, 'Cards', p. 8.
16 A. Callinicos, *The Revenge of History* (Cambridge, 1991).
17 R. Brenner, 'The Soviet Union and Eastern Europe', *Against the
    Current*, n.s., 30 and 31 (1991), and E. Loone, *Soviet Marxism and
    Analytical Philosophies of History* (London, 1992), pp. 213–31.
    I discuss Brenner's views at greater length in section 3.3 below.

18 T. Cliff, *State Capitalism in Russia* (rev. edn, London, 1988).
19 R. J. Overy, *Goering* (London, 1984). On the general trends, see C. Harman, *Explaining the Crisis* (London, 1984), ch. 2.
20 C. Harman, 'The Storm Breaks', *IS*, 2: 46 (1990).
21 Elliott, 'Cards', p. 9.
22 I. Deutscher, *Marxism, Wars and Revolutions* (London, 1984), pp. 57–8; cf. Elliott, 'Cards', p. 10.
23 Comments on an earlier version of this chapter delivered as a seminar paper given at the Centre for Social Theory and Comparative History, University of California, Los Angeles, 8 April 1993.
24 See, in addition to Callinicos, *Revenge*, C. Harman, 'Where is Capitalism Going?', *IS*, 2: 58 and 2: 60 (1993).
25 Goethe, *Faust* (2 vols, Harmondsworth, 1960), vol. 1, p. 75.
26 Fukuyama, *End*, p. 144.
27 See, on Kojève, R. Queneau, 'Premières confrontations avec Hegel', *Critique*, 19: 195–6, August–September 1963, V. Descombes, *La Même et l'autre* (Paris, 1979), ch. 1, M. Roth, *Knowing and History* (Ithaca, 1988), L. Niethammer, *Posthistoire* (London, 1992), pp. 62–8, and Y. Moulier Boutang, *Louis Althusser*, vol. 1 (Paris, 1992), ch. 7.
28 A. Kojève, *An Introduction to the Reading of Hegel* (New York, 1969), p. 259 n. 41.
29 Niethammer, *Posthistoire*, p. 64.
30 G. W. F. Hegel, *Phenomenology of Spirit* (Oxford, 1977), sections 178–96, pp. 111–19. A. V. Miller's translation talks of lord and bondsman rather than Master and Slave, but I have preferred to stick to the latter usage, which corresponds to Kojève's.
31 Kojève, *Introduction*, pp. 7, 16, 20, 44.
32 J. Hyppolite, *Logique et existence* (Paris, 1953).
33 D. Strauss, quoted in W. Kaufmann, *Hegel* (London, 1965), p. 176. The most important contemporary anthropological interpretation of Hegel is Charles Taylor's *Hegel* (Cambridge, 1975). More accurate readings are, in my view, provided by G. Lebrun, *La Patience du concept* (Paris, 1972) and M. Rosen, *Hegel's Dialectic and its Criticism* (Cambridge, 1982).
34 G. W. F. Hegel, *Lectures on the Philosophy of World History: Introduction* (Cambridge, 1975), pp. 27, 28.
35 G. W. F. Hegel, *The Science of Logic* (2 vols, London, 1966), vol. 1, p. 60.
36 G. W. F. Hegel, *Logic* (Oxford, 1975), section 212, 'Zusatz', p. 275.
37 J. Hyppolite, *Genèse et structure de la Phénoménologie de l'esprit de Hegel* (Paris, 1946), p. 47.
38 G. W. F. Hegel, *Lectures on the History of Philosophy* (3 vols, London, 1963), vol. 1, pp. 95–6; *Philosophy of World History*, p. 143.

39 Hegel, *Phenomenology*, 801, p. 487.

40 Lebrun, *Patience*, p. 115 n. 117. The *Encyclopaedia* passage to which Lebrun alludes is worth quoting more fully: 'Time, therefore, has no power over the Notion, nor is the Notion in time or temporal; on the contrary, *it* is the power over time ... Only the natural, therefore, is subject to time in so far as it is finite; the True, on the other hand, the Idea, Spirit, is *eternal*,' G. W. F. Hegel, *Philosophy of Nature* (Oxford, 1970), 258, p. 35. This passage, and that cited above from the *Phenomenology*, cast doubt on Kojève's claim that, for Hegel, 'the Concept is Time', *Introduction*, p. 148; see, generally, ibid., pp. 100–49.

41 A. Ryan, 'Introduction', *After the End of History* (London, 1992), p. 1. If the argument given in the text is correct, Cornelius Castoriadis is also mistaken when he calls the End of History 'at once Hegel's central intention and the corner stone without which the *whole* system falls into dust,' 'La Fin de l'histoire?', in B. Lefort, ed., *De la fin de l'histoire* (Paris, 1992), p. 63.

42 Hegel, *Philosophy of World History*, pp. 54, 134, 176.

43 Hegel, *Philosophy of Nature*, 258, 'Zusatz', p. 36.

44 Anderson, 'Ends', p. 292.

45 Hegel, *Philosophy of World History*, pp. 170, 54.

46 McCarney, 'Endgame', p. 38.

47 Quoted in Niethammer, *Posthistoire*, p. 65.

48 Boutang, *Althusser*, p. 276. Boutang is here discussing Althusser's views in the late 1940s, but, as he points out, they were, in this respect at any rate, close to Kojève's.

49 A. Kojève, 'Tyranny and Wisdom', in Leo Strauss, *On Tyranny* (rev. edn, also including Strauss–Kojève correspondence, New York, 1991), p. 138.

50 Ibid., p. 173.

51 Kojève, *Introduction*, p. 233 n. 27.

52 I. Deutscher, *Stalin* (Harmondsworth, 1970), p. 550; see generally ibid., ch. 14, originally written in 1948.

53 Hegel, *Philosophy of World History*, pp. 84, 89.

54 Kojève, letter to Strauss, 19 September 1950, in Strauss *On Tyranny*, p. 256.

55 Kojève, *Introduction*, p. 161.

56 Fukuyama, *End*, p. 388 n. 2. See also Anderson, 'Ends', pp. 316–18.

57 See my discussion of communism in *Revenge*, ch. 4.

58 Kojève, *Introduction*, p. 90.

59 G. W. F. Hegel, *Elements of the Philosophy of Right* (Cambridge, 1991), 260, 'Zusatz', p. 283. On civil society and its discontents, see ibid., 182–225, pp. 220–74.

60 Elliott, 'Cards', p. 6.

61 Quoted in Hegel, *Philosophy of Right*, editorial note 12, p. 16.

See also S. Avineri, *Hegel's Theory of the Modern State* (Cambridge, 1972), and Anderson, 'Ends', pp. 285–94.

62 Fukuyama, *End*, p. 291.

63 Ibid., pp. 13, 165, xxi.

64 Hegel, *Philosophy of Right*, 190, 'Remark', p. 228. See also Hegel's discussion of the concept of human nature in *History of Philosophy*, vol. 3, pp. 6–7, and K. Löwith, *Karl Marx and Max Weber* (London, 1993), pp. 91–2.

65 Kojève, letter to Strauss, 29 October 1954, in Strauss, *On Tyranny*, p. 262. See also his letter to Strauss, 19 September 1950, ibid., pp. 255–6, and Kojève, *Introduction*, pp. 193, and 212–18 (on the dialectic of nature). On the circularity of the dialectic, cf. Hegel, *Science of Logic*, vol. 2, pp. 483–4, and L. Althusser, 'Marx's Relation to Hegel', in *Politics and History* (London, 1972).

66 Kojève, *Introduction*, p. 205.

67 Fukuyama does sometimes seem to commit himself to a more unitary, and consistently idealist, version of the dialectic. Thus he attributes to Hegel the view that 'the primary motor of human history is not modern natural science or the ever expanding horizon of desires that powers it, but rather a totally non-economic drive, the *struggle for recognition*,' and declares: ' "recognition" allows us to recover a totally non-materialist historical dialectic', *End*, pp. 135, 144. But the extended narrative he gives of the triumph of liberal capitalism allocates causal roles to both the logic of modern natural science and the struggle for recognition. Elliott taxes Fukuyama with only recognizing the existence of '*inter*-systemic' contradictions in capitalism – i.e. those it had with 'historical Communism', 'Cards', p. 6. But since Fukuyama acknowledges the possibility that the two drives that he claims power capitalist development may come into conflict (and indeed fears that there may be conflicts between different forms of recognition), he does seem to give some place to what Elliott calls '*intra*-systemic contradictions', even if their relationship is under-theorized.

68 Strauss, letter to Kojève, 6 December 1948, in Strauss, *On Tyranny*, p. 239.

69 Niethammer, *Posthistoire*, pp. 91–2 n. 22.

70 McCarney, 'Endgame', p. 36.

71 Ibid., and 'Shaping Ends', p. 37. In the latter article, McCarney withdraws the distinction he had drawn earlier between the esoteric and the exoteric Fukuyama, replacing it with one between 'an official doctrine or doctrines, and the deeper logic of the arguments,' 'Shaping Ends', p. 38 n. 6. See, for those portions of Fukuyama's book supporting this interpretation, *End*, chs 20–2, and 28–30.

72 McCarney, 'Shaping Ends', p. 43.

73 Fukuyama, *End*, p. 302; and see, on the filiations of this criticism with Nietzsche's thought, ibid., p. xxii.
74 F. Nietzsche, *Thus Spoke Zarathustra* (Harmondsworth, 1969), pp. 46–7 (translation modified).
75 Strauss, *On Tyranny*, pp. 239 (Strauss, letter to Kojève, 22 August 1948), 208–9.
76 Kojève, *Introduction*, pp. 218, 225, 220 n. 19.
77 Ibid., pp. 189ff, 158 n. 6.
78 Niethammer, *Posthistoire*, p. 3; see esp. ibid., ch. 5. Niethammer (ibid., pp. 16–19) and Anderson ('Ends', pp. 294–308) have discovered in Cournot yet another precursor of Kojève and Fukuyama, but the great statistician formulates the concept of the End of History within an Enlightenment framework where, as Niethammer puts it, '[t]he new condition is presented ... as an overcoming of chaotic historicity, and as a hope of world peace and prosperity,' *Posthistoire*, p. 17.
79 Ibid., p. 50 n. 14. Jünger's influence on Heidegger is discussed in R. Wolin, *The Politics of Being* (New York), ch. 3.
80 O. Spengler, *The Decline of the West* (abr. edn, London, 1991), pp. 24–6.
81 See esp. J. Herf, *Reactionary Modernism* (Cambridge, 1984).
82 Spengler, *Decline*, p. 243.
83 Ibid., p. 244
84 Ibid., p. 347.
85 Kojève, *Introduction*, p. 159n.
86 F. Fukyama, 'The End of History?', *The National Interest*, Summer 1989, p. 18.
87 Fukyama, *End*, pp. 3, 12.
88 McCarney, 'Endgame', pp. 37–8.
89 Ibid., p. 36.
90 K. Marx, *A Contribution to the Critique of Political Economy* (London, 1971), p. 22. Althusser draws attention to this passage in a long letter to Jean Lacroix written in December 1949 and January 1950: substantial extracts are cited in Boutang, *Althusser*, pp. 314–24. The immediate object of Althusser's attack is not Kojève, but Hyppolite, presumably for the latter's discussion of the End of History in his review of Lukács's *The Young Hegel*, reprinted in J. Hyppolite, *Studies on Marx and Hegel* (New York, 1969).
91 Fukuyama, 'End', p. 18; Saint-Simon, quoted in J. B. Bury, *The Idea of Progress* (London, 1920), p. 282.
92 It is, of course, true (as Perry Anderson pointed out at the seminar referred to in n. 23 above) that Engels does envisage an end of history in the radical sense of the end of the human species when he predicts, on the basis of the laws of nature, the death of the solar system: *Dialectics of Nature* (Moscow, 1972), pp. 35–6.

But this is a very different kind of end of history from that anti-
cipated by the tradition of *Posthistoire*, whose concern is with,
as Niethammer puts it (see section 1.3 above), 'not the end of the
world, but the end of meaning'.

93 L. Althusser, 'Contradiction and Overdetermination', in *For Marx*
(London, 1969).

94 G. A. Cohen, *Karl Marx's Theory of History* (Oxford, 1978), pp.
34–5.

95 See A. Callinicos, *Marxism and Philosophy* (Oxford, 1983), chs 2
and 3. The nature of the explanations used by Marx has been a
subject of much recent controversy: see esp. Cohen, *Karl Marx's
Theory of History*, J. Elster, *Making Sense of Marx* (Cambridge,
1985), and the exchange between them reprinted in A. Callinicos,
ed., *Marxist Theory* (Oxford, 1989).

96 M. Mandelbaum, 'The Presuppositions of *Metahistory*', *History and
Theory*, 29, *Beiheft* 19 (1980), pp. 41–2.

97 Hegel, *Philosophy of World History*, pp. 42–3.

98 W. Benjamin, 'Theses on the Philosophy of History', in *Illuminations* (London, 1970).

99 Cohen, *Karl Marx's Theory of History*, p. 27.

100 Ibid., pp. 27, x. My version of the distinction between philosophies
and theories of history is thus closer to Elster's, who contrasts
Marx's 'non-empirical philosophy of history', which is teleological,
with his 'theory of history, of the successive modes of production
based on class domination', *Making Sense*, p. 107. See also Elster's
discussion of different forms of explanation in ibid., ch. 1, and
in *Explaining Technical Change* (Cambridge, 1983), part 1.

Chapter 2   History as Narrative

1 J. B. Bury, 'The Science of History', and G. M. Trevelyan, 'Clio,
A Muse', both in F. Stern, ed., *The Varieties of History* (New
York, 1973), pp. 223, 234.

2 J. Le Goff, 'L'Histoire nouvelle', in J. Le Goff, R. Chartier and
J. Revel, eds, *La Nouvelle Histoire* (Paris, 1978), p. 215. Le Goff
thus shows his fidelity to the *Annales* tradition when he describes
the great mediaeval struggle between Pope and Emperor as 'a
mere shadow play behind which the serious events took place',
Mediaeval Civilization 400–1500 (Oxford, 1988), p. 96.

3 F. Braudel, *The Mediterranean and the Mediterranean World in
the Age of Philip II* (2 vols, London, 1975), vol. 1, p. 21.

4 L. Stone, 'The Revival of Narrative', *Past and Present*, 85 (1989),
pp. 3, 17. Zeldin compares his 'kaleidoscopic vision' of modern
France to 'the paintings of the Impressionists or the Cubists',
Ambition and Love (Oxford 1979) p. viii.

Notes to pp. 46–53

5   E. J. Hobsbawm, 'The Revival of Narrative: Some Comments', *Past and Present*, 86 (1980), pp. 5, 8. See, on the *Annales* conception of society as a totality, M. Bloch, *The Historian's Craft* (Manchester, 1992), p. 155.

6   J. M. McPherson, *Battle Cry of Freedom* (New York, 1988), pp. ix, 857–8.

7   M. Arnold, *Literature and Dogma* (London, 1876), p. xiii.

8   J. Clive, *Not By Fact Alone* (London, 1989), for example, pp. 34ff.

9   Trevelyan, 'Clio', p. 229.

10 Augustine, *Confessions* (Harmondsworth, 1961), XI. 26–30; P. Ricoeur, *Time and Narrative* (3 vols, Chicago, 1984, 1985, 1988), vol. 1, p. 21.

11 Ricoeur, *Time*, vol. 1, pp. 31, 42; see generally ibid., ch. 2.

12 Ibid., vol. 3, p. 154 (and see generally ibid., ch. 6), vol. 1, p. 91.

13 Ibid., vol. 1, pp. 44, 193, 199, 200, 224–5, 209. Ricoeur's association of events with 'the life and death of structures themselves' occurs in a discussion of François Furet's *Penser la révolution française* (ibid., vol. 1, p. 224); it is, however, plainly intended to be of more general import.

14 Ibid., vol. 1, p. 225.

15 See, respectively, ibid., vol. 2, *passim*, and vol. 3, pp. 9–96.

16 H. White, *Metahistory* (Baltimore, 1975), pp. 30, 31, 34, 7.

17 H. White, *The Content of the Form* (Baltimore, 1987), pp. xi, ix.

18 White, *Metahistory*, p. 283.

19 White, *Content*, pp. 21, 87. See L. Althusser, 'Ideology and the Ideological State Apparatuses', in *Lenin and Philosophy and Other Essays* (London, 1971).

20 White, *Content*, p. 2; see also ibid., pp. 27 and 217 n. 3.

21 White, *Metahistory*, pp. 37, 38, 250–1. Tocqueville in this account is a transitional figure, seeking a 'tragic reconciliation' capable of avoiding both 'that resentment which was the basis of Gobineau's Ironic historiography and that spirit of accommodation to "things as they are" which inspired Ranke's Comic historiography': 'Burckhardt's historical vision began in that condition of Irony in which Tocqueville's ended,' ibid., pp. 223, 234.

22 F. R. Ankersmit, 'The Dilemma of Contemporary Anglo-Saxon Philosophy of History', *History and Theory*, Beiheft 25 (1986), p. 2.

23 White, *Metahistory*, pp. 427–8.

24 G. Himmelfarb, 'Telling It As You Like It', *Times Literary Supplement*, 16 October 1992, p. 14. It is typical of Himmelfarb's clumsy polemic that so busy is she in denouncing White as a red that she ignores his extraordinary treatment of nationalism and the Holocaust (discussed in section 2.3 below).

25 White, *Content*, p. 227 n. 12.
26 R. Rorty, *Contingency, Irony, and Solidarity* (Cambridge, 1989), p. xv.
27 R. Rorty, 'Postmodernist Bourgeois Liberalism', *Journal of Philosophy*, 53 (1983).
28 A. MacIntyre, *After Virtue* (London, 1981), pp. 194, 201, 203. There are important parallels between MacIntyre's 'narrative concept of selfhood', and Ricoeur's claim that personal identity must be understood on 'the model of dynamic identity arising from the poetic composition of a narrative text', *Time*, vol. 3, p. 246.
29 Ricoeur, *Time*, vol. 3, p. 246. For an account of the self analogous to MacIntyre's and Ricoeur's which draws heavily on Freud, see R. Wollheim, *The Thread of Life* (Cambridge, 1986). The relationship between narrative, on the one hand, and enlightenment and emancipation, on the other, is one of the main themes explored by Edward Said in *Culture and Imperialism* (London, 1993).
30 M. Mandelbaum, 'A Note on History as Narrative', *History and Theory*, 6 (1967), p. 417.
31 W. Dilthey, *Selected Writings* (Cambridge, 1976), p. 206.
32 A. R. Burn, Introduction to Herodotus, *The Histories* (Harmondsworth, 1972), p. 17. There is an interesting and sympathetic discussion of Herodotus, '[t]he first and greatest world historian', in O. Murray, *Early Greece* (London, 1980), pp. 27–32, 292.
33 W. H. Walsh, *An Introduction to the Philosophy of History* (3rd edn, London, 1967), p. 32.
34 A. C. Danto, *Analytical Philosophy of History* (Cambridge, 1965), pp. 135, 141; see generally ibid., chs 7, 11.
35 Ibid., p. 255.
36 E. J. Hobsbawm, *The Age of Revolution* (London, 1973), p. 11.
37 Quoted in H. Butterfield, *Man on His Past* (Cambridge, 1955), p. 70.
38 Lord Acton, *Historical Essays and Studies* (London, 1907), p. 345.
39 Thucydides, *History of the Peloponnesian War* (Harmondsworth, 1972), I. 22.
40 Polybius, *The Rise of the Roman Empire* (Harmondsworth, 1979), VI. 9.
41 Quoted in G. E. M. de Ste Croix, *The Origins of the Peloponnesian War* (London, 1972), p. 33. On 'pragmatic history', see B. Croce, *Theory and History of Historiography* (London, 1921), pp. 94–9.
42 R. G. Collingwood, *The Idea of History* (Oxford, 1970), p. 31. Collingwood isn't the only British neo-Hegelian to have made an ass of himself over Thucydides. Michael Oakeshott declares: 'With Thucydides personal character and motive is a first cause behind which, as a general rule, he does not press,' *Experience and its Modes* (Cambridge, 1985), p. 131. But Thucydides appeals to what

human beings *in general* will do, not to the quirks of personality, in his explanations. Thus the Athenians declare in the Melian Dialogue: 'Our opinion of the gods and our knowledge of men lead us to conclude that it is a general and necessary law of nature to rule where one can,' *History*, V. 105. See Ste Croix, *Origins*, pp. 5–34. Collingwood's master Croce has a far more balanced view of the Greek historians: see *Theory and History*, part 2, ch. 2.

43 C. N. Cochrane, *Thucydides and the Science of History* (London, 1965).

44 L. von Ranke, *The Theory and Practice of History* (New York, 1983), p. 137 (translation modified). See also R. Koselleck, 'Historia Magistra Vitae', in *Futures Past* (Cambridge, MA, 1985). The account of modern historiography that follows is heavily indebted to Koselleck's outstanding essays.

45 E. Loone, *Soviet Marxism and Analytical Philosophies of History* (London, 1992), p. 94.

46 Quoted in I. Berlin, *Vico and Herder* (London, 1976), p. 191.

47 Machiavelli, *Discourses* (Harmondsworth, 1974), Preface, pp. 97–8. See Croce, *Theory and History*, part 2, ch. 4, on Renaissance historiography.

48 Ranke, *Theory and Practice*, p. 53.

49 Thucydides, *History*, I. 22.

50 Collingwood, *Idea*, pp. 25–6

51 Koselleck, *Futures Past*, p. 35.

52 B. G. Niebuhr, Preface to the second edition, *History of Rome*, in Stern, ed., *Varieties*, p. 51. On the Göttingen school, see Butterfield, *Man On His Past*, pp. 39–61.

53 Koselleck, *Futures Past*, p. 143.

54 A. S. Skinner, 'Adam Smith: An Economic Interpretation of History', in A. S. Skinner and T. Wilson, eds, *Essays on Adam Smith* (Oxford, 1975). See also R. L. Meek, 'Smith, Turgot and the "Four Stages" Theory', in *Smith, Marx and After* (London, 1977).

55 J. Kenyon, *The History Men* (London, 1983), pp. 15–16. Kenyon's grossly partisan account of twentieth-century British historiography is summed up by the absence of any reference to E. P. Thompson and his work, a vulgarity only perfunctorily remedied in the second (1993) edition.

56 H. R. Trevor-Roper, Introduction to Gibbon, *The Decline and Fall of the Roman Empire* (3 vols, London, 1993), vol. 1, pp. liii, lxxviii–lxxix, and *passim*. Roy Porter stresses somewhat more strongly than Trevor-Roper does Gibbon's reservations about progress, but his overall account does not differ significantly: *Gibbon* (London, 1988).

57 Acton, *Historical Essays*, p. 346.

58 For two very different accounts which both depict the German historical school drawing on the Enlightenment and Romanticism, see Butterfield, *Man on His Past*, pp. 60–1, and H.-G. Gadamer, *Truth and Method* (London, 1975), pp. 242ff.
59 Ibn Khaldûn, *The Muqadimmah* (3 vols, New York, 1958), vol. 1, pp. 258, 249, 343.
60 *The New Science of Giambattista Vico*, ed. T. G. Bergin and M. Fisch (Ithaca, 1970), 915, 1102, and 1106, pp. 283, 380, 381. Isaiah Berlin suggests that Vico's innovations should be seen in the context of the development of historical scholarship in late Renaissance French jurisprudence: *Vico and Herder*, pp. 99–142.
61 Polybius, *Rise*, VI. 52.
62 Koselleck, *Futures Past*, pp. 277, 281.
63 J. Habermas, *The Philosophical Discourse of Modernity* (Cambridge, 1987), p. 7.
64 See esp. Augustine, *City of God* (Harmondsworth, 1984), XII. 4, pp. 487–9.
65 K. Löwith, *Meaning in History* (Cambridge, 1949), pp. 169, 19, 45.
66 G. R. Elton, *The Practice of History* (London, 1969), p. 53.
67 T. Judt, 'Chronicles of a Death Foretold', in *After the End of History* (London, 1992), pp. 113–14.
68 E. P. Thompson, *Customs in Common* (Harmondsworth, 1993), p. 431. See Bloch, *Historian's Craft*, ch. 2, and Elton, *Practice*, p. 20.
69 C. Ginzburg, 'Checking the Evidence', *Critical Inquiry*, 18 (1991), p. 83.
70 See P. Novick, *That Noble Dream* (Cambridge, 1988), chs 8 and 9.
71 S. Friedlander, Introduction to Friedlander, ed., *Probing the Limits of Representation* (Cambridge, MA, 1992), p. 2.
72 See E. Nolte, *Der Europaische Bürgerkrieg 1917–1945* (Berlin, 1987), and A. J. Mayer, *Why Did the Heavens Not Darken?* (New York, 1990). There is, as Habermas and others have pointed out, an 'apologetic tendency' in Nolte's account of National Socialism as a defensive and imitative reaction to the Russian Revolution, which is absent from Mayer's interpretation despite its faults.
73 J.-F. Lyotard, *The Differend* (Manchester, 1988), pp. xii, 3–4.
74 T. W. Adorno, *Prisms* (Cambridge, MA, 1981), p. 34.
75 Lyotard, *Differend*, pp. 88, 57.
76 S. Greenblatt, 'Towards a Poetics of Culture', in H. A. Veeser, ed., *The New Historicism* (London, 1989), p. 4.
77 White, *Content*, pp. 66, 63, 72.
78 Ibid., pp. 74–5, 77, 80.
79 C. Ginzburg, 'Just One Witness', in Friedlander, ed., *Limits of Representation*, p. 94.

80 P. Anderson, 'On Emplotment', in Friedlander, ed., *Limits of Representation*, p. 65.

81 B. Anderson, *Imagined Communities* (London, 1983).

82 See Robert Fisk's extraordinary account of the 1982 Lebanon war in *Pity the Nation* (Oxford, 1991), chs 7–11.

83 H. White, 'Historical Emplotment and the Problem of Truth', in Friedlander, ed., *Limits of Representation*, pp. 37, 38, 39–40, 50, 51. White attributes to Fredric Jameson the view that 'modernism is a cultural expression of the fascist form of social totalitarianism', ibid., p. 51. As a glance at, say, the famous opening chapter of Jameson's *Postmodernism, or, the Cultural Logic of Late Capitalism* (London, 1991) would establish, this interpretation bears no relation to his actual views.

84 Ginzburg, 'Only One Witness', p. 352 n. 21.

85 P. Haidu, 'The Dialectics of Unspeakability', in Friedlander, ed., *Limits of Representation*, p. 294.

86 M. Jay, 'On Plots, Witnesses and Judgements', in Friedlander, ed., *Limits of Representation*, p. 98.

87 White, *Metahistory*, p. 5. See Croce, *Theory and History*, pp. 17ff.

88 I. Kant, *Critique of Pure Reason* (London, 1970), A112, p. 139.

89 White, *Content*, pp. 4, 5, 10.

90 Jay, 'Plots', p. 98.

91 Walsh, *Introduction*, pp. 33–4.

92 Danto, *Analytical Philosophy of History*, pp. 137, 140.

93 F. H. Bradley, *The Presuppositions of Critical History* (Donn Mills, Ont., 1968), p. 93. Compare Collingwood, *Idea*, pp. 131–3, and Oakeshott, *Experience*, p. 100 ('There is no fact in history which is not a judgement, no event which is not an inference').

94 Quoted in Le Goff, 'L'Histoire nouvelle', p. 217. See the interesting discussion of Febvre's theoretical approach in P. Schöttler, 'Althusser and *Annales* Historiography', in E. A. Kaplan and M. Sprinker, eds, *The Althusserian Legacy* (London, 1993).

95 See Jay, 'Plots', *passim*. Maurice Mandelbaum makes substantially the same point: 'No historian is confronted at the outset of his inquiries with an *unprocessed* historical record, with a bank of data devoid of all order, to which he must import whatever order it is to possess. Rather, every historian will, from the outset, be confronted not by raw data but by earlier accounts of the past,' 'The Presuppositions of *Metahistory*', *History and Theory*, 19, *Beiheft* 19 (1980), p. 43. Just to add to the confusion, White on occasion acknowledges this fact, though he does not integrate it into his general theory of historical writing: see, for example, 'New Historicism: A Comment', in Veeser, ed., *New Historicism*, esp. p. 297.

96 E. H. Carr, *What is History?* (2nd edn, Harmondsworth, 1990), p. 22.

97   Ibid., p. 26.
98   Loone, *Soviet Marxism*, p. 61. Loone praises Collingwood for being '[o]ne of the few philosophers of history who emphasized the importance of questions, *problems*, in historiography,' p. 107. See, on the logic of question and answer, R. G. Collingwood, *An Autobiography* (Oxford, 1978), ch. 5.
99   Collingwood, *Idea*, p. 133.
100 Lord Acton, *Lectures on Modern History* (London, 1960), p. 37. Cf. Collingwood, *Idea*, pp. 281–2.
101 Schöttler, 'Althusser', p. 87.
102 R. C. Lewontin, 'Fact and the Factitious in the Natural Sciences', *Critical Inquiry*, 18 (1991), p. 140.
103 Quine's formulation of the problem is definitive: see 'Two Dogmas of Empiricism', in *From a Logical Point of View* (New York, 1963). See, for the most developed statement of Rorty's anti-realism, his *Philosophy and the Mirror of Nature* (Oxford, 1980).
104 I. Lakatos, *Philosophical Papers* (2 vols, Cambridge, 1978), vol. 1 *passim*.
105 See esp. ibid., vol. 1, ch. 3. I skate here over various logical and epistemological difficulties with the idea of a theory approximating to the truth, since they are not relevant to the argument in hand.
106 See, for example, M. Devitt, *Realism and Truth* (Oxford, 1984).
107 Rorty, *Contingency*, p. 5.
108 P. F. Strawson, 'Truth', in *Logico-Linguistic Papers* (London, 1971).
109 D. Davidson, 'The Structure and Content of Truth', *Journal of Philosophy*, 87 (1990), pp. 303, 309, 325. For Davidson's earlier views, see *Inquiries into Truth and Interpretation* (Oxford, 1984). Davidson acknowledges ('Structure and Content', p. 302 n. 40) the influence of Rorty's paper, 'Pragmatism, Davidson and Truth', in E. Lepore, ed., *Truth and Interpretation* (Oxford, 1986). Some critics believe that even Davidson's earlier position was anti-realist: see, for example, Devitt, *Realism*, ch. 10, and D. Papineau, *Reality and Representation* (Oxford, 1990), *passim*.
110 For more on these matters, see Devitt, *Realism*, and Papineau, *Reality*.
111 See the discussion of novel facts in E. Zahar, 'Why Did Einstein's Programme Supersede Lorentz's?', *British Journal of the Philosophy of Science*, 24 (1973), and the excellent discussion of the analogies and disanalogies between the physical and social sciences in R. Bhaskar, *The Possibility of Naturalism* (Brighton, 1979).
112 Collingwood, *Idea*, pp. 263–6, 282–302.
113 See esp. Dilthey, *Selected Writings*, pp. 223–6.
114 A. Callinicos, *Making History* (Cambridge, 1987), chs 1–3.
115 Gadamer, *Truth and Method*, pp. 258, 263, 272, 273.

116   Ibid., pp. 264–5.
117   See esp. C. Ginzburg, *The Cheese and the Worms* (London, 1980), and *Ecstasies* (London, 1990).
118   Gadamer, *Truth and Method*, p. 14; see more generally ibid., pp. 11–19.
119   W. H. Dray, *Laws and Explanation in History* (London, 1957), p. 126; see generally ibid., ch. 5.
120   S. Runciman, *The Sicilian Vespers* (Harmondsworth, 1960), p. 285.
121   Davidson, *Inquiries*, p. 137.
122   G. Macdonald and P. Pettit, *Semantics and Social Science* (London, 1981), pp. 29–30.
123   D. Wiggins, *Sameness and Substance* (Oxford, 1980), p. 222.
124   Bradley, *Presuppositions*, pp. 77–8, 100–1.
125   H. Delbrück, *History of the Art of War* (4 vols, Westport, 1985), vol. 1, pp. 35, 84.
126   M. Bernal, *Black Athena*, vol. 1, (London, 1991), pp. 441, 302.
127   Quoted in Gadamer, *Truth and Method*, p. 185. See Koselleck, 'Perspective and Temporality', in *Futures Past*, which argues that partisanship and objectivity at once contradict and require one another in modern historiography.
128   Bloch, *Historian's Craft*, p. 22.
129   L. Namier, 'History', in Stern, ed., *Varieties*, p. 375.
130   L. Namier, 'Human Nature and Politics', in Stern, ed., *Varieties*.
131   M. Mandelbaum, *The Anatomy of Historical Knowledge* (Baltimore, 1977), p. 157.
132   M. Heidegger, *Being and Time* (Oxford, 1967), p. 191. See J. Habermas, *The Theory of Communicative Action*, vol. 1 (London, 1984), pp. 70–2, for the idea that modernity involves a 'change in the weights' of the 'lifeworld' of 'more or less diffuse, always unproblematic, background convictions', on the one hand, and of rational critique, on the other.
133   G. M. Spiegel, 'History, Historicism, and the Social Logic of the Text in the Middle Ages', *Speculum*, 65 (1990), p. 85.
134   C. Ginzburg, 'Microhistory: Two or Three Things I Know about It', *Critical Inquiry*, 20 (1993), p. 32. This essay is a fascinating discussion of Ginzburg's method, for which see also his *Myth, Emblems, Clues* (London, 1990). Perry Anderson's review of *Ecstasies* is a model of sympathetic but firm critique: see *A Zone of Engagement* (London, 1992), ch. 10.
135   G. M. Spiegel, 'History and Post-Modernism', *Past and Present*, 135 (1992), p. 196. Spiegel acknowledges her debt for the idea of the 'alterity' of the past to Michel de Certeau.
136   Habermas's theory of communicative action has been used by some writers as the basis of an account of historical interpretation: see, for example, Jay, 'Plots', pp. 105ff. I do not, however, discuss

this theory here, having sought elsewhere to point out its defects at some length: *Against Postmodernism* (Cambridge, 1989), ch. 4. W. G. Runciman, *A Treatise on Social Theory*, vol. 1 (Cambridge, 1983) contains much of value on social theory and historical writing.

Chapter 3   History as Theory

1 See, for example, H. A. Veeser, ed., *The New Historicism* (London, 1989).
2 M. Foucault, 'Questions of Method', *I & C*, 8 (1981), p. 4. Paul Veyne brings out the philosophical underpinnings of Foucault's 'histories' in 'Foucault révolutionne l'histoire', in *Comment on écrit l'histoire* (2nd edn, Paris, 1978).
3 G. R. Elton, *The Practice of History* (London, 1969), p. 87.
4 H. R. Trevor-Roper, 'The Gentry 1540–1660', *Economic History Review*, supp., 1 (1953), and 'The General Crisis of the Seventeenth Century', in T. Ashton, ed., *Crisis in Europe 1560–1660* (London, 1965); M. Mann, *The Sources of Social Power*, vol. 1 (Cambridge, 1986), chs 14 and 15.
5 Elton, *Practice*, p. 84.
6 A. J. P. Taylor, *A Personal History* (London, 1984), p. 147. Ernst von Weizsäcker was State Secretary at the German Foreign Office under the National Socialist regime.
7 N. Stone, 'Taylorism', in K. Miller, ed., *London Review of Books Anthology One* (London, 1981), pp. 18–19, where other examples of Taylor's green fingers are given.
8 See the admirable discussion in E. Loone, *Soviet Marxism and Analytical Philosophies of History* (London, 1992), esp. part 3, ch. 5.
9 See A. Callinicos, *Making History* (Cambridge, 1987), ch. 2.
10 Loone, *Soviet Marxism*, p. 94. Among the variants of historical theory Loone lists is 'the theory that records differences in systems that belong to its referents', ibid., p. 132.
11 For example: 'All science would be superfluous if the outward appearance and the essence of things coincided,' K. Marx, *Capital*, vol. 3 (Moscow, 1971), p. 817.
12 M. Bloch, *The Historian's Craft* (Manchester, 1992), p. 140, and *Feudal Society* (2 vols, London, 1965), vol. 1, p. xviii. See also A. C. Danto, *Analytical Philosophy of History* (Cambridge, 1965), pp. 182–3.
13 For classic treatments of the concept of mode of production, see L. Althusser and E. Balibar, *Reading Capital* (London, 1970), and G. A. Cohen, *Karl Marx's Theory of History* (Oxford, 1978). What Loone, following Soviet usage, calls 'socio-economic

formations' are what western Marxists tend to name 'modes of production': see *Soviet Marxism*, part 4, ch. 2. The distinction between mode of production and social formation was first formally stated by Althusser: see his discussion in 'On Theoretical Work', in *Philosophy and the Spontaneous Philosophy of Scientists and Other Essays* (London, 1990).

14 W. G. Runciman, *A Treatise on Social Theory*, vol. 2 (Cambridge, 1989), pp. 12, 55.

15 P. Anderson, *English Questions* (London, 1992), p. 231.

16 A. J. Toynbee, *A Study of History* (abr. edn, 2 vols, ed. D. C. Somervell, London, 1960), vol. 1, pp. 76–7.

17 For a comparatively sympathetic critical discussion of Toynbee, see W. H. Dray, *Philosophy of History* (Englewood Cliffs, 1964), ch. 7.

18 Anderson, *English Questions*, p. 231.

19 Mann, *Sources*, p. 523; Mann's general theory of power is expounded in chs 1 and 16. See Runciman, *Treatise*, pp. 14–15 for a critical discussion of Mann's attempt to distinguish between political and military power.

20 See Callinicos, *Making History*, ch. 2. On the dynamics of feudal crisis, see G. Bois, *Crisis of Feudalism* (Cambridge, 1984), and Robert Brenner's essays in T. S. Aston and C. E. Philpin, eds, *The Brenner Debate* (Cambridge, 1985).

21 G. Duby, *The Three Orders* (Chicago, 1980), p. 37.

22 E. O. Wright, A. Levine and E. Sober, *Reconstructing Marxism* (London, 1992), p. 79.

23 Cf. Cohen, *Karl Marx's Theory of History*, ch. 6, and Wright et al., *Reconstructing Marxism*, ch. 2 and pp. 80–2.

24 A. Giddens, *A Contemporary Critique of Historical Materialism* (London, 1981), pp. 19–25.

25 Wright et al., *Reconstructing Marxism*, p. 85. On time–space distanciation, see Giddens, *Contemporary Critique*, pp. 90ff.

26 Runciman, *Treatise*, p. 39.

27 Mann, *Sources*, p. 524; see more generally ibid., pp. 524–7. Note that Mann here more or less explicitly gives a version of Wright et al.'s condition (1), that social forms are sticky downward.

28 M. Weber, *The Protestant Ethic and the Spirit of Capitalism* (London, 1976). Cf. A. Giddens, *The Nation State and Violence* (Cambridge, 1985).

29 Toynbee, *Study*, vol. 1, p. 253. The critical discussion of 'Deterministic Solutions' (ibid., pp. 247–54) from which this quotation is taken makes clear that Toynbee does not offer a straightforwardly cyclical theory of directionality.

30 G. W. F. Hegel, *The Science of Logic* (2 vols, London, 1966), vol. 2, p. 484.

31 I. Kant, *Political Writings* (2nd edn, Cambridge, 1991), pp. 50, 44–5.

32 Anderson, *English Questions*, p. 231.
33 Mann, *Sources*, pp. 531–2.
34 Runciman, *Treatise*, p. 296.
35 Wright et al., *Reconstructing Marxism*, p. 79.
36 Cohen, *Karl Marx's Theory of History*, p. 134.
37 See generally ibid., chs 9 and 10, Joshua Cohen, review of *Karl Marx's Theory of History*, *Journal of Philosophy*, 79 (1982), Callinicos, *Making History*, ch. 2, C. Harman, 'Base and Superstructure', *IS*, 2: 32 (1986), and G. A. Cohen and W. Kymlicka, 'Human Nature and Social Change in the Marxist Conception of History', in G. A. Cohen, *History, Labour and Freedom* (Oxford, 1988).
38 But see, for a searching recent exploration of the complex relations of opposition and dependence between Marx's and Durkheim's thought, D. Lockwood, *Solidarity and Schism* (Oxford, 1992).
39 See, in addition to Karl Löwith's classic *Max Weber and Karl Marx* (London, 1993), G. Therborn, *Science, Class and Society* (London, 1976), pp. 270–315, and *Actuel Marx*, 11 (1992), special issue on Weber and Marx.
40 See Loone, *Soviet Marxism*, p. 169, and E. Gellner, *State and Society in Soviet Thought* (Oxford, 1988), ch. 8.
41 Thus see the attempts to distance the authors from Weber in A. Giddens, *The Class Structure of the Advanced Societies* (2nd edn, London, 1981), p. 296, Mann, *Sources*, ch. 1 (though he calls Weber 'the greatest sociologist', ibid., p. 4), and Runciman, *Treatise*, pp. 47–8.
42 See A. Callinicos, *The Revenge of History* (Cambridge, 1991), esp. ch. 2.
43 C. Wickham, 'Systactic Structures', *Past and Present*, 132 (1991), p. 189 n. 2.
44 Mann, *Sources*, p. 503. See also the discussion of the comparative sociology of ancient empires, ibid., pp. 167–74.
45 Runciman, *Treatise*, pp. 155–60, 163–8, 208–31 and 285ff.
46 See Perry Anderson's outstanding discussions of Mann and Runciman, now in *A Zone of Engagement* (London, 1992), chs 4 and 7 respectively. Many of the issues raised by Mann and Runciman are explored in J. F. Haldon, 'The Ottoman State and the Question of State Autonomy', *Journal of Peasant Studies*, 18 (1991).
47 Mann, *Sources*, p. 377, part of a summary (ibid., pp. 376–8) of chs 12–16: see esp. ch. 7 on multi-power-actor civilizations, and chs 5 and 9 on compulsory co-operation.
48 A. Watson, *The Rise of International Society* (London, 1992); Heeren is quoted on p. 208.
49 Mann, *Sources*, p. 376.
50 Anderson, *Zone*, pp. 84, 85. See also, on Mann's 'hostility to

comparison', C. Wickham, 'Historical Materialism, Historical Sociology', *NLR*, 171 (1988), pp. 75–6.

51 S. Runciman, *A History of the Crusades* (3 vols, Harmondsworth, 1965), vol. 1, p. 319, vol. 3, p. 335.

52 See M. Legassick, 'The Frontier Tradition in South African Historiography', in S. Marks and A. Atmore, eds, *Economy and Society in Pre-Industrial South Africa* (London, 1980).

53 Leopold von Ranke, *The Theory and Practice of History* (New York, 1983), pp. 76–7.

54 J. L. Abu-Lughod, *Before European Hegemony* (New York, 1989), pp. 354–5. See also Wickham, 'Historical Sociology', pp. 71–2.

55 Mann, *Sources*, p. 377.

56 M. Mann, 'The Social Cohesion of Liberal Democracy, *American Sociological Review*, 35 (1970). See, more generally, N. Abercrombie, S. Hill and B. S. Turner, *The Dominant Ideology Thesis* (London, 1980), and Callinicos, *Making History*, pp. 138–57. David Lockwood, however, vigorously defends a modified version of Durkheimian sociology: *Solidarity and Schism, passim*.

57 See, for example, A. Giddens, *Central Problems in Social Theory* (London, 1979), p. 112.

58 Giddens, *Contemporary Critique*, pp. 198, 250. See also Giddens's discussion of the 'world military order' as one of the four autonomous 'dimensions of modernity' in *Consequences of Modernity* (Cambridge, 1990).

59 Mann, *Sources*, pp. 222–3.

60 Wickham, 'Historical Sociology', p. 77.

61 C. Bertram, 'International Competition in Historical Materialism', *NLR*, 183 (1990), pp. 116, 119–20.

62 Ibid., p. 21. See, on the broader debate, the exchange between G. A. Cohen and J. Elster on 'Marxism, Functionalism and Game Theory', reprinted in A. Callinicos, ed., *Marxist Theory* (Oxford, 1989), and R. Brenner, 'The Social Basis of Economic Development', in J. Roemer, ed., *Analytical Marxism* (Cambridge, 1986).

63 Bertram himself cites Y. I. Semenov, 'The Theory of Socio-Economic Formations and World History', in E. Gellner, ed., *Soviet and Western Anthropology* (London, 1980), but see also Harman, 'Base and Superstructure', p. 20.

64 Runciman, *Treatise*, pp. 449, 42–3; see generally ibid., ch. 4. Surprisingly, Bertram makes no mention of Runciman's book. Wickham, by contrast, explicitly endorses the latter's theory of social evolution: 'Systactic Structures', pp. 200–1. See Anderson, *Zone*, pp. 165–7, for criticism, directed at Runciman but applicable to Bertram, of the idea that, in line with the analogy of natural selection, social change is random.

65 Runciman, *Treatise*, pp. 20ff.

66 Bertram, 'International Competition', p. 119 n. 9. See also Cohen's

discussion, cited by Bertram, in *History, Labour, and Freedom*, pp. 27–9.

67 L. D. Trotsky, *1905* (Harmondsworth, 1973), pp. 21–2. Trotsky's interpretation was attacked by vulgar Marxist historians like M. N. Pokrovsky: see ibid., pp. 342–60.

68 This and the following paragraphs summarize the arguments of A. Callinicos, *Is There a Future for Marxism?* (London, 1982), chs 5 and 8. See also Roman Rosdolsky's fundamental commentary, *The Making of Marx's 'Capital'* (London, 1977).

69 See C. Barker, 'The State as Capital', *IS*, 2: 1 (1978), C. Luporini, ' "Politique" et "Étatique" ', in E. Balibar, C. Luporini and A. Tosel, *Marx et la critique de la politique* (Paris, 1979), and C. Harman, 'The State and Capitalism Today', *IS*, 2: 51 (1991).

70 See, for a much more extensive discussion of these issues, A. Callinicos, 'Marxism and Imperialism Today', *IS*, 2: 50 (1991).

71 What follows summarizes the argument of Callinicos, *Making History*, pp. 157–72.

72 Brenner, 'Social Basis', pp. 32, 27.

73 Ibid., pp. 31–2.

74 P. Anderson, *Lineages of the Absolutist State* (London, 1974), p. 31.

75 See, on mediaeval Europe, C. Harman, 'From Feudalism to Capitalism', *IS*, 2: 45 (1989), esp. pp. 44–65 (the entire article is a powerful critique of Brenner's account of the transition), and, on China, M. Elvin, *The Pattern of the Chinese Past* (London, 1973), part 2.

76 See Bois, *Crisis of Feudalism*.

77 G. Bois, *La Mutation de l'an mil* (Paris, 1989). The idea of a feudal revolution *c.*1000 originates in the work of Georges Duby: see, for example, *Three Orders*, ch. 13.

78 See A. Callinicos, 'The Limits of "Political Marxism" ', *NLR*, 184 (1990).

79 R. Brenner, 'Agrarian Class Structure and Economic Development in Pre-Industrial Europe', and 'The Agrarian Roots of European Capitalism', both in Aston and Philpin, eds, *Brenner Debate*.

80 See A. Callinicos, 'Anthony Giddens: A Contemporary Critique', in Callinicos, ed., *Marxist Theory*.

81 Runciman, *Treatise*, p. 3.

82 M. Sahlins, *Stone Age Economics* (London, 1974), pp. 9 (quotation), 21, 11; see, generally, ibid., ch. 1.

83 See, for example, *Revenge*, pp. 118–33.

84 Cohen, *Karl Marx's Theory of History*, pp. 150–60, and Wright et al., *Reconstructing Marxism*, pp. 80–3.

85 See Wickham, 'Systactic Structures', p. 192, for a discussion of how Runciman implicitly accords primacy to the economic.

86 See Anderson's pertinent comments on Runciman in *Zone*, pp. 152–3.
87 C. G. Hempel, *Aspects of Scientific Explanation* (New York, 1965), ch. 9. Danto has a sensible discussion of the issues; *Analytical Philosophy of History*, ch. 10.
88 Bhaskar, *Possibility of Naturalism*.
89 See W. G. Runciman, *A Critique of Max Weber's Philosophy of Social Science* (Cambridge, 1972).
90 See M. Devitt, *Realism and Truth* (Oxford, 1984), pp. 14ff, on scientific realism.
91 R. M. Unger, *Social Theory* (Cambridge, 1987), p. 109.
92 Ibid., pp. 96–120.
93 K. Marx, *Grundrisse* (Harmondsworth, 1973), pp. 100–1.
94 See A. Callinicos, *Marxism and Philosophy* (Oxford, 1983), ch. 2.
95 K. Marx, *Capital*, vol. 1, (Harmondsworth, 1976), p. 90.
96 K. Marx, *Theories of Surplus Value*, vol. 2, (Moscow, 1968), p. 174.
97 A. Rattansi, ed., *Ideology, Method and Marx* (London, 1989).
98 Respectively, Brenner, 'Agrarian Class Structure' and 'Agrarian Roots'; *Merchants and Revolution* (Cambridge, 1993); 'The Deeper Roots of US Economic Decline', *Against the Current*, n.s., 2 (1986), 'Political Effects of US Economic Decline', ibid., n.s., 3 (1986), 'The Soviet Union and Eastern Europe', ibid., n.s., 30 and 31 (1991).
99 Brenner, 'Social Basis', p. 33.
100 See esp. Brenner, 'The Origins of Capitalist Development', *NLR*, 104 (1977).
101 See esp. Marx, 'Results of the Immediate Process of Production', Appendix to *Capital*, vol. 1, pp. 1023ff.
102 See Brenner, 'Agrarian Roots' for the fullest statement of this interpretation.
103 Brenner, *Merchants*, p. 45. Though made of the first half of the seventeenth century, the statement summarizes Brenner's broader view of the dynamics of capitalist development in England.
104 Harman, 'From Feudalism', p. 46.
105 Callinicos, 'Limits', p. 112.
106 Brenner, 'Origins', p. 52 n. 43. It is not clear where plantation slavery fits into Brenner's analysis. His remarks on Caribbean sugar production (ibid., pp. 87–90) leave the question open. Elsewhere he argues that 'pre-capitalist slave economies' had 'roughly similar rules of reproduction' to those of feudalism ('Social Basis', pp. 32–3 n. 6), a formulation which seems to admit the possibility of *capitalist* slave economies.
107 See Brenner, *Merchants*, esp. chs 2, 3, 4, 7, 10 and 12.
108 P. Anderson, 'Maurice Thompson's War', *London Review of*

Books, 4 November 1993, p. 17. See also my review of *Merchants*, 'Capitalism and the English Revolution', forthcoming in *NLR*.

109 See, for example, V. I. Lenin, *Collected Works* (45 vols, Moscow, 1974), vol. 21, pp. 137–57, and vol. 22, pp. 265–76.

110 See, for the elements of such an account, P. Kriedte, *Peasants, Landlords and Merchant Capitalists* (Leamington Spa, 1987).

111 E. P. Thompson, *Customs in Common* (Harmondsworth, 1993), esp. ch. 2.

112 Loone, *Soviet Marxism*, p. 219.

113 Brenner, 'Soviet Union', p. 27. See also, for a much more detailed analysis of contemporary China that uses the same theory of 'the bureaucratic social-property form', R. Smith, 'The Chinese Road to Capitalism', *NLR*, 199 (1993).

114 Brenner, 'Soviet Union', p. 27.

115 See Callinicos, *Revenge*, ch. 2, for the analysis (with supporting evidence) on which these criticisms are based.

116 R, Overy, *Goering* (London, 1984), p. 66.

117 L. Goldner, 'Postmodernism versus World History', *Against the Current*, n.s., 45 (1993), p. 30.

118 See Callinicos, *Future*, ch. 8, for a discussion of Cliff's interpretation of Stalinism which puts it in the context of the Marxist tradition of writing about imperialism.

119 M. Klare, 'The Next Great Arms Race', *Foreign Affairs*, 72: 3 Summer 1993.

Chapter 4   History as Progress

1 A. C. Danto, *Analytical Philosophy of History* (Cambridge, 1965), pp. 155, 18, 8–9; see also ibid., ch. 8, on narrative sentences.

2 J. Morgan, 'Rip Van Winkle's New World Order', *Financial Times*, 25 April 1992.

3 Danto, *Analytical Philosophy of History*, pp. 166–7: see also chs 5 and 6, where Danto criticizes various forms of scepticism and relativism about the past.

4 The concept of causality appropriate to historical inquiry is notoriously controversial. I ignore this issue here, but, for what it's worth, Roy Bhaskar offers what seems to me the best available account of causal explanations of the social world: see *The Possibility of Naturalism* (Brighton, 1979).

5 See D. Davidson, *Essays on Actions and Events* (Oxford, 1980), esp. Essay 7, for a defence of the claim that intentional explanations are causal.

6 Hegel might seem to represent a counter-example to this assertion, since he notoriously describes philosophical knowledge as retrospective, the *Erinnerung* – remembrance by internalization – of the

past course leading up to the moment of Absolute Knowledge: see, for example, the famous conclusion to the Preface to the *Philosophy of Right*. But recall that, for Hegel, the attainment of Absolute Knowledge is an escape from time: the End of History, I suggested in section 1.2 above, lies outside the historical process. Another way of putting this is to say that, though the author of a *Philosophy of History*, Hegel is only in an approximate way a philosopher of history, and it is therefore difficult to fit him into the kind of clear-cut distinctions drawn in the text.

7 Hegel, *Lectures on the Philosophy of World History: Introduction* (Cambridge, 1975), pp. 42–3, 68 (translation modified).

8 Lord Acton, *Lectures on Modern History* (London, 1960), p. 39. See also Acton's essay, 'German Schools of History', in *Historical Essays and Studies* (London, 1907).

9 Acton, *Historical Essays*, pp. 504, 505. See Hugh Tulloch's discussion of Acton's philosophy of history in *Acton* (London, 1988), ch. 5.

10 See, *inter alia*, A. MacIntyre, *After Virtue* (London, 1981), S. Lovibond, *Realism and Imagination in Ethics* (Oxford, 1983), B. Williams, *Ethics and the Limits of Philosophy* (London, 1985), and C. Taylor, *Sources of the Self* (Cambridge, 1990).

11 E. Gibbon, *The Decline and Fall of the Roman Empire* (3 vols, London, 1993), vol. 1, p. 89.

12 J. B. Bury, *The Idea of Progress* (London, 1920), chs 4 and 5. This study seems to me of far greater value as intellectual history than Löwith's more philosophically sophisticated essay.

13 K. Löwith, *Meaning in History* (Chicago, 1949), p. 212.

14 See, for example, Bryan S. Turner's preface to K. Löwith, *Max Weber and Karl Marx* (London, 1993), p. 24.

15 W. Blumenberg, *The Legitimacy of the Modern Age* (Cambridge, MA, 1983), pp. 30, 48–9.

16 Ibid., p. 32.

17 R. Koselleck, *Futures Past* (Cambridge, MA, 1985), pp. 239, 281, 282: see generally ibid., part 3.

18 R. Schacht, *Nietzsche* (London, 1983), p. 254; see generally ibid., pp. 251–66.

19 K. Löwith, 'Nietzsche's Revival of the Doctrine of Eternal Recurrence', Appendix II to Löwith, *Meaning*.

20 Nietzsche, *The Will to Power* (New York, 1968), section 635. See Schacht, *Nietzsche*, pp. 207ff.

21 See T. W. Adorno, 'Spengler after the Decline', in *Prisms* (Cambridge, MA, 1981), and section 1.3 above.

22 A. J. Toynbee, *A Study of History* (abr. edn, 2 vols, ed. D. C. Somervell, London, 1960), for example, vol. 2, pp. 271, 273, 322ff.

23 J. Bidet, *Théorie de la modernité* (Paris, 1990), pp. 294, 297–8.

24 J. Bidet, 'Capitalisme, communisme, marxisme, socialisme', in J. Bidet and J. Texier, eds, *Fin du communisme? Fin du marxisme?* (Paris, 1991), p. 17.

25 A. Callinicos, 'Le Socialisme et les temps modernes', in J. Bidet and J. Texier, eds, *L'Idée du socialisme a-t-elle un avenir?* (Paris, 1992).

26 R. M. Unger, *False Necessity* (Cambridge, 1987), p. 66.

27 R. M. Unger, *Plasticity into Power* (Cambridge, 1987), pp. 6–8. There are other cyclical theories around. Paul Kennedy's theory that dominance in the international state system is a consequence of relative economic strength which is then undermined by the military expenditures required to maintain this position could be seen as one: *The Rise and Fall of the Great Powers* (London, 1989); Kevin Phillips's account of the oscillation between right and left in American politics is another: *The Politics of Rich and Poor* (New York, 1991).

28 Unger, *False Necessity*, pp. 52, 36.

29 Ibid., p. 103.

30 A. Giddens, *Central Problems in Social Theory* (London, 1979), and A. Callinicos, *Making History* (Cambridge, 1987).

31 H. A. L. Fisher, *A History of Europe* (2 vols, London, 1935), vol. 2, p. vii.

32 Quoted in N. Stone, *Europe Transformed 1879–1919* (London, 1983), p. 15.

33 W. Benjamin, *Illuminations* (London, 1970), pp. 259, 263 (translation modified). See the discussion of Benjamin's 'Theses' in L. Niethammer, *Posthistoire* (London, 1992), ch. 6.

34 S. Buck-Morss, *The Dialectics of Seeing* (Cambridge, MA, 1989), p. 108.

35 For example, G. W. F. Hegel, *Lectures on the History of Philosophy* (3 vols, London, 1963), vol. 1, p. 346. See J. Elster, *Making Sense of Marx* (Cambridge, 1985), pp. 107–18, 302–3.

36 *CW*, vol. 6, p. 487.

37 F. Jameson, *Postmodernism, or, the Cultural Logic of Late Capitalism* (London, 1991), p. 47. For some reservations about how Jameson puts this insight to work, see A. Callinicos, *Against Postmodernism* (Cambridge, 1989), pp. 128–32, and 'Drawing the Line', *IS*, 2: 53 (1991).

38 *CW*, vol. 12, pp. 126, 132.

39 E. Said, *Orientalism* (Harmondsworth, 1985), p. 154.

40 R. Young, *White Mythologies* (London, 1990), p. 3.

41 But see Elster's discussion of this article in *Making Sense*, pp. 111–12.

42 P. Anderson, *Lineages of the Absolutist State* (London, 1974), p. 494, see generally ibid., pp 462–549, A. M. Bailey and J. Lobera, eds, *The Asiatic Mode of Production* (London, 1981),

and B. O'Leary, *The Asiatic Mode of Production* (Oxford, 1989). O'Leary, in the most systematic treatment of this topic, makes some peritinent criticisms of Anderson's arguments (pp. 225–34), but these are not intended to help rehabilitate the concept of the Asiatic mode.

43 B. Warren, *Imperialism: Pioneer of Capitalism* (London, 1980), p. 134. Warren's views are summarized in the first chapter, 'Capitalism and Historical Progress'. See, on the Great Bengal Famine, A. K. Sen, *Poverty and Famines* (Oxford, 1982), ch. 6 and Appendix D.

44 *CW*, vol. 12, pp. 217–18, 221, 222.

45 A. Ahmad, *In Theory* (London, 1992), pp. 227–8; see generally ibid., ch. 6.

46 G. Therborn, *Science, Class and Society* (London, 1976), pp. 355–6.

47 K. Marx, *Grundrisse*, (Harmondsworth, 1973), p. 488.

48 J. Schumpeter, *Capitalism, Socialism and Democracy* (London, 1976), ch. 7, and M. Berman, *All That is Solid Melts into Air* (London, 1983).

49 R. Grundmann, 'The Ecological Challenge to Marxism', *NLR*, 187 (1991), p. 111. For a different view, to which Grundmann's article is a response, see T. Benton, 'Marxism and Natural Limits', *NLR*, 178 (1989).

50 T. Eagleton, *The Ideology of the Aesthetic* (Oxford, 1990), p. 221.

51 *CW*, vol. 6, p. 506.

52 See, in addition to Eagleton, *Ideology*, ch. 8, G. A. Cohen, 'Reconsidering Historical Materialism', and N. Geras, 'The Controversy about Marx and Justice', both reprinted in A. Callinicos, ed., *Marxist Theory* (Oxford, 1989), and W. Kymlicka, *Liberalism, Community and Culture* (Oxford, 1989), ch. 6.

53 Marx, *Grundrisse*, p. 162.

54 *CW*, vol. 12, p. 221.

55 Ahmad, *In Theory*, pp. 236, 229.

56 Benjamin, *Illuminations*, pp. 265, 262.

57 E. P. Thompson, 'History Lessons', in 'Powers and Names', *London Review of Books*, 23 January 1986, p. 10. See, on Benjamin's theory of revolution, Callinicos, *Making History*, ch. 5.

58 *CW*, vol. 6, pp. 482, 496.

59 Callinicos, *Making History*, chs 2 and 5.

60 E. O. Wright, A. Levine and E. Sober, *Reconstructing Marxism* (London, 1992), pp. 79–80.

61 E. Loone, *Soviet Marxism and Analytical Philosophies of History* (London, 1992), pp. 179, 184, 185; see generally ibid., part 4, ch. 4.

62 J. Cohen, review of G. A. Cohen, *Karl Marx's Theory of History*, *Journal of Philosophy*, 79 (1982), p. 271.

63 W. G. Runciman, *A Treatise on Social Theory*, vol. 2, (Cambridge, 1989), pp. 310, 311, 312, 320, 321.

64 Quoted in Buck-Morss, *Dialectics*, p. 92.

65 O'Leary, *Asiatic Mode*, pp. 3 (a statement repeated incessantly throughout the book), 201, 175.

66 Critiques of 'political correctness' exist in abundance, and are generally more effective (rhetorically at any rate) than the response from the left: for three examples representing, respectively, the New Right and right- and left-of-centre liberalism, see D. D'Souza, *Illiberal Education* (New York, 1991), A. Schlesinger, *The Disuniting of America* (New York, 1991), and R. Hughes, *Culture of Complaint* (New York, 1993). For two sensible contributions from the left, see L. Selfa and A. Maass, *PC* (Chicago, 1991), and J. Molyneux, 'The "Politically Correct" Controversy', *IS*, 2: 61 (1993).

67 Hegel, *Philosophy of World History*, p. 176.

68 H. Butterfield, *Man On His Past* (Cambridge, 1955), p. 110.

69 L. von Ranke, *The Theory and Practice of History* (New York, 1983), pp. 46, 162–3. See also Butterfield, *Man on His Past*, ch. 4.

70 G. G. Iggers and K. von Moltke, Editors' Introduction to Ranke, *Theory and Practice*, p. lii.

71 Acton, *Historical Essays*, p. 380.

72 L. von Ranke, *The History of the Popes*, vol. 1 (London, 1891), p. 242.

73 Quoted in B. Davidson, *Africa in History* (rev. edn, London, 1991), p. xvii.

74 P. Novick, *That Noble Dream* (Cambridge, 1988), pp. 229, 77. See also ibid., pp. 68–80, the concluding chapter, 'The Propaganda of History', of W. E. B. Du Bois, *Black Reconstruction in America* (New York, 1969), and the Preface to E. Foner, *Reconstruction* (New York, 1988).

75 H. R. Trevor-Roper, *The Rise of Christian Europe* (rev. edn, London, 1965), p. 9.

76 Schlesinger, *Disuniting*, p. 78.

77 L. Vail, 'Introduction: Ethnicity in Southern African History', in Vail, ed., *The Creation of Tribalism in Southern Africa* (London, 1989), p. 3. See also R. Oliver, *The African Experience* (London, 1993), pp. 147–8, 184–5.

78 Toynbee, *Study*, vol. 1, p. 54.

79 Ibid., vol. 2, pp. 302–3, 353.

80 W. H. McNeill, *Plagues and Peoples* (Harmondsworth, 1979), p. 189.

81 See, for example, Christopher R. Browning's discussion of the issue in *Ordinary Men* (New York, 1992), pp. 159–62. Browning cites John W. Dower's terrifying account of the pervasive racism

expressed, and the widespread atrocities practised, by the western Allies during the Pacific war with Japan: *War without Mercy* (New York, 1986), esp. parts 1 and 2.

82 See, for an example of Afrocentric historiography, A. Diop, *Civilization or Barbarism?* (New York, 1991).

83 R. W. Southern, *The Making of the Middle Ages* (London, 1967), pp. 64–6.

84 L. Goldner, 'Postmodernism versus World History', *Against the Current*, n.s., 45 (1993), esp. pp. 31ff.

85 Perry Anderson criticizes Michael Mann for focusing almost exclusively on the development of social power in the west, but argues that this is a consequence of Mann's methodological hostility to comparative explanations rather than of 'any familiar kind of Eurocentrism', *A Zone of Engagement* (London, 1992), pp. 84–5. See also section 3.2 above.

86 T. W. Mason, *Social Policy in the Third Reich* (Providence, 1993), p. 1.

87 *CW*, vol. 24, p. 200. See also Marx's letter to Vera Zasulich of 8 March 1881 (and his discarded drafts of the letter), ibid., pp. 346–71.

88 There is an interesting discussion of these issues in P. Q. Hirst, *Marx and Historical Writing* (London, 1985), ch. 5, a critical review of Anderson's *Lineages of the Absolutist State*.

89 S. Amin, *Unequal Development* (Brighton, 1976), pp. 18–19, 15, 58, 55.

90 L. D. Trotsky, *History of the Russian Revolution* (3 vols, London, 1967), vol. 1, p. 22.

91 S. Amin, *Eurocentrism* (New York, 1989), p. 26; see also ibid., pp. 15–59, 79ff. For the role of Platonism in the scientific revolution, see A. Koyré, *Etudes Galiléenes* (Paris, 1966).

92 E. M. Wood, *Peasant-Citizen and Slave* (London, 1988), p. 83; see generally ibid., chs 3 and 4. It is regrettable that Wood over-eggs her cake, seeking systematically to play down the role of slavery in the Athenian economy: see G. E. M. de Ste Croix, *The Class Struggle in the Ancient Greek World* (London, 1981), and A. Callinicos, 'The Foundations of Athenian Democracy', *IS*, 2: 40 (1988). The economic and military presuppositions of classical antiquity are well treated in O. Murray, *Early Greece* (London, 1980), chs 8–10, and M. Mann, *The Sources of Social Power*, vol. 1 (Cambridge, 1986), chs 6 and 7.

93 C. Wickham, 'The Uniqueness of the East', *Journal of Peasant Studies*, 12 (1985), pp. 170, 168, 187, 185. O'Leary's attempt to use non-European precapitalist societies as a *reductio ad absurdum* of historical materialism is greatly weakened by his failure, in the course of a discussion which acknowledges the strengths of the concept of the tributary mode, to consider

Wickham's fundamental essay: *Asiatic Mode of Production*, pp. 197–200.
94 Wickham, 'Uniqueness', pp. 185–6.
95 Ibid., pp. 168, 184.
96 C. Wickham, 'The Other Transition', *Past and Present*, 103 (1984), pp. 36, 6, 19, 20, 24.
97 Wickham, 'Uniqueness', p. 169. Wickham's restriction of feudalism to Europe is, however, strongly disputed by other historians: see, for example, H. Berktay, 'The Feudalism Debate: The Turkish End', *Journal of Peasant Studies*, 14 (1987).
98 It is a matter of great controversy whether premodern Japan is also an instance of the feudal mode as, for example, Anderson argues: *Lineages*, pp. 435–61. The argument in the text is, of course, the merest sketch, which isolates for discussion some aspects of a much more complex story. Developed networks of international trade in which mercantile capitalism could prosper are by no means a strictly European phenomenon. Janet Abu-Lughod has painted a compelling portrait of a world economy bound together by circuits of exchange stretching from western Europe to China which reached its apogee between AD 1250 and 1350. She argues that the development in the sixteenth century of a European-dominated world economy was a consequence both of the development of a temporary power vacuum in south and south-east Asia, and of the intrusion into, and exploitation of, the old circuits by 'players interested in short-term plunder rather than long-term exchange' – Portugal, Holland, England. The emergence of this 'new European approach to trade-cum-plunder', however, once again poses the question of the peculiarities of European development: *Before European Hegemony* (New York, 1989), p. 361 and *passim*.
99 P. Buhle, 'Letter to the Editors', *Against the Current*, n.s., 46 (1993), p. 5, a response to Goldner, 'Postmodernism'.
100 Southwest Parks and Monuments Association, *Frijoles Canyon* (1991). The decline of Anasazi society is discussed in Brian M. Fagan, *Ancient North America* (London, 1991), ch. 15.
101 D. N. Beach, *The Shona and Zimbabwe 900–1850* (Gwelo, 1980), pp. 50–1.
102 See G. Bois, *The Crisis of Feudalism* (Cambridge, 1984).
103 See M. Haynes, 'Columbus, the Americas and the Rise of Capitalism', and M. Gonzalez, 'The Myths of Columbus', both in *IS*, 2: 57 (1992).
104 I. Clendinnen, *Aztecs* (Cambridge, 1991), pp. 2, 262.
105 G. Bois, *La Mutation de l'an mil* (Paris, 1989), pp. 186, 263.
106 Young, *White Mythologies*, p. 2. Though presented as a summary of claims made by Hélène Cixous, Young's formulations here state the position he defends throughout his book.

107 A. Callinicos, *Against Postmodernism* (Cambridge, 1989), esp. chs 3 and 5.
108 Young, *White Mythologies*, p. 19.
109 Goldner, 'Postmodernism', pp. 31–3. The importance of classical Greece to Foucault's thought is evident to anyone who reads *L'Usage des plaisirs* (Paris, 1984).
110 See *October*, 61 (1992), a special issue devoted to 'The Identity in Question', and consisting in the transcript of a symposium on this subject held at the City University of New York in November 1991.
111 E. Laclau and C. Mouffe, *Hegemony and Socialist Strategy* (London, 1985) is probably the main attempt to spell out the connections between poststructuralism and 'left' identity politics.
112 E. Laclau, 'Universalism, Particularism, and the Question of Identity', *October*, 61 (1992), pp. 85–7.
113 Young, *White Mythologies*, p. 3.
114 A. Callinicos, *Marxism and Philosophy* (Oxford, 1978), chs 2 and 3.
115 See R. Bhaskar, *A Realist Theory of Science* (2nd edn, Hassocks, 1978).
116 H.-G. Gadamer, *Truth and Method* (London, 1975), p. 111.
117 Amin, *Eurocentrism*, p. 33.
118 Quoted in F. Rosenthal, Introduction to Ibn Khaldûn, *The Muqadimmah* (3 vols, New York, 1958), vol. 1, p. cxv.
119 Trevor-Roper, *Rise*, p. 12.
120 Y. Lacoste, *Ibn Khaldûn* (London, 1984), part 2.
121 Toynbee, *Study*, vol. 2, p. 263.
122 Blumenberg, *Legitimacy*, pp. 385, 369, 373.
123 Marx, *Grundrisse*, p. 706.
124 C. Taylor, 'Rationality', in M. Hollis and S. Lukes, eds, *Rationality and Relativism* (Oxford, 1983), pp. 102–3.
125 M. Devitt, *Realism and Truth* (Oxford, 1984), pp. 107–8. The arguments are not identical, since Devitt's concern is with explaining 'theoretical success' – the case where the world is as if a theory's assertions are true – rather than technological success.
126 'Congress Debate on Colonial Policy', in J. Riddell, ed., *Lenin's Struggle for a Revolutionary International: Documents 1907–1916* (New York, 1984), pp. 10, 11. Laclau refers briefly to this debate in support of his argument that Marxism is Eurocentric: 'Universalism', p. 86.
127 A. Callinicos, 'Marxism and Imperialism Today', *IS*, 2: 50 (1991).
128 L. D. Trotsky, *The Struggle against Fascism in Germany* (New York, 1971), p. 203.
129 See F. Claudin, *The Communist Movement* (Harmondsworth, 1975), and D. Hallas, *The Comintern* (London, 1985).
130 D. Chakrabarty, 'Marxism and Modern India', in *After the End*

of History (London, 1992), p. 83. The theoretical significance of *Subaltern Studies* is, in any case, a complex issue: see, for example, R. Guha and G. C. Spivak, eds, *Selected Subaltern Studies* (New York, 1988).

131 H. Batatu, *The Old Social Classes and the Revolutionary Movements of Iraq* (Princeton, 1978).

132 M. Naison, *Communists in Harlem during the Depression* (New York, 1984).

133 R. D. G. Kelley, *Hammer and Hoe* (Chapel Hill, 1990).

134 See, for example, A. Horne, *A Savage War of Peace* (Harmondsworth, 1979), pp. 136–7.

135 For some sketchy attempts to do this for one very important liberation struggle, see A. Callinicos, *South Africa between Reform and Revolution* (London, 1988), esp. ch. 3, and my interview with Jeremy Cronin in A. Callinicos, ed., *Between Apartheid and Capitalism* (London, 1992), ch. 3. Edward Said's statement that '[m]uch of Western Marxism, ..., is ... blinded to the matter of imperialism', *Culture and Imperialism* (London, 1993), p. 326, is true enough if applied, as it is by him, to the Frankfurt school and its chief heir, Habermas, but it should be clear from the foregoing that it cannot be extended to other variants of Marxism.

136 L. Goldner, 'Europe and Freedom', *Against the Current*, n.s., 47 (1993), p. 40. I criticize Goldner's undifferentiated concept of 'statism' in section 3.3 above.

137 Ibid., p. 41, and Blumenberg, *Legitimacy*, p. 518. Blumenberg calls Bruno '*the* significant "heretic" of the beginning of the modern age', ibid., p. 563. See also A. Koyré, *From the Closed World to the Infinite Universe* (Baltimore, 1970).

138 This is one reason, among many, why Goldner's attempt to devalue the French Revolution relative to the English is misguided: see Goldner, 'Postmodernism', pp. 29–30, and, for a discussion of the proper significance of 1789, P. McGarr and A. Callinicos, *Marxism and the Great French Revolution* (London, 1993).

139 K. Marx, *Capital*, vol. 1 (Harmondsworth, 1976), pp. 272–3.

140 This line of thought suggests that it should be possible to give a ranking of class societies according to the degree to which they realize human freedom. Intuition indicates that slavery would come at the bottom; the feudal and tributary modes of production would share the same level, since both involve the political subjection of peasant communities in at least partial control of the soil; and capitalism would come next. An obvious objection to this ordering is that some of the slave societies of classical antiquity offered a high degree of individual and collective freedom to citizens: see Wood, *Peasant-Citizen*.

141 *CW*, vol. 3, pp. 154, 168.

142 J. Habermas, 'Modernity – An Incomplete Project', in H. Foster, ed., *Postmodern Culture* (London, 1985).

143 I. Kant, *Political Writings* (2nd edn, Cambridge, 1991), pp. 54–5.

144 E. Balibar, ' "Droits de l'homme" et "droits du citoyen" ', *Actuel Marx*, 8 (1990), pp. 20, 21, 22. Marx's discussion of the Declaration of the Rights of Man and of the Citizen is in *CW*, vol. 3, pp. 60–8.

145 Balibar, ' "Droits" ', p. 23.

146 Ibid., p. 23. There are interesting parallels between Balibar's interpretation of the Declaration and Gary Wills's argument that Lincoln's Gettysburg Address amounted to a Transcendentalist rereading of the American Constitution in the light of the egalitarian opening lines of the Declaration of Independence: *Lincoln at Gettysburg* (New York, 1992).

147 Balibar, ' "Droits" ', pp. 28, 31.

148 J. Habermas, *Autonomy and Solidarity* (2nd. edn, London, 1992), p. 155.

149 S. Lovibond, 'Femininism and Postmodernism', *NLR*, 178 (1989), pp. 11, 28.

150 R. Rorty, *Contingency, Irony, and Solidarity* (Cambridge, 1989), p. 191.

151 Ibid., p. 192.

152 *Observer*, 25 July 1993.

153 Take, for example, Michael Walzer's odious argument in favour of denying immigrant workers citizenship rights and insistence that 'the deepest meaning of self-determination' lies in a state's right, 'more basic' than any other, 'to choose an admissions policy' that will preserve nations as *'communities of character'* (the last formulation is Otto Bauer's): *Spheres of Justice* (Oxford, 1983), pp. 60–2. It is astonishing that someone expressing such views can be regarded as a theorist of the *left*.

154 E. J. Hobsbawm and T. Ranger, eds, *The Invention of Tradition* (Cambridge, 1983).

155 See, for example, Laclau, 'Universalism', pp. 88–9.

156 E. Laclau, in 'Discussion', *October*, 61 (1992), p. 79.

157 See, for example, J. Habermas, 'The Second Life-Fiction of the Federal Republic', *NLR*, 197 (1993).

158 E. S. Said, panel discussion, *States of America*, Channel Four TV (UK), 19 April 1993. See, on the tensions of Said's work, Young, *White Mythologies*, ch. 7, and Ahmad, *In Theory* ch. 5. Said's latest book, *Culture and Imperialism*, seems to represent a step beyond these tensions.

159 See, for a broader discussion of the issues raised here, C. Harman, 'The Return of the National Question', *IS*, 2: 56 (1992).

160 See H. K. Bhabha, *The Location of Culture* (London, 1994).

161 P. Gilroy, *The Black Atlantic* (London, 1993), p. 3 and *passim*.

162 See P. Buhle, *C. L. R. James* (London, 1989), though this biography is weak precisely on James's universalism, my brief discussion in *Trotskyism* (Milton Keynes, 1990), pp. 61–6, and Said, *Culture and Imperialism*, pp. 288–340.

163 *CW*, vol. 3, pp. 186–7.

164 S. Aronowitz, 'Reflections on Identity', *October*, 61 (1992), pp. 101, 102–3.

165 For extended discussions of the issues raised here, see A. Callinicos and C. Harman, *The Changing Working Class* (London, 1987), L. German, *Sex, Class and Socialism* (London, 1989), A. Callinicos, *Race and Class* (London, 1993), and C. Harman, 'Where is Capitalism Going?', II, *IS*, 2: 60 (1993).

Conclusion

1 R. Rorty, *Contingency, Irony, and Solidarity* (Cambridge, 1989), pp. 73–4.

2 Quoted in C. Jencks, *What is Post-Modernism?* (London, 1986), p. 18.

3 R. Rorty, 'Thugs and Theorists', *Political Theory*, 15 (1987), p. 566.

4 C. V. Woodward, 'Clio with Soul', in F. Stern, ed., *The Varieties of History* (New York, 1973), p. 490.

5 See P. Novick, *That Noble Dream* (Cambridge, 1988), chs 13 and 14.

6 C. V. Woodward, 'Freedom and the Universities', *New York Review of Books*, 18 July 1991.

7 F. Moretti, *Signs Taken for Wonders* (rev. edn, London 1988), pp. 242–3, 246–7. See C. Schmitt, *Political Romanticism* (Cambridge, MA, 1986). Compare also Paul de Man's remark: 'it is a historical fact that irony becomes increasingly conscious of itself in the course of demonstrating the impossibility of our being historical,' *Blindness and Insight* (2nd edn, London, 1983), p. 211.

8 G. W. F. Hegel, *Elements of the Philosophy of Right* (Cambridge, 1991), §140 and 'Zusatz', pp. 170, 180, 184.

9 H. White, *Metahistory* (Baltimore, 1975), p. 121.

10 K. Burke, *A Grammar of Motives and A Rhetoric of Motives* (Cleveland, 1962), p. 512. (I am grateful to Christina Britzolakis for pointing me in Burke's direction.) Hegel does recognize the connection between irony and dialectic, but subordinates both to the Absolute. Thus he praises Plato, 'who was so far from treating the dialectic in itself, let alone irony, as the ultimate factor and as the Idea itself that, on the contrary, he ended the to and fro of thought, and particularly of subjective opinion, by submerging it in the substantiality of the Idea,' *Philosophy of Right*, §140, p. 180.

11   Burke, *Grammar*, pp. 512–13.
12   Ibid., p. 514.
13   E. S. Said, *Culture and Imperialism* (London, 1993), p. 4.
14   For a shrewd poststructuralist critique of Jameson, see R. Young, *White Mythologies* (London, 1990), ch. 6.
15   Said, *Culture and Imperialism*, p. 4.
16   F. Jameson, *Late Marxism* (London, 1990), p. 251. See also Jameson, *Postmodernism, or, the Cultural Logic of Late Capitalism* (London, 1991), pp. 331–40.
17   J.-F. Lyotard, *The Postmodern Condition* (Manchester, 1984), p. 60.
18   White, *Metahistory*, p. 329.

INDEX